The Hiding Place:
The Sinner Found in Christ

by
John Macfarlane

"Thou art my hiding place."
– Psalm 32:7

REFORMATION HERITAGE BOOKS
Grand Rapids, Michigan

Reprint 2006
REFORMATION HERITAGE BOOKS
2965 Leonard St., NE
Grand Rapids, MI 49525
616-977-0599 / Fax 616-285-3246
e-mail: orders@heritagebooks.org
website: www.heritagebooks.org

10 digit ISBN #1-892777-78-9
13 digit ISBN #978-1-892777-78-2

Originally published
LONDON: JAMES NISBET & CO., 1855

For additional Reformed literature, both new and used, request a free book list from Reformation Heritage Books at the above address.

TO THE

VENERABLE AND REVEREND

WILLIAM KIDSTON, D.D.,

GLASGOW,

THE OLDEST MINISTER OF ALL DENOMINATIONS,

AND THEREFORE

𝔗𝔥𝔢 𝔉𝔞𝔱𝔥𝔢𝔯 𝔬𝔣 𝔱𝔥𝔢 𝔆𝔥𝔲𝔯𝔠𝔥 𝔬𝔣 𝔆𝔥𝔯𝔦𝔰𝔱 𝔦𝔫 𝔖𝔠𝔬𝔱𝔩𝔞𝔫𝔡,

THIS VOLUME IS,

WITH MUCH RESPECT AND AFFECTION, DEDICATED,

BY HIS SON-IN-LAW,

THE AUTHOR.

PREFACE.

My object in writing and publishing this volume, is to put before the reader such a simple and comprehensive view of 'the way to the Father by Jesus Christ,' that if he be at all in earnest about his soul's salvation, he must rise from the perusal, if not convinced and converted, at least in no doubt of the place where, and the manner in which lost sinners are to be ' delivered from the wrath to come.' The plan of the following work is determined by the order of those new covenant titles given to our Lord in the Old Testament, which have the prefix JEHOVAH. It is exceedingly interesting to find, that, by the proper arrangement of such titles, we have the entire scheme of the gospel in a *system*, so that the serious student can obtain from their study clear and connected ideas of ' the will of God in Christ ' concerning his conversion, pardon, purity, peace, and prospects. There is necessarily repetition of idea. This I do not regret, as I desire my book to fall into the hands of thoughtless or indifferent professors of religion. It is for their benefit that *the one mediation* should be viewed repeatedly and from different points. My fervent prayer is, that in all such cases the result may be, their awakening from nominalism, and their cordial espousal of the truth as it is in Jesus.

Until of late, authors of plain and moderate pretensions were discouraged. 'Why,' it was asked, 're-publish what has been given to the world over and over again? if you have nothing *new*, keep your manuscript in your desk, or throw it into the fire.' I regard it as one of the greatest of privileges, that in these days other sentiments upon this subject prevail, and that the most humble amongst us are now welcomed, as well from the press as from the pulpit. By this means, too, we have our sphere of doing good enlarged; and to an honest christian minister, no object can be dearer or more desirable. Taking advantage of this boon (for I am willing to regard it as such), I venture to lay this volume before the public, in the hope that God will condescend to honour it, to do its own appointed work on the great field of christian usefulness and enterprise. The men of erudition, and genius, and mighty intellect in the church are comparatively few, and have their own august work to attend to. A more humble class of theological students constitutes the majority. To them also a peculiar work is in these days assigned; and as 'fellow-workers' with the former, though at some distance, they cannot fail to promote the best interests of their fellow-men, by doing 'what they can,' and offering as they have to give. There was provision made under the law for the 'turtle doves' of the poor, as well as for the costly sacrifices of the rich; and the Saviour has assigned no undistinguished place in his gospel church to such things as the mite of the widow, the tears of the penitent, and the prayers of the saints.

Since going to press, the venerable man to whom this volume is dedicated has entered upon the 'rest that remains for the people of God.' Intended as a mark of respect for living excellence, it remains a tribute sacred to departed worth.

GLASGOW, IBROXHOLM,
November, 1852.

NOTE TO THE SECOND EDITION.

DULY impressed with gratitude to 'the Father of Lights' for the acceptance which this work has met with, in the rapid sale of a large impression, the Author sends forth this Second Edition, in the humble hope that his book may continue to do good.

GLASGOW, *Oct.*, 1854.

CONTENTS.

INTRODUCTION.

	Page
'The principles of the doctrine of Christ,'	9

CHAPTER I.
JEHOVAH.

'I am JEHOVAH, that is my name,' - - - - - 29

CHAPTER II.
JEHOVAH-JESUS: THE LORD OUR GOD.

'I am the Lord thy God,' - - - - - - - 39

CHAPTER III.
JEHOVAH-JIREH: THE LORD WILL PROVIDE.
PART I.

'And Abraham called the name of that place JEHOVAH-JIREH; that is, The Lord will provide,' - - - - - - 54

CHAPTER IV.
JEHOVAH-JIREH: THE LORD WILL PROVIDE.
PART II.

'Take no thought for the morrow,' - - - - - - 67

Chapter V.

JEHOVAH-TSIDKENU: THE LORD OUR RIGHTEOUSNESS.

PART I.

'This is his name whereby he shall be called, JEHOVAH-TSIDKENU: the Lord our righteousness,' - - - - - - 87

Chapter VI.

JEHOVAH-TSIDKENU: THE LORD OUR RIGHTEOUSNESS.

PART II.

'Bring forth the best robe, and put it on him,' - - - - 100

Chapter VII.

JEHOVAH-TSIDKENU: THE LORD OUR RIGHTEOUSNESS.

PART III.

'Put ye on the Lord Jesus,' - - - - - - - 118

Chapter VIII.

JEHOVAH-ROPHI: THE LORD MY HEALER.

PART I.

'I am JEHOVAH-ROPHI, the Lord that healeth thee,' - - - 139

Chapter IX.

JEHOVAH-ROPHI: THE LORD MY HEALER.

PART II.

'Is there no balm in Gilead? is there no physician there?' - - 166

CONTENTS. xiii

Chapter X.

JEHOVAH-SHALOM: THE LORD OUR PEACE.

Part I.
Page

'Then Gideon built an altar there unto the Lord, and called it JEHOVAH-SHALOM, the Lord our peace,' - - - - 193

Chapter XI.

JEHOVAH-SHALOM: THE LORD OUR PEACE.

Part II.

'Let the peace of God rule in your hearts,' - - - - 216

Chapter XII.

JEHOVAH-NISSI: THE LORD MY BANNER.

Part I.

'And Moses built an altar, and called the name of it JEHOVAH-NISSI, the Lord my banner,' - - - - - - 245

Chapter XIII.

JEHOVAH-NISSI: THE LORD MY BANNER.

Part II.

'In the name of our God we will set up our banners,' - - 267

Chapter XIV.

JEHOVAH-SHAMMAH: THE LORD IS THERE.

Part I.

'The name of the city from that day shall be, JEHOVAH-SHAMMAH, the Lord is there,' - - - - - - - - - 294

Chapter XV.

JEHOVAH-SHAMMAH: THE LORD IS THERE.

PART II.

'He endured as seeing him who is invisible,' - - - - 320

Chapter XVI.

JEHOVAH-SHAMMAH: THE LORD IS THERE.

PART III.

'Thou God seest me,' - - - - - - - - 339

Chapter XVII.

THE IMPROVEMENT.

'I flee unto thee to hide me,' - - - - - - - 359

THE

HIDING PLACE.

INTRODUCTION.

'THE PRINCIPLES OF THE DOCTRINE OF CHRIST.'

HEB. vi. 1.

THERE are, in these days, frequently issuing from the press, contributions to the science of religion, upon a great variety of topics, more or less intimately connected with the necessity and importance of vital piety. This is a hopeful sign of the times, and if a wise use be made of such books by professing christians, 'there cannot fail, ere long, to be an extensive revival of religion in the land. Nor is it the least encouraging element in this state of things, that the publications referred to unite in giving homage to the *Bible*, as the divine source of truth and the only 'rule of faith and manners.' Until recently, there were comparatively few modern books that bore directly and exclusively upon the great doctrines of the cross of Christ. Hence the lukewarm christianity that prevailed, and to a painful extent still prevails among many nominal disciples of Jesus; and hence the dwarfish and feeble specimens of christian stature which will indispose our future historian to record that 'there were giants in these days.' True godliness, among any people, is not to be formed and maintained otherwise than by a humble and thorough searching of scripture—this being the only way to a just appreciation of the doctrines of the person and sacrifice of the Redeemer. Books of religious consolation and excitement are useful in their own place and at their own time; but books which purposely confine the attention to Christ as the 'wisdom of God, and the power of God unto salvation,' are the only elementary ones, in the study of which we are taught and trained by the Spirit of God, until we all 'come unto a perfect man, unto the measure of the stature of the fulness of Christ.' There may be a christianity which is effeminate, and which allows itself to evaporate in the dreamy regions of mere sentimentalism. To construct a christianity which shall be sturdy, athletic, and enterprising, there must be a long, an earnest, and an enlightened curriculum of study at and in the Cross itself. The lessons may be somewhat abstract and comparatively common-place, but, like the bread, which is the staff of human subsistence, they are indispensable to christian character and usefulness. To the repeated study of such lessons the reader is here invited.

To become apt scholars in this school, the *subject* itself must be held in the highest estimation, and until it is mastered, all others must be kept in abeyance. Other subjects may present more fascinating charms to unrenewed minds, but *this* alone has ever charmed men out of their sins, their miseries, and their unavailing struggles after reconciliation with God. In other words, it is 'by the foolishness of preaching' Christ and him crucified that men must be saved. Nor can there be a revival of religion while such a theme is neglected as an old-fashioned theology, and while the morbid craving for crude novelties is unintentionally perhaps, but fatally pandered to in public instruction. To such a style of imparting christian knowledge as reared our giants in theology, and inspired the martyrs to our faith, there is certainly, on many hands, a lamentable dislike amongst us. Progress, it is said, is the order of the day; the anchors of ancient usages and principles are being lifted on every side, and everything is hastening forward with a velocity which must soon carry the world far out of sight of the ancient landmarks. Applied to mundane art or science, there is truth in this; but to the philosophy of the cross it has no just reference. Christian doctrine is eternal and immovable. Improvements there may be in the principles of mere biblical criticism, and in the most approved methods for handling the gospel plan; but upon the great first principles themselves, by the faith of which men are saved, addition or improvement is impossible. The idea is preposterous; it is profane. Are we to expect some christian philosopher to be born who shall be a wiser expounder of truth than was Jesus himself? Are we to expect the rise and endowment of a college of men, who shall teach the way of salvation more effectively than did the college of the apostles? Assuredly not—the christian temple of truth is built already—nothing can be added to, and nothing can be taken from its stately proportions. If men allow their appetite for what is new to carry them away, they must abandon principles for chimeras, substance for shadows, the light of day for the glare of meteors, and God himself for man. In these pages, therefore, we seek not to amuse by the mere poetry of ideas, or the artistic touches of fancy, or the laboured artillery of argument dragged by the horses of Egypt over the Palestine of gospel story. Here, the materials and achievements of unadorned truth are not retired to give place to the grimaces and whinings of a sensual devotion, or to gratify carnal desires for the spices of speculative discussion. Truth is not served up in the dress of sceptical harlotry or of academic rationalism. Here, the wisdom of God, it is hoped, is in no degree hid behind the wisdom of man. Human learning is all very well in its own place, and its progress must enrich and improve the world; but though it goes on to put to the blush even the learning of angels, it can never equal, much less outstrip, the teaching of the fishermen of Galilee. And so it shall appear in the end. Everything that exalts itself here must and shall be brought low, and all the triumphs of mere mind, having served their little day, shall dissolve with the elements of nature. But as the Lord liveth and reigneth, every eye shall yet see, that from amid the ruins of all systems, and the conflagration of worlds, the solitary survivors that shall rise to meet the Judge in the air shall be THE CROSS on which he himself died, and the people who lived and died glorying only in him and in it. Let us, then, under these impressions, proceed to the study and contemplation of that wonderful and soul-saving system of truth, which has for its object the incarnate Son of God; for its subject the doctrine of his great atonement for sins; and for its aim the bringing back of a lost world to God. And may God grant that while we muse, the fire of divine love may burn, and that the beauties of holiness may be imparted, together with 'the peace of God that passeth all understanding!' Before entering directly upon the grand subject of CHRIST OUR 'HIDING PLACE,' let us glance cursorily at some of 'the principles of the doctrine of Christ,' which may be said to be foundations upon which this 'hiding place' is reared.

FIRST PRINCIPLES require to be both submitted

and admitted before any science can be understood. What axioms or postulates are to mathematics, principles are to philosophy and to religion. To know and appreciate the fundamental principles of the Baconian or Newtonian systems, secures a readier assent to the inductions of the one and the elevated speculations of the other. He would be esteemed a fool who should try to explain the firmamental wonders in ignorance of the law of gravitation; and any project to illustrate the analogies of reason, or explain the laws of mind in utter disregard of the approved principles of modern light, would be universally ridiculed.

Applied to *religion*, these remarks rise to unspeakable importance. Surely, if anywhere, it must be within the province of divine things that acquaintance with first principles is indispensable. In his epistle to the Hebrews, the apostle evidently lays great stress upon what he describes to be 'the first principles of the oracles of God,' or, 'the principles of the doctrine of Christ.' In the following pages, doctrinal, experimental, and practical religion is to be illustrated and enforced; but, before entering upon this wide field, we must first lay the foundation, or state the *principles* to which the apostle refers. From these principles the christian system is a deduction, and the more simply and clearly they are stated, the more probable is the assent to christianity as a divine revelation—the more certain is the conversion of the soul to God through faith in its Saviour, and the more secure is the convert against the suggestions of Satan, the plausibilities of the infidel, and the temptations of the world. Let us glance then for a moment at first principles:—

I. THERE IS ONE GOD. This is of all principles the 'Alpha,' or the first. It is the 'be all and the end all' of religion. If there be no God there is no religion, because all religion has its reference to his existence and his will. On this supposition, sin and holiness are insignificant terms, and it becomes the duty of the creature to disregard any consideration but what contributes to his own interests: a selfish prudence, not a religion, is binding upon him. But, if there be a God, then it is clear he ought to be loved and adored. His favour must be life; his displeasure must be death. His favour should never be lost, and his anger, if ever incurred, should be, if the thing be possible, without delay appeased, for 'it is a fearful thing to fall into the hands of the living God.'

II. THE EXISTENCE OF GOD CAN BE PROVED. Atheism is an absurdity. 'It has no foundation,' says Dr Parr, 'in the common sense of men, no superstructure from their general habits, no cement from their nobler affections, no embellishments from their unperverted imaginations, nor pillars from their social virtues. It starts up but to vanish; it towers but to fall.' All philosophic principles, therefore, discard atheism, because it can be shown, from incontrovertible reasoning, that God must exist. For example,—1. *Belief in his existence is natural to man.* Conscience is a power in every human heart, and it uniformly declares for a God. 'The *invisible* things of God from the creation of the world are *clearly* seen, being understood by the things that are made, even his eternal power and Godhead.' An atheist, then, if there be one, is a monster—he is blind to what can be 'clearly seen.' 2. *There is the ascending and the descending proof*, or, the argument *a priori* (by Dr Clarke,) and *a posteriori*, by which we mean that a supreme existence can be proved either by reasoning from the effect upwards towards the cause, or from the cause downward to the effect—from the visible up to the invisible, or from the invisible down to what is seen. We prefer, for edification, the argument *a posteriori*, because it conducts the mind, by easy and natural stages, from the *finite* or the creature, to the *infinite* or the Creator; *thus*, 3. *As something exists now, something must have existed from eternity.* Even infidels admit that, if there ever had been a time when nothing existed, nothing could have been in existence now. To get quit of the idea of a designing power, Epicurus resorts to that manifest absurdity about the universe having been formed out of a 'fortuitous concourse of atoms,' and that these atoms must have existed from all eternity. 'I will no more believe,' says Swift (borrowing the idea from Cicero,) 'that the universe was formed by a fortuitous concourse of atoms, than that the accidental jumbling of the letters of the alphabet could fall by chance into an ingenious and learned treatise of philosophy.' Apply the argument of the atheist to *man*—he exists now, he must have always existed—therefore there never was a *first* man. But, asks Dr Dick, 'how could a succession be eternal although all its parts had a beginning? How could all its parts have a beginning, and yet the whole be without a beginning?' Atheism tells us that there can be 'a chain which has only one end.' Again, 4. *Design implies a designer.* There are proofs of *design* everywhere in creation, therefore there must be an intelligent Creator. Enter one of our large manufactories or engineering yards, where stands, in the beauty and symmetry of a perfect finish, one of the grandest pieces of machinery— enter the 'Great Exhibition of the Works of the Industry of all Nations'—point to the gorgeous manifestations of a world's art within its crystal walls, and then announce that, though there we have proofs of intelligence and genius of the highest order, yet there never was a designer—that the whole came together by mere chance, and that the structures and their contents are lucky concourses—you would be set down by the veriest tyro as a mocker or a madman. And yet, though from the mechanism of the heavens to the meanest insect, from the angel to the worm, from the ocean to the rimpling stream, from the cedar of Lebanon to the hyssop on the wall, there be proofs without number of the highest wisdom and power, there are men who say in their hearts 'there is no God.' 5. *The general consent of mankind to the existence of God* is also a fair argument here. The idea of a presiding Deity has been found in the human mind, in every age of the world, and among the rudest and most barbarous of the race. 6. *The proofs of a Providence* superintending and controlling all creatures, and all their actions, are also brilliant and impressive advocates for the existence of one supreme Deity, in whom all 'live and move and have their being.' To call these providences 'the laws of nature,' only puts the question one step farther back; laws imply a lawgiver, and who is he? Who but the God of the Bible? And, in one word, 7. *The Bible testimony* is the sufficient and the convincing one to the disciples of Jesus. The inspiration of the scriptures is, of course, in this respect, taken for granted. But, even admitting this, there is, to the serious inquirer, no stronger proof of the existence of the 'one only, the living and the true God,' than what is afforded in the express and sublime revelations of that Lord himself. We stand at the foot of Sinai, and take our creed from the mouth of the Lord God of Israel, who commands, 'Thou shalt have no other gods before me;' 'Hear, O Israel, the Lord our God is one Lord.'

III. THERE ARE THREE PERSONS IN THE GODHEAD. These three are distinct—each is a divine person—and yet there is only 'one true and living God.' This is one of the mysteries of *revelation*. The knowledge of it does not appear to be necessary to the religion of innocence. Adam was perfect when formed, but it is questionable if he had any idea of the *triune* Jehovah. Men have ridiculed it. How ungrateful! How impious! God was under no necessity to reveal it; and when he did so, it was because of man's fall, and especially because of the purpose to restore him. This could not be done except by a *divine mediation;* hence the necessity of revealing the Father who sends the Son, the Son who gives himself, and the Holy Ghost who applies the blessings of their united salvation.

IV. THERE IS BUT ONE RELIGION. This is a consequence from the doctrine or principle of *one* God. All intelligent creatures owe to him what is called a *religion*—which means, pure love and perfect obedience. God himself is love, and religion itself is love; which love includes perfect assimilation to God's nature, and entire submission to God's will. This is invariably the religion of innocence. The holy angels, and all uncorrupted intelligences, possess and practise it. Consequently their intercourse with God is direct. Of mediation they know nothing, because of sin they are guiltless. Theirs is the religion of nature.

V. SINFUL MAN HAS NO RELIGION. He is godless, or 'without God.' He was created holy. He broke God's law, became a sinner, and was condemned to die. His likeness to God, his satisfaction in God, and his love for God, all took their flight from his soul, when he ate of the forbidden tree. He is by nature 'dead in trespasses and in sins,'—*spiritually* dead, for holiness has died out of him; *judicially* dead, for God has condemned him; and *eternally* dead, for 'the wages of sin is death,' not only now, but for ever and ever. Left, then, to himself, man not only has no religion, but religious he never can become. Has God, then, withdrawn his claims upon his love and obedience? By no means. His rights are unaffected by any moral or judicial change in man's condition. Holiness the creature is still bound to cultivate, and obedience he is still bound to give; but, alas! to neither is he now equal. He cannot be holy, because he is 'shapen in iniquity, and in sin did his mother conceive him;' and he cannot obey, because he hates the very thought of God, and it is written, 'Love is the fulfilling of the law.' Eternal separation from God, and everlasting wrath, must be his doom. Is there no hope for him? There is.

VI. THERE IS A MEDIATOR BETWEEN GOD AND MAN. This is Jesus Christ, the Son of God. This is the revelation of the Bible. This is the religion, not of *nature*, but of *christianity;* for 'God so loved the world, that he gave his only-begotten Son, that whosoever believeth in him should not perish, but have everlasting life.' This same Jesus 'God hath set forth to be a propitiation, through faith in his blood, to declare his righteousness for the remission of sins that are past, through the forbearance of God.' The Son of God from all eternity, this Mediator became man in the fulness of the time; for 'verily he took not on him the nature of angels, but he took on him the seed of Abraham;' which means that he assumed the human into union with his divine nature: 'The Word was made flesh,' and 'the Word was with God, and the Word was God—all things were made by him.'

VII. THE MEDIATOR IS GOD. It is evident that *redeeming* power implies *creating* power. Redemption is accomplished by mediation, but mediation supposes that sin has been atoned for, that the Lawgiver is satisfied, and that pardon, peace, purity, and paradise are placed in the option of the sinner. Now, God must not only have approved of this work, bu God alone must have accomplished it. True, sin was imputed to the humanity of the substitute, and from that humanity alone was exacted the penalty of sin—death; but what was it that imparted to the humanity *strength* sufficient to bear the mighty load of human guilt? and what was it that gave to the sufferings of Jesus their infinitely meritorious righteousness? It was the *divinity* of the surety. Under the law it was the altar that 'sanctified the gift;' till the gift came into contact with the altar it was not a sacrifice. Under the gospel there is also an altar which sanctifies the gift, and that altar is the divine nature of the Redeemer; which, in mysterious union with his humanity, imparts to his offering all its propitiatory value. The deity and the atonement of Christ are inseparable. If he be not God, then there is no atonement, and if there be no atonement, then for the sinner there is no hope whatever. But the Bible affirms that he is divine, and hence he becomes to the christian 'all his salvation and all his desire.'

VIII. THERE IS ONLY ONE MEDIATOR. 'For other foundation can no man lay than that is laid, which is Jesus Christ.' There can be no other. None other has satisfied the law for man, and none other can plead on his behalf: 'him *only* the Father heareth always.' Jesus Christ the righteous, and none but he, is our 'Advocate with the Father.' This excludes all human merit. This proves that salvation is by grace, and not by works. Repentance, however sincere; reformation, however radical; charity, however munificent; and prayers, however earnest, are in this relation 'refuges of lies.' These things are only duties—they are not, and cannot be atonement for sins that are past. Besides, in all these things, even at their 'best estate,' there is imperfection; and with imperfection of any kind, or in any degree, God, as the just and offended Lawgiver, can have nothing to do. The principle then is,—*none but Christ, and nothing but his one sacrifice of himself,* form the basis on which a guilty sinner can ask, or a holy God grant pardon and acceptance.

IX. FAITH IN THIS GOSPEL PLAN OF MERCY IS THE ONLY AND THE GRACIOUS CONDITION OF SALVATION. 'Without faith it is impossible to please God.' 'He that believeth shall be saved.' Faith is just a simple taking of God at his word, or the acceptance of pardon from him for Christ's sake. This, of course, includes the assent of the understanding to his remedial scheme, the embrace by the heart of his beloved Son as surety, and the consecration of all we have and are from that moment to God's service. Is there merit in this faith? None whatever. It is a condition of *grace* merely, not of *merit.* God *freely* puts belief and pardon together in the economy of grace, and is just as sovereign in this as in the choice and mission of his Son to die in our room. The principle is, 'faith is the gift of God.' He gives his Son, and with him he freely gives all other good things.

X. THERE IS ONE SPIRIT. The Holy Spirit took part with the Father and the Son in the councils of peace, when human redemption was decreed. He is the author of the Bible—for 'holy men of old spake as they were moved by the Holy Ghost.' He is the father of Christ's human nature—for said the angel to his mother, 'The Holy Ghost shall come upon thee, and the power of the Highest shall overshadow thee: wherefore also that holy thing, which shall be born of thee, shall be called the Son of God.' He brings the sinner to Christ, renews the heart, enlightens the mind, and carries forward the work of sanctification, till at death that work is consummated, and the soul is received up into glory. The principle is, 'not by might, nor by power, but by my Spirit, saith the Lord.'

XI. JESUS CHRIST IS THEREFORE THE 'FOUNTAIN OF LIFE.' He is the *head* of the church. From him all spiritual blessings flow. Through him the sinner gets back to God; through him the Holy Ghost reaches conscience, and converts the sinner. The prediction of Zechariah is fulfilled: 'In that day there shall be a fountain opened to the house of David, and to the inhabitants of Jerusalem, for sin and for uncleanness.' Sin, on the other hand, is the fountain of death, out of which are poured upon the world the elements of moral disorder and unutterable woes. It can discharge no other materials. Sin cannot cure sin: death cannot produce life: justification cannot flow from condemnation. From amid this appalling desolation rises up *a fountain of life*—Jesus Christ—to whom all may come and draw thence copious draughts of living water, without money and without price.

The one grand inference which we draw from this magnificent finding is, that there is, after all, to every guilty sinner 'a hiding place from the wind, and a covert from the tempest' of the divine indignation; and this hiding place is '*in Christ Jesus.*' 'There is therefore,' says the apostle, 'now no condemnation to them who are in Christ Jesus.' This phrase, '*in Christ Jesus,*' is very emphatic and comprehensive. You have in it *all* that Christ did for us, and *all* that we must do with him. Contemplating him thus, as the 'all in all' of our salvation, we address him in the beautiful language of the Psalmist, 'THOU ART MY HIDING PLACE.' And such indeed he is to every sinner that flees to him by faith. From the very beginning does the Bible represent him to us in this winning aspect. In the Old Testament, especially, are such titles given to him as cannot fail, if they are spiritually discerned, to fill the mind with adoration and confidence in him as the *all* of a sinner's hope, and the *in all* of the graces of a christian's life. From these titles we make the following selection, for the purpose of opening up the whole subject of the way of salvation, and of imparting to it unity of purpose and variety of illustration. We shall view him as 'JEHOVAH-JESUS,' the Lord our God;—as 'JEHOVAH-JIREH,' the provider of all the good things of the covenant of grace, and of all the loving-kindnesses that overflow the cup of blessing;—as 'JEHOVAH-TSIDKENU,' 'the Lord our righteousness,' the righteousness indeed of every guilty soul, by which it is pardoned, and is at last accepted ;—as 'JEHOVAH-ROPHI,' 'the Lord my healer,' the sanctification of every sin-sick soul, 'the balm of Gilead, and the physician there;'—as 'JEHOVAH-SHALOM,' 'the Lord our peace,' the reconciliation, the pacifier of God towards man, and of man towards God;—as 'JEHOVAH-NISSI,' 'the Lord my banner,' who fights and wins for us all our battles, and who receives the service and the homage of all our hearts and lives;—and as 'JEHOVAH-SHAMMAH,' 'the Lord is there,' everywhere present to bless and to do us good.

Such, then, are the great principles of the christian religion, upon which the illustrations and discussions of the following pages are to be raised; and such are the sublime titles given to the Mediator of the new covenant—'the hiding place' of souls—from which the richness and fulness of his grace are to be proclaimed. Repetition of truth there must be, inasmuch as 'there is no other name under heaven given among men whereby we must be saved.' Notwithstanding there is propriety in concentrating the mind upon such a theme, and in causing it, under a variety of figures and illustrations, to become intimately acquainted with its august, divine, eternal element. The views of our Saviour to be obtained through this treatise shall thus resemble those of the kaleidescope. By the revolutions of this optical instrument, while there is continual change in the arrangement of the pebbles, the pebbles themselves are invariably the same. In like manner, by the successive illustrations of the Mediator's work, through the medium of these new covenant titles, there is afforded endless configurations of truth, though the substance of that truth remains unchanged. To become quite familiar with the gospel plan is a precious attainment which, however, is not to be acquired by a mere occasional or hasty contemplation. It is to be feared that but too many rest satisfied with such a superficial study of its inestimable doctrines; and to counteract the baneful effects of this evil, is one of the objects sought in the present mode of handling the subject.

CHAPTER I.

JEHOVAH.

'I am JEHOVAH, that is my name.'
ISAIAH xlviii. 8.

IN 'looking unto Jesus' as the sinner's 'hiding place,' we are at once invited to the study of that mysterious Being who is revealed in scripture as the supreme and independent Deity. It is of himself that Jehovah speaks when he says, 'My people have committed two evils; they have forsaken me, the fountain of living waters, and have hewed them out cisterns, broken cisterns, that can hold no water.' By the beautiful figure of this text we are to understand all the blessings of Christ's salvation; and it is clear that every one of these must be traced to the speaker as their procuring cause, or the source from which they flow. And who is he who thus charges his people with sin? He is called the Lord, or Jehovah. Now, as Jesus Christ is the 'author and finisher of our faith,' and as Jehovah here claims to be the fountain of life, we must infer that the Jesus of the New, is the Jehovah of the Old Testament.

This is an august theme; and when we sit down to study it, there cannot be a more appropriate prayer than that of the psalmist, 'Open thou mine eyes, that I may behold wondrous things out of thy law.' The 'wondrous thing' to be sought for at present is, not the silent and vital stream, but the remote and hidden source of spiritual life in the soul; it is not the light itself, but the Father of lights; it is not man under grace, nor yet grace in man, but the God of all grace himself. And who is sufficient for this? We are but the creatures of a day, and this is He who 'inhabiteth eternity.' We are the children of darkness, and know nothing, and this is he who 'dwelleth in light that is inaccessible.' We cannot 'see God and live;' and yet here we are invited to the contemplation of that awful Being whom 'the heaven of heavens cannot contain,' and who is of 'purer eyes than to behold iniquity.' Notwithstanding, this 'wondrous thing' we must search for; and if we do so under the guidance of scripture, and with humble and docile minds, we are sure to be rewarded with such a sight of Him whose name is Jehovah, as shall thrill us with joy unspeakable, and inspire us with hope that 'maketh not ashamed.' Let us then consider the following points:—

I. THE NAME OF GOD IS JEHOVAH. It is the name given to him in the Bible, and it is peculiar to the Bible. Its meaning is, *underived, necessary, and eternal existence.* The other names applied to God in the scripture are official, or expressive of some of his perfections; but Jehovah is his incommunicable name, and is descriptive of that which is, and must be, his especial Deity. Elsewhere he calls himself 'I am that I am,' which means, 'I exist because I exist.' He cannot but exist; and for that existence he is dependent upon none, being in this, as in everything else, absolutely sovereign.

The critical student of the original Hebrew discovers that another name is given by Moses to the Deity, kindred to, but not identical with, Jehovah— a name, indeed, which is anterior to that of Jehovah, and which is not necessarily of an economical character. This is the name ELOHIM, which is just the abstract term for *Deity,* irrespective of anything that may be revealed concerning his nature or works. It is only when we come to the divine intercourse with man that we are permitted to think of him as *Jehovah.* Before any creature whatever existed, he is Elohim; even after man is formed and has fallen, he is Elohim. But when he condescends to break silence upon his purpose of mercy through an atonement, then he appears as the 'Jehovah.' Let this be well considered. The *revealed* name of God is Jehovah; that is, this is the name which, from the very first of his gracious manifestations to man, he took to himself. Does not this place in a most delightful and encouraging juxtaposition the *Deity* and the *Redeemer?* It is also noticeable that Moses uses these two names quite discriminately—in no instance arbitrarily. He uses *Elohim* when he refers to *Deity,* and he uses *Jehovah* when he represents the Deity in gracious fellowship with man.

The name Jehovah directs attention to certain attributes which exclusively belong to Deity. He is a being who never began to exist. He exists of necessity. He must exist for ever. He is that God who 'was, and is, and is to come.' He 'was' in all the past; he 'is' in all the present; and he 'is to come,' or exists, in all the future. His existence is not affected by what is called time, for he exists in '*an everlasting now.*' We cannot associate *succession* with his being. There is a difference between the eternal existence of angels and that of God. Theirs regards only the future, whereas his embraces both the future and the past. Hence the words of the man of God: 'Before the mountains were brought forth, or ever thou hadst formed the earth and the world, from everlasting to everlasting thou art God.'

II. THE NAME JEHOVAH IS REVEALED FOR A SPECIAL OBJECT. It was intended to convey to man some impression of the Elohim's purposes of mercy to him. Hence, in speaking to Moses, God says: 'I appeared unto Abraham, unto Isaac, and unto Jacob by the name of God Almighty; but by my name *Jehovah* was I not known to them.' In this language there appears to be reference to the *gradual* mode of unfolding himself as the God of salvation—faint and comparatively indistinct at first to the patriarchs, a little more clear and specific to the Jewish church, and next to a perfect or full-orbed disclosure in the gospel times. To the patriarchs there is the one grand idea of 'God Almighty,' enshrined behind some awful and unapproachable cloud. Before the eye of the Jews this cloud partially separates, and a special condescendence reveals *one* of the persons of Elohim, who takes the name of *Jehovah*. Under that name he is to be worshipped, by that name he is to be appropriated, and in that name he and they are to covenant together: 'You only,' he says to Israel, 'have I known (or appropriated) of all the families of the earth.'

III. THE NAME JEHOVAH IS GIVEN TO THE MESSIAH. In some scriptures it is applied to the first and third persons of the Godhead. It is much oftener very pointedly and emphatically given to the Messiah, or to him whom we know and love as the Lord Jesus Christ; in other words, the Jesus of the New, is the Jehovah of the Old Testament. This is one of the solid and indestructible foundations on which we build our faith in the supreme divinity of our Saviour. He is God as well as man, because he is called in scripture '*Jehovah*,' a name which cannot be applied to any mere creature. We know him to be the 'Mediator of the new covenant;' and what therefore can be conceived more probable than that he should act and be revealed in this character, even from the 'councils of peace' downward? Hence he appears in the very beginning as Creator, for by him we know 'all things were made;' then he is seen as '*the Word*,' in the intimations of mercy which he gave to our first parents immediately after they fell; then he holds from generation to generation those interesting interviews with patriarchal families, which serve as forerunners to the Mosaic organisation; and then, from prophet to prophet, he communicates more and more clearly his advent and atonement as the promised 'seed of the woman.' The scriptural proofs here are very valuable. There is a very interesting emendation of the common translation of the words of Eve at the birth of Cain. She said, 'I have gotten a man from the Lord,' which should be rendered, 'I have gotten *a man-Jehovah*.' It is probable that our first parents associated the promised seed with Deity, and on the sight of this first and beautiful infant, Eve gives expression to her hopes that *now* this *divine Saviour* was born. Again, in those passages in which he is spoken of as 'the angel of the Lord,' the literal meaning is 'the angel-Jehovah,' or 'Jehovah-angel;' or, that he who was the person sent was also the person sending—that the sender was Jehovah, and Jehovah was the messenger. It was '*the angel-Jehovah*' that appeared to Moses in the burning bush of Horeb, and said to him, 'I am the God of thy father, the God of Abraham, the God of Isaac, and the God of Jacob.' In Isaiah he is represented as thus addressing his people: 'Thus saith the Lord thy Redeemer, the Holy One of Israel, *I am the Lord thy God.*' In examining the context of this passage, we find that this same person claims to be 'the first and the last,' and to have laid 'the foundation of the earth,' while yet he represents himself as being 'the messenger of the Lord Jehovah and his Spirit,'—words which the best critics explain as conveying the information, that the person sending and the person sent is alike *Jehovah*. In the forty-third chapter of this same book he proclaims himself thus: 'I, even I, am *Jehovah*, and beside me there is no Saviour.' By Isaiah he is called '*Jehovah* our righteousness,' and in Zechariah he says, 'They shall look upon me, *Jehovah*, whom they have pierced.'

It is remarkable that there are only *two* passages in scripture where the *first* person of the Godhead is said to speak; in those, namely, where the baptism and the transfiguration of Christ are narrated. It has been inferred from this, that in all other passages where God is represented as speaking, we must understand them of the *Son*. Jesus Christ, then, must be God, for he is Jehovah; and God says, 'I am Jehovah, that is my name, and my glory I will not give to another.' Yes, delightful truth! Jesus is the Lord our God, the Elohim who alone should be worshipped, and the Jehovah who has been revealed in order to be worshipped; in short, the 'man-Jehovah,' or the Lord incarnate, by whom we have access to, and through whom we have power with, the Father. Thus the idea of Deity becomes inseparable from the idea of Mediator between God and man. In that mediation there must be God, not approving or accepting merely, but God himself actually making and offering the atonement. This necessarily produces the thought of there being friendship or mercy in the Elohim or Deity for sinful man, which is just the evangelical meaning of these words, 'I am the Lord *thy* God.' He is the revelation of God as the God of love, and is in this respect the only 'image of the invisible God' to us. It is not the *power* of that God that he reflects, but his smile; it is not the menace that he proclaims, but the promise; it is not the law that he commands, but the gospel.

Upon this one sublime principle rises the magnificent structure of Christianity. To see and admit this truth is indispensable to salvation. Sin has withdrawn us from our Creator, hence its evil and our misery. But it is the object of the remedial scheme to deliver us from both. In order to do so, the power and the disposition to worship and love God must be restored; and this can never be accomplished except by our believing that the Lord Jesus Christ is at one and the same time 'the Lord our God.' It was commanded in heaven, 'let all the angels worship him;'

and we know that on earth he received homage of men. Now in so doing, he taught men, and won them to himself; he taught them to worship God, and won them over to himself as Jehovah, or God revealed; this being the very object for which man was at first created, and is redeemed. It is scarcely possible not to be overcome by the contemplation of such a sublime piece of heavenly wisdom as this. To be unimpressed by it is a proof of ignorance and alienation from God, which is indeed the natural condition of man. If, then, we be at all desirous to rise from it, and be again upon the happiest and holiest terms of friendship with our Maker, we must anticipate all by believing that Jesus is Jehovah, that he who was born of Mary was also the only-begotten of the Father; yea, 'the brightness of the Father's glory, and the very image of his person;' in other words, 'Lord over all, and blessed for ever.'

'Without controversy, great is the mystery of godliness; God was manifest in the flesh.' Without controversy, let us add, great also and unspeakably important is this doctrine of the divinity and humanity of our Lord, alike to our understanding of and our comfort in the Bible. We lay it down as the foundation principle of the whole system of redemption; we point to it as the 'hiding place' to the souls of men, and we glory in it as the very charm and essence of the divine pity for lost souls. It has been well said, that 'there is no such book of contradictions as the Bible, if there be no person who was both human and divine. Nothing but such a combination will make sense of the Bible, or rescue it from maintaining a vast mass of inconsistencies. Some may think that it would simplify the christian theology to remove from it the mystery that two natures coalesced in the one person of Christ; but as the divinity of our Lord is the foundation of our hope, so is it the key to the Bible. We acknowledge, reverently, a great mystery, but not the thousandth part as great as the whole Bible becomes on the supposition that Christ was only man.'*

* Henry Melville.

CHAPTER II.

JEHOVAH-JESUS: THE LORD OUR GOD.

'I am the Lord thy God.'
Exod. xx. 2.

It is impossible to exaggerate the misery of a guilty conscience. When allowed to rise upon the sinner in all its terrific power, the darkness that sets in upon him is 'darkness that may be felt,' and the hopelessness that grasps his heart is despair in agony. There is a God, and he believes it; there is a law of that God, and he has broken it; there is a penalty, even death itself, attached to the breach of that law, and he has incurred it. What shall he then do? He cannot appease the wrath of the Lawgiver; the idea of atonement he cannot form, for that is an idea which must be posterior to the revelation of the purpose of mercy. His first thought is to arise and hide himself from the presence of God; and he hides himself—so he thinks for the moment—till conscience calls aloud to him to look around, and then he sees that he is seen: 'Whither,' he exclaims, 'shall I go from thy Spirit? or whither shall I flee from thy presence?

If I say, Surely the darkness shall cover me, even the night shall be light about me; yea, the darkness hideth not from thee, but the night shineth as the day; the darkness and the light are both alike to thee.'

What can pacify such an accusing conscience as this? It is evident that nothing whatever can do so but a reply from that sin-avenging Deity, assuring the sinner of his continued friendship, and of his purpose to pardon him in a way most harmonious with all his perfections. Has the sinner, then, received such a reply? He undoubtedly has. Behold him *hiding!* He fears the divine approach; the tread of *Jehovah's* foot in the garden makes him tremble exceedingly. He hears the voice of God, and prepares for the execution of the sentence, 'The soul that sinneth it shall die.' When, hark! what sound is this which falls upon his ear? its accent is kindly, its note is love; and lo, what stream of light is this which enters his retreat? It is the ray of God's smile, the dawn of God's mercy. Now is the birth-time of Hope; she speaks but in a whisper, still the very movement of her lips tells that God is coming, more in pity than in anger—that He, and pardon, and reconciliation are all on the ground together, and that soon the guilty and terror-stricken shall be reassured and at peace. The silence is at length broken, and these glorious words are irrevocably placed in the everlasting covenant, 'I AM THE LORD THY GOD.'

I am indeed Jehovah, whose kindness has been abused and whose law has been violated; but, notwithstanding, 'I am the Lord thy God;' I am still thy friend; yea, I am thy Saviour from sin and all its woes; I, even I alone, am thy 'hiding place.' Such is the aspect which the doctrine of the Incarnation at first presents to the mind. Here is Jehovah himself. True, he appears in the likeness of sinful flesh—he obeys, suffers, and dies; notwithstanding, this Jesus is Jehovah—this is God in our nature—this is *Jehovah-Jesus in our stead.* The knowledge and belief of this give assurance to the sinner, that after all that has occurred, in God himself he has still a friend. Now, as the divinity of Christ is the very essence of christian doctrine, so the idea on the guilty mind that the Deity is friendly to its pardon, is the very life of its repentance, and the very soul of its movement towards holiness and heaven. In other words, as it is the harsh and despairing thought of God that maintains hatred to and fear of him, so it is the gospel thought of his compassion, and the gospel belief that 'God is love,' that restores confidence and ensures peace. We see, then,

I. IN JEHOVAH BECOMING JESUS, THE ASSURANCE IS GIVEN THAT GOD HIMSELF IS THE SINNER'S FRIEND. How can it be otherwise? Behold *he* comes to us in our low and lost estate, and yet there is no frown upon that look—no curse from that lip—no sword in that hand—no fire in that train. He passes by, but the 'time is a time of love,' and he drops into the soul the seed of the tree of life, as he says, 'I am the Lord thy God.' Pardon, then, is not only probable; it is certain. The Lawgiver himself has come to obey his own law, and in the end he suffers its penalty, though 'he knew no sin.' Such is the strongest of all proofs that God is 'not willing that any should perish, but that all should return unto him and live.' If this do not beget hope in the sinner, he must remain for ever the child of despair. God can do no more than this—can add no more to evidence like this. Our Redeemer is now in heaven, at once the pledge of the divine acceptance of his sacrifice, and of their perfect safety who offer it to God for their own sins. Man cannot now be forgotten in heaven. The Lamb that was slain is his memorial there. Our great High Priest has the most exalted of all natures, and is the best of all beings, and therefore it seems but suitable that the vilest of all men can be saved by this the greatest of beings, and that the chief of sinners may hope, when the Lord of angels has died for him.

What proof can be added to this? Do you say, let us *see* Jesus, and let us *hear* him saying, 'I am the Lord thy God,' then we will believe? We reply— He has been seen and heard already by competent witnesses when he sojourned among men, and you have their testimony written on the inspired page.

Do you rejoin—We would have the full assurance of God's friendship within ourselves? Why have you it not? This is your sin as well as your loss. How ungrateful and how profane to doubt the divine interest in you—an interest written in letters of love upon every page of the Bible! If that evidence does not convince you, neither would you believe though upon the blue firmament it were written in letters of electric light, or upon the black arch of midnight, in letters of living fire. No, you would not believe though Moses and all the prophets, Stephen and all the martyrs, Paul and all the apostles, were to re-appear and re-assert that God is now the friend of man for Christ's sake, and that 'if any man sin, he has an advocate with the Father, Jesus Christ the righteous.' The important, indeed the awful fact of the case is, that the whole story of the divine friendship for man is wrapped up in the small but precious volume of the gospel; there we have it, and there alone. This method of assuring the sinner may be offensive to his natural pride, but God will never consent to gratify any craving after glorious signs in the heavens or marvellous signs on the earth. We must listen to it in the 'still small voice' of the simple truth as it is in Jesus; we must take it on his bare word, and be as persuaded of his sincere and precious love for us, as if no sin had ever alienated us from him, as if there was no law to be pacified nor any penalty to be endured.

II. IN THE FRIENDSHIP OF GOD SINFUL MEN HAVE IN THEIR OFFER THE MOST PRECIOUS OF ALL BLESSINGS. This is not the opinion of the unrenewed mind. Sin has perverted the judgment and reversed in it every truthful proposition. God is regarded as an enemy; holiness is offensive, and the divine favour is despised. Hence men act a corresponding part; they seek to forget God, they indulge in sin, and search for happiness everywhere but in the loving-kindness of their Maker. It is a most melancholy thought that there is not one instance of success on record; every man has failed. Pretended success there has been, but it is a dream; there is a worm that never dies, and there is a fire that is never quenched within them, while they depend for happiness upon the contributions of this vain world. Admitting that all is gained that is sought after, the 'one thing needful' to make the soul happy is awanting—conscience is not appeased—sin is not pardoned—the sense of God's love is not felt. These are fearful wants, covering as with a deadly shade every possession, causing perpetual restlessness in every faculty, and agitating without abatement the dread question, 'What shall I do to be saved?' It was natural to be happy when the soul was holy, but now that the soul is in sin, this is unnatural; this opposes first principles and contravenes the original law of our constitution. A human soul can no more be happy without the favour of God, than a human body can be comfortable with raging disease and racking pain. Is he not a fool who calculates on safety while he carries fire in his bosom—or on health while he inhales infection—or on riches while he folds his hands in sloth? And what is he who expects peace within, while he stirs up wars against God, casts and keeps him out of his heart, and woos and weds sin as his dearest associate? He must be the victim of delusion; for certain it is, that, separated from God, the sinner is a 'wretched man.' He may not be conscious of it, for sin is an opiate, and deadens moral sensibility; sin is a poison, and kills spiritual life; sin is a lie, and deceives all who trust in it. But this opiate by and by loses its power, and sensibility returns; this poison loses its virus, and consciousness is restored; this lie has its hour, and the delusion vanishes. The re-appearance of *truth* on the dark canopy of a sinner's death-bed is indeed a frightful vision. The farce of life is now played out; the spiritual delirium comes on apace, and in the agonies of an unpurged conscience he discovers the hollowness of the world, and admits the great and indestructible truth of the exclusive adaptation of the soul's happiness to a sense of the divine friendship. The worldling himself is often a reluctant witness here, when he is heard reproving mammon and pleasure for befooling him. It is truly a pitiful sight, when even he spits upon his minion slaves, and kicks away from him the ladders on which he would have clambered to independence, and howls over the beggarly return of a lifetime's labour, as beasts of prey do when they scour the forest and find no food.

There are many unsolved enigmas in human life, and this is one of them,—the difficulty of getting men to believe that God is their friend, and that they cannot be happy till they rest in that conviction. This is indeed a puzzle, which only becomes more intricate from the consideration that this very friendship of God, which they will not have, is the most precious of blessings. It cost God more than a thought or a word. Nothing he has ever done for or given to any creature has cost him so much as this. He gave away himself for it. He simply passed his word, and men were formed and reason was bestowed; but to restore to them his favour after it had been forfeited, his own blood must flow on his own altar. In itself his *friendship* is our highest honour. All other relationships, honours, and possessions, are poor compared with it. These must be surrendered at death, but this is to last for ever; and after sanctifying all other connections, sweetening every earthly trial, dignifying every position in life, and enriching the poorest lots, this will speak peace for us in our extreme hours, and after death, will gladden and glorify us with the unclouded vision of God himself.

III. To appropriate the friendship of God is therefore the first duty, as it is the highest privilege of man. Jehovah-Jesus says,

'I am the Lord thy God.' It is our duty to reply with Thomas, 'My Lord and my God.' Surely what *He* offers, a sinner should take, though it were but a crumb of bread. And when he offers *himself*, there should be instant appropriation. No silly hesitation, no weak cavilling, no muttered excuses are admissible here, for salvation and consolation await the belief of this sublime gospel. This idea of *appropriation* was more frequently elucidated in the days of our fathers than it is now. We hope that it will soon return to favour, for it is just the very marrow of genuine piety. 'All consolation in religion,' says Wilkinson, ' is connected with appropriation.' Many will say, 'Lord, Lord,' but it is not the privilege of many to say with Thomas, '*my* Lord and *my* God.' What is it all worth to the poor guilty sinner if this God be not *his* God? God must either be for him or against him; if against him, then perish he must; if for him, then why not embrace him at once in the soul's affectionate belief? Why refuse to say, 'this God is *my* God?' Read the sayings of the godly :—' I know that *my* Redeemer liveth,' said Job; ' the Lord is *my* salvation, and *my* God,' said David ; '*my* beloved is *mine*,' said the spouse ; ' He loved *me*, and gave himself for *me*,' said Paul.

The warrant to appropriate is the same to all, even the authority of God himself: '*I am the Lord thy God.*' Who, then, dares dispute it? He alone knows the state of his own heart, and as he is the God of truth, as well as the God of love, our assent to his declarations ought to be immediate and hearty. It is true, we are not worthy of such an unparalleled blessing. Still, if he be willing to give *himself* to us, it becomes us to take him at his word. How inspiriting is this to a good man! Not only is he innocent of presumption in the matter, but it is positively his duty to take Jehovah for his God—his friend, 'his buckler, and the horn of his salvation.' In this view, it becomes a sin not to appropriate the divine favour. Surely it must ever be right to obey God, to believe in Christ, to get the precious soul into amiable relationship with its own Father, and ever right to secure, through this union, all the benefits that accompany or flow from the redemption purchased by the blood of his Son.

It is our highest privilege to 'avouch' Jehovah-Jesus for our God. 'The beauty of scripture,' said Luther, 'consists in pronouns.' O! blessed above compare is that man who can use the '*my*' and the '*me*' of appropriation in reply to the '*thy*' and the '*thee*' of the covenant. Is it not, indeed, a precious state of mind to have *unbelief* banished from it? It is; and such is the state of that man's mind who gives God a welcome when he comes to him in the kindness of his love. It is peculiar to unbelief to put God away, to refuse to open when he knocks, and to despise his gifts when offered. Is it not a valuable attainment, then, to feel *personally* interested in the great salvation? It is; and such is the attainment of every appropriator. There is a 'holy selfishness' in his closing with Christ's 'giving love,' for belief is necessarily, in the first instance, selfish. It takes mercy *to itself*, and the feeling that it is rich in that mercy is a foretaste of heaven. There is no impropriety in such a selfishness as this: would God every sinner had it!—for then every sinner would himself be saved, and the selfishness of sin would flee away before the rising orb of universal love.

IV. TO REFUSE THE DIVINE FRIENDSHIP IS, THEREFORE, THE MOST HEINOUS SIN MEN COMMIT. It is the capital crime under the christian dispensation: 'If any man love not the Lord Jesus Christ, let him be Anathema Maran-atha.' Men have perpetrated great crimes; crimes of rampant and dominant wickedness; crimes which make us feel that where sinners dwell, devils dwell, and that where sin is, hell is not distant; crimes, at the very mention of which the delicate mind shrinks back, and the noble spirit of humanity rises up in wrath; crimes which most men conceive it impossible for them to commit, and which must ever remain unmeasurable and indescribable till a plummet has been found to sound the bottomless, and some fiend has appeared capable of the revolting analysis. Can it be that there is a character of crime, a phasis of sin, outdistancing such extremities? There is; and all have it who refuse to take the Lord for their God. All sins are, no doubt, against God, but there is a speciality in the antagonism of this one, which stamps it with peculiar enormity. Surely there is daring insult in the contemptuous rejection of his marvellous love, boundless mercy, and unmatched condescendence. We cannot think charitably of treason within the sanctuary of the heart's affections and claims. We feel righteous indignation at ingratitude among men, and do not hesitate to hiss it out of our sight. If it be so in the nature of man, how think you is it in the nature of God? If created love, if finite kindness, if vitiated moral sympathies, such as ours, thus feel towards the scornful rejection of our overtures of kindness, what must be the grief, the hurt, the anger of the uncreated, the infinite, and the Holy One, who comes from his 'secret place' to sing of mercy rather than of judgment; and who, in all his dealings with his rebellious creatures, condescends, on the basis of a finished atonement, to beseech them to be 'reconciled!' Is it so that He has done all *he* could do in the way of scheming, and working, and suffering, and dying; that he has added for men's benefit every beautiful and blissful mean of grace, and constituted every one of his providences as co-operators with himself in completing their happiness; and is it so, that, notwithstanding all this, they trample his gifts under the foot of unbelief, or merely gambol with them from the hand of hypocrisy into that of formalism? How, then, can it be otherwise, but that fearfulness shall surprise, and unfaithfulness bring upon them swift destruction? How often are 'the terrors of the Lord' seen upon such gospel despisers in this world! They are left to judicial blindness; they have eyes, but they see not—to judicial deafness; they have ears, but they hear not—to judicial hardness; they have hearts, but they feel not—to judicial searedness; they have consciences, but they sting not. Is there not enough in this to make any man pause and ponder? Who is more to be pitied than the poor blind man, who walks amid the grandeurs of creation, but sees neither smile on the face of God nor beauty on the fields of nature;—or than the deaf man, on whose ear the winning cadences of affection's voice never fall, and who knows not the joy that charming music gives;—or than the heartless man, who never gave and never received a blessing, to whom the sweets of kindness are as bitters, and from whom all the best emotions keep sternly apart;—or than the petrified wretch, who can do all manner of cruelty, and never own to one pang of remorse, to one blush of shame? What is more pitiful? *Your* condition, O despiser of the kindness of God in Jesus Christ,—your condition is far more pitiful than any, or than all of these. You are in the midst of God's tender mercies, and yet you 'see no beauty in them that they should be desired;' you are serenaded with the gospel halels of heaven's own orchestra, and yet you hear them not; you are near, very near, to

Gethsemane and Calvary, and know their blood, their agony, their cries, their death, and yet you pale not, weep not, repent not. The wisdom of the Godhead, the processions of everlasting love, the very incarnation of divine compassion, and the whole appliances of high heaven for your soul's redemption, go for nothing with you, and are disregarded as the idle paraphernalias of a vain show. Be induced to think over such a sin as this; the iniquity of it is very great. Be not deceived: you may be a kind father or mother, amiable in disposition, courteous in manners, honest in business, useful in society, and perhaps of influence within the church itself; but if you have never taken, by solemn and believing covenant, the Lord to be your God; if his friendship be not prized and accepted, and if you are not, under its powerful attractions, drawn into intimate communion with him, and led into those paths of piety and philanthropy wherein the followers of God are found—then in this sin you are living; and if in this sin you die, you are lost for ever.

These pages being written to persuade the unthinking to believe in the loving-kindness of Jehovah, to cast away not only indifference, but all fears as to his merciful intentions, and to lie down and take quiet rest to their souls in the rich pastures of gospel grace and truth, we must now, in order to this, proceed to strike the rock from whence all living waters flow; to call in and detail the evidence that the great 'I am' has made most ample provision for the spiritual needs of the whole world, and to employ all the ordinary evangelical remonstrances with the thoughtless and the Christless, that they no longer betake themselves to 'refuges of lies,' but unto Jesus as their 'HIDING PLACE,' singing as they gaze and flee,

> 'Rock of Ages! cleft for me,
> Let me *hide* myself in Thee;
> Let the water and the blood,
> From thy riven side which flowed,
> Be of sin the double cure;
> Save me from its guilt and power.

> 'Not the labour of my hands
> Can fulfil the Law's demands:
> Could my zeal no respite know,
> Could my tears for ever flow,
> All for sin could not atone;
> Thou must save, and Thou alone.

> 'While I draw this fleeting breath,
> When mine eyelids close in death
> When I soar to worlds unknown,
> See Thee on thy Judgment throne;
> Rock of Ages! cleft for me,
> Let me hide myself in Thee.'

CHAPTER III.

JEHOVAH-JIREH: THE LORD WILL PROVIDE.

PART I.

'And Abraham called the name of that place Jehovah-Jireh; that is, The Lord will provide.'

GEN. xxii. 14.

GOD IS LOVE. Such is the Bible account of the divine nature. The words fall very sweetly upon the ear. The description is alike comforting and encouraging. This abstract idea of God, however, is not enough for sinful men. It may be very true that 'God is love,' but the question occurs, Does he love us—and if so, where is the proof? It were only to tantalise us to let it be known that in our Creator there was abundance of friendship, while no embodiment of that friendship was offered to our reception. The name given to him by Abraham when the ram caught in the thicket was most seasonably provided for a sacrifice, suggests such answers to the question as cannot fail to be satisfactory. This God of love is JEHOVAH-JIREH, HE 'WILL PROVIDE;' not only does he pity his children in their wants, but he supplies these wants,—the whole of them,—and that both for body and for soul, for time and eternity. This title, therefore, is alike applicable to God in his dispensations of providence and of grace. We shall proceed to illustrate this:—

I. IT IS APPLICABLE TO HIM IN HIS DISPENSATIONS OF PROVIDENCE. We are emphatically dependent creatures—dependent because our existence is derived. This truth is not affected by our moral condition; it applies to every creature, whether holy or guilty—to Adam before, as well as after the fall. It is as true of an angel as of a devil. This condition of dependence, therefore, is not originally a sinful one. We cannot tell whether, if sin had not entered, man would have had, in any degree, suspense or anxiety about the future, but certainly sin must have effected a very serious change both in the matter and in the feeling of his dependence. By losing every claim on God's kindness, its sphere is enlarged, and a new element entirely is added to the feeling; it may be racking solicitude, or fear, or despair. How emphatic are the words of the curse pronounced upon Adam!* The labour was to be painful, and the very enjoyment of it was to be embittered with sorrow. All those griefs, then, that go amongst us under the name of 'worldly cares and anxieties,' must be traced

* Gen. iii. 17.

to sin; they are parts of the curse, or the fruits of transgression. Man would have had more than it was God's will to give him, and henceforth man shall be tormented with the fear that he shall have less even than what God actually provides. Putting these two things together—our dependence and our guilt—we may expect to find man everywhere an unhappy creature, and prone to apprehensions of evil—in short, of an unquiet spirit.

This natural anxiety has its accessories; these are the observation and experience of the vicissitudes of life, and our conscious unworthiness. Every day produces illustrations of the original curse. We see that man himself is not abiding, and that the whole fashion of this world is unstable. We live in a Sodom, where wickedness of all kinds abounds. Our holiday is a vanity fair where everything is vexation of spirit; we see our fellows daily carried to the grave, and the mourners going about the streets; we see the most flattering hopes disappointed, the most stately structures overturned, wealth becoming poor, and poverty becoming rich, and hard labour and honest industry making nothing of it, either for present demands or future needs. Furthermore, we discover that judicious plans, prudent policies, economical habits, and unwearied patience, do not necessarily ensure success, and that often after a protracted prosperity, disaster and ruin bring up the rear of life. Even virtuous activity says, there is no certainty, and merry-laughing vice alone seems to be careless,—but hers is the caper and cantrip of a maniac, and ends the same. Nor does it alleviate the anxieties hence begotten, to notice that whereas the good and upright among men often toil hard and gain little, the idle and unprincipled do little and gain much. This extraordinary providence only adds weight to the fear, that if want does not await us, we are continually liable to it. And then, there is this *conscience*, that 'makes cowards of us all,' for ever whispering that we have not a vestige of claim on the divine clemency, and that at any moment, and in any circumstances, God should only be acting righteously if he were to leave us to become the victims of every ill of life. In vain we seek relief from others—all are under the same condemnation, for all 'have sinned.' But let the origin and analysis of worldly solicitudes be what they may, one thing is sure, not one is free from them; they grieve our very existence, and embitter such bounties of providence as we have. Here is the catalogue of them from the mouth of Christ himself: 'What shall we eat, and what shall we drink, and wherewithal shall we be clothed?' Such are the staple of human anxieties, the carnal powers that move the human machine, the moral tenantry that possess and work the human heart, the irresistible levers that stir the globe.

The most painful element in this worldly-mindedness is the utter disregard which it implies of the very existence of God, and consequently the withdrawment of all confidence in him as the friend of sinners. Is this not bordering upon Atheism? There might indeed be no God for any good the doctrine of his existence does to such minds. They pant, toil, and sweat as if it all depended on themselves, as if God were a fiction, and providence a farce. In this mental imbecility we have one of the most humiliating proofs of the fall; for what can be conceived more deplorable than a state of feeling in the creature, where the very idea of a God becomes useless, and where He is indeed entirely forgotten, or if remembered, is rather repugnant than attractive? Contrast with this the ready opening of the same mind to the idea, that for mere moral or spiritual blessings some degree of dependence may be had on God, but that for temporal and perishing mercies, it cannot be that He should be implicitly trusted. What a sad reversal of the famous argument of Paul, 'He that spared not his own Son, but delivered him up for us all, how shall he not with him also freely give us all things?' and what an equally profane antagonism to the sublime proposition of our Lord, 'If ye then, being evil, know how to give good gifts to your children, how much more shall your Father who is in heaven give good things to them that ask him?' We present, then, this new covenant title of our Lord, 'Jehovah-Jireh,' as an answer to all unbelieving cares about this life.'

(1.) *He alone can provide.* A dependant like man cannot be his own provider. For many earthly good things he depends on the laws of nature—on the light and heat of the sun, on the rain and dews of heaven, and on the fertility of the soil. Now these laws are God's laws, and these things are God's property. If he suspend any of these laws, where is the provision? Then as to the providences called *events*, all of them are under his control: 'The lot is cast into the lap, but the disposal thereof is the Lord's. Even things meant for evil he converts into good, and things meant for good into evil. If he were not at the helm, everything would get into confusion; for it is his wisdom, power, and love that manage all things well. Bad as it is, God has not yet withdrawn from our world: his providence still presides over men and their affairs.

(2.) *He alone has provided.* There is something very sublime in the thought, that in all the past all things 'have lived, and moved, and had their being in God;' 'by him all things consist,' and, he 'preserveth man and beast. When an epitome of animal and rational creation was shut up in the ark, all were provided for by him. This ark is the world—the universe in miniature. The universe is just one vast enclosure of animate or inanimate being, constantly maintained out of his parental bounty. Hence all the past providences of God are illustrations of the faithfulness of Jehovah-Jireh. Every good gift in its own place, in its own season, and for its own end, has come down from him. No creature of God has ever had just cause of complaint against him. Certainly there is want, and many are in misery, but folly and reckless disregard of God's will are the causes thereof. To associate discomfort or destitution with defects in the principles of a supreme and sovereign government, may be natural to us, but in this connection it is most iniquitous. It ought never to be forgotten, that if God had had his will, all his creatures should have continued perfectly happy; and even yet, if they would only give him his will with them, he would speedily bring order out of confusion, and joy out of grief. If there be a chaos anywhere in matter or in mind, this cometh not from the Lord. Nature, it is said, abhors a vacuum; so does Jehovah. To him it is grievous to see want where he arranged for plenty, and tears bedewing the cheek on which he impressed the smile of contentment. It is no pleasure to him to hear the cry of distress, where he expected the song of gratitude, and to receive the groanings of grumbling, instead of the offerings of gratified children. To read aright the character of God from the past history of providence, we should find that so far as his plans have been adopted, there has been abundance provided for man of all good things for all necessary purposes.

(3.) *He now provides.* Let the present exigency be what it may, direst poverty or deepest distress,

God himself *is* 'ever a present help.' He has always supply at hand for every want and woe. Of his grace it is written, not that it *may* be, or *shall* be, but that it '*is* sufficient.' In those laws of benevolence which he has framed, and in those principles of sympathy which he has implanted in our natures, he has stored up an abundance of consolation for man even in his neediest condition. But after all, when the heart has been taught to choose himself as its portion, *in him* it has always its chiefest property and choicest joy. Does this seem to mock the ills of life, the griefs of humanity, the devastation of fond hopes, and the rivers of tears that run down the pilgrim's cheek? It really does not do so, inasmuch as there is actually provided for the unhappy, what is in itself sufficient for present straits; and if they have lost the way to, or their taste for God, this only corroborates our proposition. If, when the night is at the darkest, and the storm is at its height; if, when every source appears to be dried up, and all props to have given way; if, when the spirit of a man is made to feel as if *alone* in some vast and dreary solitude of condition; if, we say, the most miserable of beings would only then and there open his eyes to what a kind Father provides, he would see even in the wilderness of Beersheba an encompassing angel and streams of water; Baca itself is made a well, and 'the rain also filleth the pools.'

(4.) *He will provide.* The fears of a dependant

naturally wend into futurity—a futurity which may never be reached, and which, though reached, may be found innocent of the apprehended ills. It is man *as he is,* to forecast his own destiny. It is man *as he ought to be,* to 'take no thought for to-morrow.' God cannot change. That fatherly care that has supplied in the past, has also provided resources for the future. To these, however, many refuse to go. They suspend themselves upon torturing solicitude. And yet they know that it is God's nature to be kind. He has purposed to be generous, for 'his anger is turned away' from sinners, *in Christ.* Yea, it is his actual work to have perpetually ready for his children, all that may be required for help and comfort. It is equally wicked, then, to doubt the purposes of his goodness for the coming exigencies, as it is to deny that in all the past he has been proved to be 'the faithful promiser.' Most men are prone, notwithstanding, to use their *future* as if it were some portentous horizon upon which fancy may draw deep and deadly the shadows of nearing calamity. They exist among self-created spectres, and by an unnatural effort to live over that future in the present, they are the pitiful victims of a poverty that never comes, and of changes they are never to see. But man may rest assured that what God has done, he shall do, and that what he has been, he will ever be; for he is 'the same yesterday, to-day, and for ever.' The most impressive sermon Jesus ever preached gives point and emphasis to this view of providence; while, at the same time, there never was read to timid, distrusting man, such a rebuke for his little faith. With what admirable propriety did the great Teacher summon 'the lilies of the field,' and 'the birds of the air,' to testify against 'worldly anxieties!'*

II. 'JEHOVAH-JIREH' IS ESPECIALLY APPLICABLE TO GOD IN HIS DISPENSATIONS OF GRACE. Man has greater wants than what pertain to the body. He has a soul—a precious and deathless soul; and yet that soul is 'dead in trespasses and in sins.' His greatest want, then, is a Saviour for that soul. All other wants are absolutely as nothing. So important is this one, that in relation to its requirements Jesus himself said, 'one thing is needful.' So peculiarly great, indeed, is his *spiritual* necessity, that not one solitary point in its awful vastness is supplied by all the riches, pleasures, and honours of time. Heaps of such things upon a man whose soul is yet '*dead*,' is a melancholy sight, and more revolting to a pure and pious intellect than the gaudy robing of a corpse, or the gilding of the charnel-house. He most assuredly is not that man's friend who confines his regards for him merely to pushing him forward in this world, or in inducing others to laud his praises in the gates. He is not his friend who would lead him through life ignorant of his grand concerns, or

* Matt. vi. 25.

teach him to be at ease and happy, independent of pardon now, and peace with God. But as no man can provide *grace* for his brother, so this honour also appertaineth to the Lord. In this, as in everything else, he is alone. He alone is our provider; for when we were perishing in our sins, he proclaimed, 'I have found a ransom,' and forthwith sent his own Son into our world to die in our room, which leads us for a moment to contemplate God in his *greatest gift*.

Place any gift of God whatever beside man, as a rebel, and it instantly becomes great—great as a proof of his generous liberality, and eminently proving that no man is worthy even of the least of all God's mercies. But what are all the gifts of God compared with Jesus Christ? He is emphatically God's 'unspeakable gift'—not that he is never to be spoken about, but that no language can ever do him justice. What are man's greatest wants? He is a transgressor, and needs pardon; he is depraved, and needs renewing; he is wretched, and needs peace; he is weak, and needs strength; he is friendless, and needs a confidant; he is pursued by offended law and justice, and needs a 'hiding place;' he is immortal, and needs an eternal home. Now, to all these, the Jesus of God's providing is perfectly adapted. Through him, as our propitiation, the sinner at once gets pardon, purity, peace, strength, the best of all friends, a dwelling in Christ here, and a mansion in Christ's Father's house hereafter. Through him, besides, every other good gift finds its way to our outcast world. But for Christ, not even our bread, and water, and raiment, or any earthly enjoyment whatever could ever have blessed our lot. And through him, we may add, come to us all the means of grace, and every spiritual aid; the sanctuary, with its excitements and contributions; the Bible, with its doctrines, promises, and laws; the Sabbath, with its hallowed rest; the holy sacraments, with their symbolic memorials; and above and beyond all, the influences of the Holy Ghost himself, who regenerates, quickens, sanctifies, establishes, and finally glorifies the soul. And then cometh the end—for it is also through him that we enter and take possession of heaven itself, with its blissful and boundless life.

Surely, O man, thou art no more an insignificant being, when thou art so well taken care of and provided for by Jehovah-Jireh! When wilt thou learn properly to estimate thine own importance, especially the worth of thy precious soul? Remember thou wert made in the image of God; thou wert in his thoughts from eternity; in the fulness of the time he came and lived and died for thee. If, then, thou wouldst properly estimate thyself, hate sin and love holiness; embrace God as thine only and true friend, and believing with all thine heart in his parental love, go and inscribe on the lintels of thy door-posts, and on the palms of thy hands, the blessed and cheering name of 'Jehovah-Jireh.'

The more full illustration of the applicability of this title to Jehovah's dispensations of grace, is left to succeeding chapters. Meanwhile, it is proper to add, that though in the foregoing the direct reference appears to be to God the Father rather than to God the Saviour, yet in the strict and substantial sense of the words, the title Jehovah-Jireh must be held as belonging to the Son—inasmuch as but for his voluntary and unparalleled love and condescension, no such promise as that of a Saviour could ever have been given to mankind sinners: 'Being made perfect, he became *the author* of eternal salvation to all that obey him.'

CHAPTER IV.

JEHOVAH-JIREH: THE LORD WILL PROVIDE.

PART II.

'Take therefore no thought for the morrow.'
MATT. vi. 34.

THE startling precept which is placed above, is the fair and forcible inference from the foretaught doctrine. If 'God will provide,' then it is our duty to trust implicitly in him, and to 'take no thought for the morrow.' Let us, *first of all*, consider what are the sentiments and feelings which are due to Jehovah-Jireh, as the God of providence and of grace; and then, *secondly*, specify some conditions of life in which these sentiments and feelings ought to be cherished.

I. CONSIDER OUR DUTY TO JEHOVAH-JIREH AS THE GOD OF PROVIDENCE AND OF GRACE. 'Take therefore no thought for the morrow,' is Christ's description of this duty. But there is surely some modification to be made upon his words. We cannot suppose that he meant them to be literally understood—that he gave countenance to our leading an idle, sauntering life, or taught, like the fatalist, that as all things are decreed, it is useless for us to scheme or work, and that we ought to leave the necessary supplies for the morrow to the laws of nature, just as we trust to the rising of the sun, or the flowing of the tides, over which we have no control. Neither can we suppose that there is any prohibition in this precept against what is called a 'provident spirit,'—a spirit that is, which takes the proper measure of future obligations, and 'lays by in store' against these. A competence is in general the lot of the industrious—a superfluity is rare. With the former, the possessor has to do three things; he has to make provision for the present wants of himself and family, he has to contribute to the support of religion and charity, and, having done his duty in these respects, he has to put aside so much for future exigencies, whether of a secular or sacred nature. It befools the duty of trusting in Providence to say that every penny must be used up, and nothing laid aside for any future purpose whatever. We admit there is danger in what is called '*hoarding*.' Hoarding makes misers, and misers cheat themselves and others and God out of their due. This, however, is the abuse of a good principle. Herein lies its proper use. If a man have dependants, and know that demands are to be made upon them perhaps after he is dead, he ought, if he can, to make some provision for such contingencies. Every sober-minded person knows that life is short, that property is fickle, and that family wants may greatly increase; hence it becomes duty, if God permits, to see to it that we are so far prepared for the evil day. This rule applies to *religious* claims in the future, as well as to secular. A really good man has an eye to both. There are vicissitudes in religion as well as in the world. There are times when help to the cause of God is much needed,—critical seasons when, by extra efforts, much suffering may be relieved, and much good done. By a christian conservative policy, these exigencies can be met and relieved—relieved out of the moderate savings of those who fear God, and to whom God had given the superfluity (as it is then made evident) for this very purpose. What amazing advantages must have accrued to the best objects, had all professors of christianity practised economy with such views! When pious men act in this way, they are in reality trusting in Providence. It is that Providence that enables them to lay by, and if they should leave behind them widows and orphans, they are virtually casting them upon God, when they thus, with wise frugality, use their competence of this world's good things.

It may still be rejoined, ought we not, in all these things, to trust so implicitly in God, as literally to 'take no thought for to-morrow?' Are not *present* demands always so pressing as to require from us all we have to spare? We think not. It appears to be rather a mean abuse of the precept to use up all we have to gratify the claims of the passing hour, saying, 'Let God attend to the future; let other benevolent persons subscribe out of their abundance.' This sounds well, but it is unsound. There is nothing to hinder a good man from exercising self-denial here. Let him keep within the bounds of moderation, and preserve somewhat of his means, upon the principle that he is personally bound to provide for his household. He thus becomes a subscriber to the support of his own widow and children, who have the first claim. The christian religion is eminently a reasonable one, and nothing seems to be more reasonable than this arrangement. It has been argued against this view, that we are commanded to leave our widows and fatherless children upon God. But this scripture has certainly a reference, in the first instance, to the poor, and is therefore scarcely applicable. Admitting, however, that it is binding on all in easy circumstances, it is consonant with the spirit of the commandment, when they leave to their families what God has enabled them to save; this is really leaving them 'upon him.' It ought not, however, to be forgotten here, that we are thus to commit those near and dear to us to our Father in heaven, for far more important blessings than temporal support, namely, for spiritual and eternal life.

The plain import of our Lord's precept is just this, that we are not, in labouring for the 'meat that perisheth,' to be so absorbed in our business as to forget more important things, nor to be so perplexed and anxious as to distrust the God we worship and love, nor to make our happiness dependent on our obtaining worldly prosperity. The maxim of Christ goes against *worldly-mindedness*. He breaks this maxim in spirit and in letter who is distrustful of the future, even while all is dark, and who is carnally confident when all is bright. Now, there is a proneness in human nature thus to sin; and a more sure counteractive than Christ's plain admonition, cannot be conceived. The apostle caught the spirit of his Master when he thus exhorted the Philippians: 'Be careful for nothing;' or, as it may be read, be anxious for nothing; 'but in everything, by prayer and supplication, with thanksgiving, let your requests be made known unto God;' which means, that we ought to give our minds pleasantly to present duties, and leave consequences to God; and thus, while we attend to God's work, God will look after our necessities. He who receives grace thus to live, is not likely to be ever anticipating the future care; for it is impossible for a finite mind to be occupied at the same time with what is and is to come. Besides, in keeping *this*, as in keeping every commandment of

God, we are securing a blessing—'a great reward;' in *fearing God* we are made to 'prosper;' and it is further said, 'the hand of the diligent maketh rich.' There is an impressive enforcement of this principle in these words, '*now* is the accepted time; behold, now is the day of salvation.' If, therefore, even God's richest mercy be as it were shut up within the *present* moment, so must it be with his common bounties. The man who in either case does his duty, is sure to get both bread and grace for present needs. He is so fulfilling the law, that he secures for all his future the promise of God; for his temptations, sufficient grace; for his trials, abounding consolation; for his death-bed, peace; and for his eternity, life that shall never end. Let us leave, then, the future in God's hand, and take the present into our own, while we commend the past to his forgiving love.

The same argument holds good when we view God as the *God of grace*. As we ought not to be idle in temporal things, so we ought not to be triflers in spiritual. As we ought not to be sinfully or sordidly anxious in the one, so we ought not to be the victims of inward fears in the other; and as we ought not to be improvident or spendthrifts in this world's substance, so we ought not to be selfish or ungenerous in our religious privileges. With all propriety we must attend, in the first instance, to our own conversion and sanctification; but we are also bound, so to speak, to lay by grace for others, and especially for those whose spiritual interests are entrusted to our care. We do this when we exemplify our religion, and when we pray much and fervently for others, for the house of God, for the coming of the kingdom of his Son, and when we do what in us lies to maintain at home and abroad his gospel cause. While thus engaged, however, we are not 'to take thought for the morrow'—we are not to fear for the cause of Christ. It shall survive us—it shall survive all. We must have great faith that all will end well. Neither must we fear for our own religious comfort and well-being: 'As thy days, so shall thy strength be.' We should remember that grace always comes with the extremity that needs it; and as a good man often finds that his means increase with his relative obligations, so he also often discovers that trials bring with them the promised help. It would be ridiculous for a man with plenty for all present demands, to be killing himself with anxiety, because he has not as much as would meet others of twenty-fold greater amount, but which have not, and never may have, any existence. Let us be assured, then, that the duties, tribulations, and temptations of future life shall all be accompanied with a corresponding supply of heavenly aid, sufficient to do all, and bear all the will of God. Thus shall we fulfil the law of Christ, and 'take no thought for the morrow.'

II. Let us now specify some conditions of life in which these sentiments and feelings should be cultivated. There are of constant occurrence in this fitful world, events, and combinations of events, in which the spirit of a man is sorely beset, and where, if not on his guard, he is sure to go wrong—to sink under despondency, or to become presumptuous—to practise deceit, or to pant for revenge—to become vain, or to affect modesty. Spiritual men are not exempt from these; hence their painful and oft-repeated inconsistencies while undergoing the buffettings and trials of life, and hence also the sneers of the enemies of religion, and their taunting query, 'Where is thy God?' The following are a few of those conditions in which unflinching confidence in Jehovah-Jireh is incumbent:—

1. *When we are prosperous and happy.* Prosperity is perilous to piety. When a man has nothing but a good name and a good will to work honestly for his bread, when he is fighting his way with difficulty through the world, when the tide is against him, and tongues vilify him, and when all the future looks big with evil, it is not then that he is most in danger. It is when he has crossed the bar, and is riding safely moored in the harbour of plenty; when he has mastered difficulties, and secured honour and influence, and when he sees no dark spot on the horizon to remind him of dependence, and to regulate desire—it is then that he has need to practise circumspection.

Why? Because he must be more than man, if he can pass through such a season uninjured. Let his sagacity and self-control be what they may, he is indeed nigh to self-complacency, and is in danger of putting on ridiculous airs. But the principal danger is, that he forgets God, and ascribes his success to himself, or to some of those lucky hits, as they are called, which are as tides in the affairs of men, and, if 'taken at the height, lead on to fortune.' Most worldly men make no secret of this; they avow it, they glory in it, and are unconscious of any danger from their elevation and opulence. A pious man is of a different opinion. He is persuaded that without divine grace he is sure to become carnally confident, and to bring upon himself and his estate the curse due to heartless ingratitude. He consequently sets about serious jealousy of himself, and fills his spirit with lowly thoughts, while God fills his cup with plenty. He knows that weak humanity is not to be trusted in any of the extremes of life, and hence he prays with Agur, 'Give me neither poverty nor riches.' He knows that present success is apt to engender pride and presumption, and that even one of the best of men once confessed, 'In my prosperity I said, I shall never be moved;' hence, his low estate at the first, his great demerits still, and the vanity inseparable from man, even at his best estate, are often placed before his mind. He knows also that prosperity is apt to induce the feeling that we shall close life in the midst of the present, or even of greater abundance, and hence, remembering 'the man of Uz,' he takes care not to say with him, 'I shall die in my nest.' To preserve himself from such sins, he determines to bid his affections sit loose to the world, to exercise as much trust in God as ever, and to cherish the feeling of dependence as strongly as when he was poor and unknown, when the pressing claims of *to-day* were such as almost to exclude from his thoughts the very idea of a to-morrow.

A meek and lowly spirit is inseparable from piety. You can no more separate these, than you can divorce justice from equity, or charity from love. Hence you will ever find a pious rich man 'poor in spirit.' If, then, in your happy days, you would insure their continuance, and, at the same time, your growth in grace, keep down natural propensities, rein in vain fancies, and put out self-importance. Consider yourselves more in need than ever of submitting your souls to all the means and ordinances of grace, secret and public. It has been well said by South, that 'they who lie soft and warm in a rich estate, seldom come to heat themselves at the altar;' but be it your firm purpose to live nearer to God, the more you enjoy of his providential bounty. As an additional motive, never forget that the tenure by which you hold any present good is very frail—the first puff of adversity may snap it in twain. Alas! how crowded are the shelves of the world's library with tales of its own fickleness and failures! He is but a sorry observer who has not in his eye some instance thereof, wherein one was, but a short time ago, lolling in easy affluence, and is now in the dust and dirt of poverty. What wisdom and kindness are in these words, 'Boast not thyself of to-morrow, for thou knowest not what a day may bring forth?' Who can tell what is to befal him ere he is 'gathered to his people'—what mortifications await his pride, what scenes of distress are to rend his heart, what thundering avalanches of this life's calamities are to fall upon and crush him? Reader, be humble: 'before honour is humility;' 'a haughty spirit goeth before a fall.' If you be prosperous, and wish to continue so, 'love not the world, nor the things that are in the world;' 'be not conformed to this world;' and resolve thus, with the apostle, 'God forbid that I should glory, save in the cross of our Lord Jesus Christ, by whom the world is crucified unto me, and I unto the world.' But if you are prosperous, and wish that it be cursed to your interests, or that God may take it all away, then lie at ease in your nest; let the self-complacency of getting on in life supplant the meekness of the christian; let your hearts grow fat and kick—only just live for yourselves, and your children, and your citizenship, and you may depend upon it, that the last chapter of Job's life must, to be true of you, be read backwards, for your latter end shall be less than your beginning.

2. *When straitened and wretched.* The best of men

are often the most straitened. Their piety does not always succeed in taking their affections from this world. Hence they must suffer; for, as Newton says, 'If a man will make his nest below, God will put a thorn in it; and if that will not do, he will set it on fire.' Now, there is peril in such a state. Man is oftener in straits and difficulties than in ease and plenty. As in the latter he is apt to become self-confident and forget God, so in the former, if not decidedly pious, he is apt to make himself the victim of some false moves in order to right himself, or, to sink into despondency. The remedy in both cases is the same—still 'trust in God;' even now, when all is dreary and forbidding, hope in him who is 'the health of thy countenance, and thy God;' for though 'no creature can be a substitute for God, God can be a substitute for every creature.' Meditate frequently on such truths as the following:—You deserve it all, you need it all, you will be the better for it all, and out of it all God shall yet deliver you. If you are able to 'take no thought for the morrow,' and to 'cast all your cares' upon Christ, it is evident that the greatest weight of the *present* care must be removed, namely, fear for the future. Only try to keep *thought* within the current twenty-four hours, and you will find that, though the case be as dire as catastrophe can make it, you will at least be relieved of the anxiety that grieves the spirit. Light is sweet: darkness is not agreeable. Hence we enjoy the day, and we sleep during the night. How unreasonable would it be not to enjoy the day, because the night with its sombre shades draws nigh! True, it is of the *dark days* we now speak; but then there is seldom, if ever, in the good man's life a day so very dark as to exclude every glimmering ray from his eye or his path. Let that light be used, and the 'way out' of straits shall be discerned. And, dingy though every day be, there is still beyond it a darker night. Duty and interest, therefore, call upon us to use such lights as we have—to walk as the children of such light, and to believe that 'sufficient unto the day is the evil thereof.' Let us keep at a distance from our minds the coming night. O, it is ever this *coming night* that chafes the temper, and sinks the soul of man! But what have we to do with the coming night? Let the trials and duties of the present day engross us, and when this night comes, we shall find that it has at least a moon to walk amid its firmament, or some twinkling star to cheer with its radiance. And even though our worst fears come true, what then?—time is short at the longest, and it will soon be all over. Our trials are summer storms, severe while they last, but quickly off; yea, the more tempestuously they rage, they all the sooner dash our frail bark across the stream to Canaan's happy shore, where all 'the days of our mourning shall be ended.' Truly we attach too much importance to our adversities and afflictions, when we allow them the weight and authority of real evils, and so expose our spiritual joys to their bitter blasts, as to endanger their being blown completely out. Trials are blessings in disguise. They are sent to *hasten* us home. Otherwise we should linger in this world's plain, and perish in the fires of Sodom.

> 'Sweet are the uses of adversity,
> Which, like the toad, ugly and venomous,
> Wears yet a precious jewel in his head.'

A merchant, we are told, lost his all in a storm, and then went to Athens to study philosophy. He soon discovered that it was better to be wise than to be wealthy, and said, '*periissem nisi periissem*'—I should have lost all, unless I had lost much. In like manner, the christian finds out that there is a blessing in affliction, and says, 'It is good for me that I have been afflicted, that I might learn thy statutes.'

3. *When doubtful as to the path of duty.* The present duty has often a direct bearing upon the future one; hence the necessity, after all, of sometimes 'taking thought for the morrow.' It is often difficult to know what present duty is, in which case we are, like Raselas, 'afraid to go forward, lest we go wrong.' Now is the time to appreciate Jehovah-Jireh. He can, and he will give the needed direction; for it is written, 'In all thy ways acknowledge him, and he will direct thy steps.' Happy indeed is that man who knows at such times what to do. He goes and tells Jesus all about it, and leaves him to

determine the matter. Of course, he uses his own reason to ponder all the circumstances, and to discover the steps that he should take. But sometimes, after all this has been done, the difficulty remains. This is a very common, it is an every-day predicament with most men. A good rule here to walk by must be of great importance. It is this,—cherish confidence in the wisdom and goodness of Jehovah-Jireh, and leave the case in his hands, after earnest prayer that the path of duty may be soon opened up. Multitudes never think of doing this; hence their ridiculous and often humiliating positions. When this is done, and done rightly, divine direction is sure to come. The heavens may not be opened—no audible voice from above may speak to us; but circumstances speedily occur, by which the mind is assured, and a path is opened up to the view, where all before was thicket and maze; it is then that we feel as joyful and confident in stepping into it, as if we had actually heard a voice saying, 'This is the way; walk ye in it.'

4. *When provoked or injured.* The regulation and control of temper is an important moral obligation. In the whirls and bustles of the world, temper is often fretted, and if not under the influence of christian principle, it is certain to be lost. The proper management of our emotional nature requires the presence and power of the sternest principles of religion. Where these are awanting, or are kept in abeyance,

the results become baneful to ourselves and others. When injured, then, or irritated, our best plan is to remember Jehovah-Jireh; and if we believe that he will provide compensation or justification, we can afford to be cool. Sinful anger begets a passion for revenge. To obviate this, let God be appealed to, and his answer will be, 'Vengeance is mine; I will repay.' With regard to ordinary provocations, our safety and consistency are best consulted by suppressing every desire for retaliation; and remembering that there is a God who reigns in justice, let us leave it to him to inflict punishment—to bring forth our righteousness in due time, and to indemnify us, as he sees proper, for losses sustained. In this, Christ is our pattern. He endured, without murmuring, injuries of all kinds; when 'reviled, he reviled not again;' and on the cross his latest prayer was for pardon to his murderers. We too must forgive 'until seventy times seven.' Not to do so, imperils our safety when we pray, 'forgive us our debts, *as* we forgive our debtors.' Again, when suddenly and grievously provoked, and when the desire of vengeance becomes very strong, we are still bound by the same rule, and must not take the matter out of God's hands. We do so to our loss. When Jehovah-Jireh sees us bent on revenging ourselves, he lets us alone, and so arranges his providence that even success does not gratify us. But it is seldom that he permits us to succeed. It is *his* law that has been broken, and he alone has the right to punish. The best retaliation, then, any man can make, is to hand over his case to the Judge of all the earth, and think no more about it. This is the way to bridle temper, to quench passion, and even to 'heap coals of fire on our enemy's head.'—Thus do we please God—thus do we preserve our integrity and commend our religion—and thus we may be the means of subduing the enmity of others, and of bringing them to their right minds. It is thus God himself deals with men. He forbears with them—he suffers long and is kind; and it is only when all his mercy is obstinately rejected, that he allows them to taste the folly of their own devices. It is thus that he wins back his own rebel children; not by threats, but by promises; not by anger but by love; not by the law, but by the gospel; not by the ministers of his wrath, but by the mission and mediation of his beloved Son. Let us then 'be followers of God, as dear children.'

5. *When tempted to heinous sins.* Not to look to God to provide the grace needed at such seasons, is alike foolish and wicked; for if we look to ourselves or to others, we look in vain, and fall. But if we trust to him, and lean upon him with all our heart, we are sure to have a door of escape opened to us. When at any time grievously beset—when the fascinations of holiness are losing their power—when we feel the moral and religious structure within us shaking to its foundations—when brought, as we may be,

into circumstances where a breath is enough to upset our most sturdy purposes, *then* is the time to use Jehovah-Jireh. Our instant appeal must be made to him for the necessary supplies of holy thoughts and desires, otherwise we are lost. He alone, in his holiness and mercy, is the gracious provider of all the antagonistic motives to sin. Arguments drawn from other sources, such as the fear of man, the care of our character, and the preservation of our worldly interests, cannot, and do not stand before such terrible invations of impure desires; they become as chaff on the summer thrashing-floor, and are swallowed up in a moment, in the whirlpool of maddened lust. But he who remembers God, and makes his powerful appeal to him for help in the hour of such trials, is sure to grapple successfully with the tempter, and return from the combat 'more than a conqueror.'

6. *When laid on a death-bed.* No character of life can put off death. Our race is, after all, to the grave. We may gallop over the course in the hey-day of mirth, or drag our slow length along in misery; we may be Dives, or we may be Lazarus, or we may have been both—all is ended in the grave. And what a solemn sound is the drawing of the latest breath! It matters not now whether the man has been great or mean, loved or hated, prosperous or unfortunate. He is dead now. But it greatly matters to him *how* he is to die. Time is gone. Eternity is at the door, and with eternity, the Judge of all. Who is blessed

then? They only who have loved and known him as Jehovah-Jireh, and who can now plead a new covenant right to his favour. Many of God's people sin by '*taking thought*' of their death-bed, as if his merciful provisions for them should then be withdrawn or exhausted. Impossible! Then, if ever, is he present with abundance. Their God and their guide unto death, he gives them enough of dying grace for their dying work; and hence it is that many christians have testified that the death-bed they dreaded never came. Still, even with the best, it is felt to be an awful thing to die—to die, and to have our everlasting destiny *fixed*. And who is sufficient to face it? He is whose sole trust is in Jehovah-Jireh—to whom the Lord has given grace to believe in the atonement made for sin. He can commit his spirit unto God, as into the hands of a faithful Creator; and this is one of the highest privileges of the saint. But God never throws away such a privilege upon mere nominal christians, or upon cowardly terrorism. He gives it them who can, and who do trust that he will be faithful to his promise. When, then, it comes to your turn to die, O unbelieving man, you shall be paralysed with fear! God has been the witness of all your conduct, and is now to be your Judge! What shall you answer him? You shall be speechless! Now is the time to settle all such matters. Believe *now* in Jehovah-Jireh, and when you die, you shall in reality only begin to live. If you believe now, you may trust then; and if you so trust, all will be well. Trusting God puts him upon his honour—it tests his faithfulness—it brings near his abundant provision of grace for the hour of need. All may then forsake —*he* remains. He will lead you safely through the waters; he will afford you what are called manifestations of his love, which will make your dying pillow the softest you ever slept on, your dying exercises the most delightful you ever experienced, and your dying moment the most glorious in your existence. Only let it never be forgotten that your death-bed trust shall be the same in kind with your life-long trust. If you have perfect confidence that the Lord will provide *now*, you will hold that confidence fast to the end; but if you withhold it from him at present, it is almost certain that trusting in him then shall be impossible—hoping in him then a mere delusion—and dying in him then a fancy which death itself shall dissolve.

CHAPTER V.

JEHOVAH-TSIDKENU: THE LORD OUR RIGHTEOUSNESS.

PART I.

'This is his name whereby he shall be called, JEHOVAH-TSIDKENU, THE LORD OUR RIGHTEOUSNESS.'
JEREMIAH xxiii. 6.

THAT man is altogether destitute of personal righteousness, is a doctrine which pervades the Bible. The frequency with which it is repeated, and the stress laid upon it, afford abundant evidence that it is God's wish that the sinner be deeply impressed with it—a conviction thereof being indispensable to the believing appreciation of the mediatorial righteousness of the provided surety. Jesus Christ can never be prized as long as one thought of personal merit remains in the human heart. While, then, it begets a general confidence in God, as Jehovah-Jireh, that he will give us all good things, the most illustrious instance of his right to this title, is his having mercifully provided for us that of which we stand most in need—'the righteousness of Christ.' The guilt and depravity of man constitute the bane of his existence; the justifying righteousness of Jesus constitutes the antidote—the blessing—the first and last of all the divine manifestations of love. He that possesseth this righteousness, is saved; he that liveth and dieth without it, is for ever lost. We fear that many gospel hearers do not understand what this righteousness means. Familiar with the expression itself, which occurs, and is so often insisted upon in every gospel appeal, they are in danger of settling down under the impression that they know what it is; but on subjecting them to examination, their ignorance becomes painfully evident. Let us then endeavour to ascertain its exact import, and to point out the mode of its application. A more weighty or important subject cannot be handled by the teacher, nor investigated by the earnest pupil of religion. It has often been discussed after an abstract or metaphysical manner; but we shall do so with studied simplicity, under the following heads of method:—The *mediatorial* elements in, the *divine* use of, and the *human* action upon this righteousness. Let us examine—

I. THE MEDIATORIAL ELEMENTS IN JUSTIFYING RIGHTEOUSNESS. We are disposed to take it for granted that man is totally destitute of personal righteousness. The point could be easily proved by an appeal to scripture and to human experience; but we waive the discussion. The reader, it is hoped, is conscious that 'by the deeds of the law no flesh living can be justified;' that 'there is none that doeth good; no, *not one;*' and that 'the carnal mind is enmity against God: for it is not subject to the law of God, neither indeed can be.' Who is he that hath ever succeeded in obtaining pardon on the ground of 'good works?' yea, who is he that can produce such works? By nature man is depraved and condemned, because he has broken the law of God; *innocence,* therefore, is out of the question; so also must be the *life* of the fallen creature; 'for all have sinned and come short of the glory of God.' The impossibilities in the way of our becoming reconciled to God are appalling, the difficulties insurmountable. *As to God,* he is holy, and he is true to his threatenings as well as to his promises. *As to the law,* it must be satisfied for *past* breaches; and how can *present* obedience, which is always due, supplement the past, the guilt of which remains uncancelled? Besides, there is now inherent deficiency in all attempts to obey it, and it cannot accept of anything short of *perfection. As to man* himself, being thoroughly corrupted by sin, or, as the apostle states it, 'without strength,' he will not, and therefore cannot fulfil the divine precepts. To these he must give all, or nothing; for the law cannot relax—his obedience must be absolutely perfect—he must love God with all his heart, and soul, and mind, and strength, and his neighbour as himself. A momentary suspension, then, or the least abatement of love, must be fatal to him. It is not with the mere *form*, but with the *spirit* of love that he must 'run in the way of God's commandments.' His conformity to them must be uninterrupted every moment, and in every circumstance, to the last breath he draws. Who is sufficient for these things? Man *as he was* in innocence: but not man *as he is* in sin. Hence we discard all idea of his justification on the ground of his own works. Must he then suffer the penalty? No; God be thanked, the righteousness of another is provided for him, offered to him, and put down to his account by the great Lawgiver himself. How, then, was this righteousness procured, and by whom? *The Son of God undertook to work it out.* In order to this, he was 'made of a woman, made under the law, to redeem them that were under the law.' The necessity of his becoming man is apparent. It was man that sinned, and it must be man that obeys; it was man that was condemned, and it must be man that suffers and dies. Jesus Christ therefore, put himself, of his own free will, exactly in the sinner's place—under the law as a rule of life, and under the penalty as due to transgressors.

(1.) *He gave himself to the law to obey it.* 'Pay me that thou owest,' is the inflexible demand of that law, not 'one jot or tittle' of which can be abated. So it speaks to the sinner, who cannot pay one farthing of his debt. But so it also speaks to Jesus, who is

JEHOVAH-TSIDKENU. 91

that sinner's substitute, and who replies, 'I will pay thee all his debts;' and immediately he places himself 'under the law.' He made it the *rule* of his life— he, the very lawmaker and lawgiver, subjected his whole conduct to the requirements of his own law. The divine commandments, therefore, met him every day, every moment of his sojourn on the earth; each claimed for itself sincere and perfect obedience, and all were ever satisfied. All his feelings, and sentiments, and desires were in strict conformity with its spiritual nature; and all his words and actions 'magnified the law and made it honourable.' Nor was this owing to his freedom from temptation; for as 'never man spake,' so never man was tempted 'like unto this man.' He lived and moved amid abounding iniquity. Devils assailed and man oppressed him, but none ever succeeded in causing him to sin. His obedience was *cheerful;* he said, 'I delight to do thy will, O my God.' It was as *extensive* as the law itself, and comprehended perfect love both to God and man. It was *perpetual*—by night and by day—from childhood to manhood—in the scene of social friendship, or amid the insults and cruelties of infatuated men— upon the top of the mountain, when 'all the kingdoms of the world and the glory of them' were offered to him, and at the foot of the cross, when they 'gave him vinegar to drink mingled with gall.' His obedience was *uninterrupted*, in every sense, up to the hour of death. Never was law, human or divine, so honoured as this! The laws under which angels and other holy creatures live, no doubt receive a perfect obedience from them; but their condition of existence is submission to their Creator—they are commanded to obey, and must obey, else they cease to live. But the Son of God was under no such necessity: he, as divine, is above all law. When, therefore, he is found under any law, it must be an act of condescension on his part, for which only one reason can be assigned—the reason, namely, that existed for his appearance in our nature and in our stead, as guilty sinners, to *obey* for us; and thus to have at his command an amount of *obedience* or *righteousness* which he could dispose of according to his pleasure, seeing that he had no need whatever for any of it to himself. All that grand and glorious life of holiness, then, which he led on earth is his disposable property; he can do with it what he pleases—give it to whom he pleases; and the sinner to whom it is given is, from that moment, held as righteous, or as having obeyed the law, and is pardoned and received accordingly. But we spake of his having fulfilled the law of God up to the hour of his death. *His death!* What means this? What has death to do with a perfectly righteous man, who in his nature was holy, and had all his life been 'harmless, undefiled, separate from sinners?' Is not death, under the moral government of a just God, the punishment due to sin? How, then do we find it associated with the sinless? What has such a life as Christ's to do with death? O, what mean the agony of Gethsemane and the tragedy of Calvary? The explanation follows:—

(2.) *He gave himself to the penalty of the law to suffer it.* 'The soul that sinneth, it shall die'—'cursed is every one that continueth not in all things which are written in the book of the law to do them'—are the judicial determinations of the Holy One. As, then, man had to obey, and could not—which inability disposed Christ to obey for him—so man having disobeyed, and come under condemnation, Christ decided also to 'suffer' for him. The law has two favourites, and it can overlook neither. It is very fond of *homage to its precepts,* and must have it; and it is very inflexible in exacting the *penalty* from every one who violates it, whether in thought, word, or deed, and cannot forego it. *Our* Mediator having given it the first—*homage,* must needs also give it the second —*death;* and as he lived for us, so 'he died for us.' Absolutely, there was no necessity for him living or obeying; but neither was there any for his suffering and dying in our stead. Having undertaken, however, to pay *all* our debts, he had to satisfy the demands of divine *justice,* as well as those of divine law. As, then, it was not for himself he obeyed, so it was not for himself that he died. Yes; *for us* he lived, and *for us* he died: 'He hath given himself for us, an offering and a sacrifice unto God, for a sweet smelling savour.' The law was offended with *our* unsavoury transgressions, but it scented a sweet smell from the beautiful conformity of Jesus to its *spirit* and its *forms;* the law was indignant at our wickedness and impiety, and would have taken vengeance on us, but the incense of his sacrifice on the altar of divine justice appeased its wrath, and pacified it towards us for ever. 'Sing, O ye heavens, for the Lord hath done it! Shout, ye lower parts of the earth: break forth into singing, ye mountains, O forest, and every tree therein; for the Lord hath redeemed Jacob, and glorified himself in Israel.' It was indeed *thy life,* O man, that was thus redeemed, and at such a price. Christ's life and Christ's death were paid for thee. Thus it is his life that is the 'fountain' of thine. No doubt this mediatorial stream appears as if it were lost in the *death* of the cross. But it is neither lost nor arrested; its passage was for a time dark and subterranean, but in his glorious rising from the tomb it re-appeared, and sprang up into life everlasting. It shall never be hid again; for 'in that he died, he died unto sin once; but in that he liveth, he liveth unto God.' His language to every sinner now is the same as it was to the disciples: 'I am come that ye may have life, and that ye may have it more abundantly;' and, 'because I live, ye shall live also.'

What, then, did Jesus Christ do for sinners? The general reply to this is—'*he died for them.*' This, however, is only half of the truth. God be praised, he *died* for them, but did he not also *live* for them? He did. For more than thirty weary years, he was 'under the law' for them, subjected, during that long period, to all manner of temptation and indignity. It was not at the end, but at the beginning, and throughout the entire course of his life, that he was 'the man of sorrows, and the acquaintance of grief.' We are told that he 'bare our sins in his own body on the tree;' that is, *our* liabilities in consequence of sin were laid upon, or borne by him '*to* the tree,' or onwards from the cradle to the cross. From the moment he was capable of suffering, he 'bare our sins;' 'his obedience was up to death, even the death of the cross.' Let us beware, then, when we think of our obligations to the blessed Saviour, not to exclude his holy, patient, and kind life; or, when we read, or hear, or think of what is called his '*righteousness*,' let us not put asunder what God hath joined together—Christ's life and Christ's death—Christ's life for our life, and Christ's death for our death. The law still demands perfect obedience, but it is *his* it takes, not ours; still exacts death for transgression, but it is *his* it gets, not ours. 'There is therefore now no condemnation to them which are in Christ Jesus, who walk not after the flesh, but after the Spirit.'

(3.) But a highly important question must be here considered. Holy as his life was, and precious as his blood is, was it not after all but the life of *one* and the death of *one;* and how can these be in the stead of the millions upon millions of lives and deaths to which the violated law of God lays claim? We have but to think of the *divinity* of the Saviour, to be perfectly satisfied on these points. He who was the Son of Mary was also the Son of God. Hence the righteousness which he wrought out is a *divine* righteousness, and being divine, its intrinsic value is infinite. This imparts to every act of his obedience, as well as to every tear he shed, and to every agony he endured, both before and at his crucifixion, a boundless worth sufficient to satisfy the law and justice of God 'to the uttermost.' Had he been only man, all he did and suffered would have been of no avail as a propitiation, and must have classified him only among the foremost of martyrs to truth. His divinity is therefore the grand atoning element that gives to his mediation its law-honouring and justice-satisfying power; it makes his one life and his one death, as propitiating for sin, more valuable than all the lives and deaths of the ransomed. But this is not all. His obedience unto death was *entirely voluntary*: 'I lay down my life, that I might take it again. No man taketh it from me, but I lay it down of myself. I have power to lay it down, and I have power to take it again.' And here we cannot fail to be deeply affected with the marvellous character of his love for our souls. Had there been the slightest constraint upon him, the atoning merit of his righteousness must have been a fiction, and we could not have trusted in it as sufficient to meet the demands upon us. As it was altogether free, however, so is it altogether worthy of our unlimited confidence. This gave to it the charm that pacifies the angry law, and this gives to it the influence that enchains our hearts. Added to this, was the *vicarious* or *suretyship* character of his righteousness : 'He loved us and gave himself *for us*'—'He suffered the just for (or in the room of) the unjust'—'He was wounded for *our* transgressions, he was bruised for *our* iniquities : the chastisement of our peace was upon him; and with his stripes we are healed.' If Christ was not a *substitute*, then he is not a Saviour; if he was not in the sinner's place, then the sinner has not only no righteousness of his own, but none anywhere else available for him. But blessed be God, we know and believe that he came in our nature to stand in our place; hence our sins were laid upon him, and with our sins, our punishment. There is not a more awful truth in the Bible than this, that he was 'made a curse for us.' Nor can we exclude from this analysis the *nature of the death* to which he was subjected. It was an *accursed* or shameful one—crucifixion : the penalty paid for crime by the most abject and worthless. It was a *painful* one—beyond conception excruciating, and altogether so abhorrent to nature, that the very sun hid his face from it, and the very rocks broke their hearts when he 'cried with a loud voice, and gave up the ghost.'

Above and beyond all, his life and death were not only *appointed by*, but actually *accepted of the Father* as a suitable righteousness for the chief of sinners. He had lain in that Father's bosom from eternity, 'rejoicing always before him.' Angels had done him homage; and when sent into the world to do that Father's will, he had made it his 'meat and his drink' to do so. With all he did and suffered, then, Jehovah was perfectly satisfied, yea, infinitely delighted. Hence, as the proof of his complacency in him as the sinner's substitute, he 'raised him from the dead, and set him at his own right hand in the heavenly places, far above all principality, and power, and might, and dominion, and every name that is named, not only in this world, but also in that which is to come.'

Such, then, is the righteousness of Christ, which is offered freely, 'without money and without price,' to mankind sinners in the glorious gospel. God is pleased with it, and it now only remains for men to be pleased with it, and make it their own. It is *needed* by them all, for 'there is none righteous;' it is *suited* to them all, for it meets every case and answers every claim; it is *offered* to them all, for it is written, 'Look unto me, and be ye saved, all ye ends of the earth;' and again, 'He is the propitiation for our sins, and not for ours only, but also for the sins of the whole world.' What a magnificent thing, then, is the mediatorial righteousness of Jesus Christ! How astonishing that any should despise it, and that any should perish with it lying at their very door! O that every one had a just sense of what is meant by these well-known and often-used words, '*for Christ's sake!*' When used by faith, these are the very words that enter into the heart of God, and move him to pity and pardon the most wicked of transgressors. But for 'his sake,' God could have no merciful dealings with men. On the ground, however, of his righteousness, God is well pleased with every poor penitent who has the wisdom to appreciate and the heart to use it. Come hither, then, thou naked, guilty, and condemned soul! O come to the Saviour, and when thy conscience accuses thee, refer it to the bountiful holiness of thy Surety, and it will be silenced in a moment;—when the law thunders upon thee, look to the 'Lamb of God,' and its intonations will die away among the heights of Calvary;—and when stern and inflexible justice raises its sword to strike thee, put it in remembrance that it once awoke upon 'the man that was God's fellow' and thy substitute, and instantly it will be sheathed. Be this thy constant aim, from this time forward, 'to win Christ, and be found in him, not having thine own righteousness, which is of the law, but that which is through the faith of Christ, the righteousness which is of God by faith;' and then thou mayest sing with all thy heart, 'Thou art my hiding place, O God;' for it is at length a glorious truth that, thy 'life is hid with Christ in God.'

CHAPTER VI.

JEHOVAH-TSIDKENU: THE LORD OUR RIGHTEOUSNESS.

PART II.

'Bring forth the best robe, and put it on him.'
LUKE xv. 22.

HAVING examined the Mediatorial elements in justifying righteousness, we now proceed to consider what may be described as—

II. THE DIVINE USE OF JUSTIFYING RIGHTEOUSNESS. The obedience and sufferings of Jesus Christ were the fulfilment of a 'commandment' which, he says, he 'received from the Father.' In the economy of redemption, the *Father*, or the first person of the holy Trinity, represents the Godhead. As sin was an offence to all the three persons *equally*, they must be held as *equally* interested in its punishment or in its pardon. Hence the Father spares not, but sends his Son; the Son spares not, but gives himself; and the Holy Ghost spares not, but condescends to dwell in human hearts, for the purpose of quickening and applying to them all the blessings of the redemption purchased by Christ. At the same time, the Father is uniformly represented as, for the others, receiving the satisfaction rendered to violated law and insulted justice. While, however, the first and chief end of the whole mediatorial arrangements contemplated the vindication of the divine faithfulness, and the upholding of the divine government in the pardon of the guilty, we must not forget, that but for that intended pardon, no such arrangements would have been required. Now, then, that they are made— that is, now that Jesus Christ has *lived* and *died* for sinners—it follows that *divine action* must be taken upon the propitiatory righteousness constructed out of that substitutionary life and death. When Jesus Christ was 'received up into glory,' he entered heaven in a *public* character, as the '*forerunner*,' and sat down upon his throne as the representative and 'advocate' of his people; 'for Christ is not entered into the holy places made with hands, which are the figures of the true; but into heaven itself, *now to appear in the presence of God for us*.' And what was it that he did when he made this appearance in the presence of God? He delivered up, so to speak, the sum total of that holy life he had been leading on earth, and the propitiatory excellence of that accursed death he had died on the cross, into the hands of his Father, that by him all might be *used* for the benefit of sinners of mankind—used according to the good pleasure of his will, primarily for that Father's glory, and ultimately for these sinners' salvation. Having now, then, at his free and sovereign disposal a kind and amount of righteousness sufficient for the justification of the most guilty, what remained for the great Lawgiver to do, but to use it for the purposes for which it was 'brought in;' that is, to apply, or put it down to the credit of sinners? Let us, therefore, attentively consider the nature of the divine use of, or action upon, the righteousness of our Saviour.

(1.) We have a very beautiful and impressive illustration of this action in the address of the angel regarding Joshua the high priest :* 'Take away the filthy garments from him. And unto Joshua he said, Behold, I have caused thine iniquities to pass from thee, and I will clothe thee with change of raiment.' In the application of this to the sinner, we have an easy access to the divine mode of dealing with him in this matter. Under the figure of 'filthy garments,' we have represented to us our personal merits, or rather demerits. Our own works are to the soul what unclean and tattered raiment is to the body— neither comely, nor comfortable, nor in any way suitable. Humiliating, indeed, is such a description to our natural pride; but scripture everywhere corroborates the representation: 'What is man, that he should be clean? and he which is born of a woman,

* Zech. iii. 4.

that he should be righteous? Behold, *He* putteth no trust in his saints; yea, the heavens are not clean in his sight; how much more abominable and filthy is man, which drinketh iniquity like water?'* 'They are all gone aside, they are *all* together become filthy.'† 'We are all as an unclean thing, and all our righteousnesses are as filthy rags.'‡ Now, it is in reference to these most miserable outfittings of sin, that our heavenly Father gives the order to 'take them away'—which order implies a *right, a will, a power,* and a *purpose,* on God's part, to do so. The order implies his *right* to do so. Certainly no other has such. Justification, even in its incipient and earliest, as well as at its latest and most glorious developments, is the act of God alone: 'Christ is made of God unto us righteousness.' It was *his* law that was broken, and the pardon cannot possibly come except from himself. But it is his right specially and exclusively, because the righteousness, on the ground of which that pardon is in any case issued, is emphatically *his.* No doubt the Father did not live nor die for sinners; but he who did so was his only-begotten and well-beloved Son; *he* sent that Son; *he* anointed and qualified him; *he* raised him from the dead, and exalted him to honour and power; to *him* the righteousness of the Mediator was offered, and *he* accepted of it;—therefore, from henceforth *he* is the sovereign proprietor thereof, to do with it 'as

* Job xv. 14. † Ps. xiv. 3. ‡ Isa. lxiv. 6.

it seemeth good in his sight.' It is for these reasons that the righteousness of the Son is so often called by the apostle 'the righteousness of God.' The Son gave it to the Father, from love to his glory; the Substitute gave it to the Lawgiver, from love to the law; and the Lawgiver gives it to the sinner, from love to the Son, and those for whom that Son atoned;—which proves that he has the *will*, as well as the *right* to do so. One may have a right, and be indisposed to avail himself of it. It is not so in this case: God is 'not willing that any should perish, but that *all* should come to repentance.' Indeed, if he had not had the *will*, he never would have so arranged as that he should have the *right* to pardon. It is because he loved and pitied sinners, that he provided such a righteousness for them—that righteousness being alike God's title to give, and the sinner's title to ask pardon. Let us never entertain a doubt of God's willingness to be 'the justifier of him which believeth in Jesus.' To secure this blessing in harmony with his own attributes, he has done everything which it was required should be done; and more convincing proof than this cannot be led of the profound regard he bears to our best interests. Many believe in his *ability* to save, but fear concerning his *willingness*. Let them remember that but for his willingness, he never should have been able. It is *love*, not *power*, that is the source of human redemption; so that if we can trust God's *heart,* we need not fear his *hand.* Farther, having the right and the will, he has also the *ability:* 'He is mighty to save.' One may have the two former, and lack the latter; but Jesus has the *power:* 'He is able to keep that which is committed to him against that day.' He knows no adversary now who can successfully oppose him in his merciful intentions upon any sinner. The world, the devil, and the flesh may all withstand the order, and fight to *keep on* the filthy garments; but whenever he wishes them off, they fall, one after the other, till not one rag is left. How, or by what agent this is done, will be adverted to afterwards. Meanwhile it is enough to state, that neither in the condition of the sinner himself—he may be a Manasseh, or a thief, or a Saul of Tarsus— nor in the nature of God, or of God's government, nor in the hostility of any evil principality whatever, does there exist one solitary element of what could successfully resist his will in this business of everlasting love. And all this, because he has the *purpose* to save. The denuding of the sinner of his 'filthy garments,' and his being arrayed in 'the garments of salvation,' are decreed—decreed in those councils of peace which were held from eternity, and every one of which must and shall be carried into effect; hence that magnificent hosannah of Paul: 'Blessed be the God and Father of our Lord Jesus Christ, who hath blessed us with all spiritual blessings in heavenly places in Christ;. according as he hath chosen us in him before the foundation of the world, that we should be holy and without blame before him in love: having predestinated us unto the adoption of children by Jesus Christ to himself, according to the good pleasure of his will, to the praise of the glory of his grace, wherein he hath made us accepted in the Beloved.'

(2.) In executing this order to 'take away the filthy garments,' how does God proceed? Is it with or against the will of the sinner? It is unquestionably with his will. David long ago prophesied: 'The Lord shall send the rod of thy strength out of Zion: rule thou in the midst of thine enemies. Thy people shall be *willing* in the day of thy power;' and while the apostle admits to the Philippians that 'fear and trembling' ought to be mixed up with the working out of their salvation, he explicitly states that 'it is God which worketh in them both to *will* and to do of his good pleasure.' This *willingness* has of course a general reference to the whole energy and life of faith in the christian; but it is also true of every particular period or act of that life. Its beautiful pliability is never seen to better advantage than in the first stripping that goes on, when the prodigal, in penitence, hies him home to his father. Having embraced him in the arms of reconciling love, the order is given, 'Take away his filthy garments,' and that order is instantly obeyed. By the opening of his eyes to see that his own clothing is not the gorgeous or comely apparel that he fancied; that in fact he is covered with rags—with filthy rags—and these even not concealing his nakedness, he himself is in haste to cast them away, saying, 'I have heard of thee by the hearing of the ear; but now mine eye seeth thee: wherefore I abhor myself, and repent in dust and ashes.' His proper senses are now restored to him, and hence he is offended with the stench, shivers from the scantiness, and is ashamed of the exposure of such filthy habiliments. He therefore readily yields himself up to this process of disrobing, for ever renounces all complacency in himself, and gratefully submits to be washed in the fountain, and clothed anew from the gracious wardrobe of his pitying and generous parent. To drop the figure: having been convinced by the truth as it is in Jesus, that righteousness of his own he has none, and that the things which he thought meritorious are utterly repudiated as such, in the estimate of that God with whom he has to do, he renounces at once and for ever all dependence on them for salvation, and forthwith 'submits himself to the righteousness of God,' setting to his seal that 'Christ is the end of the law for righteousness to every one that believeth.' Now what is chiefly to be noticed here, is the *divine action* in the whole procedure. Without such action or interference, this revolution in mind and conduct could never have taken place. Filthy as his own works are, man thinks most overweeningly of them, and would never consent to brand them with disgrace; and perfect as Christ's righteousness is, he despises to take mercy solely for its sake. So soon, however, as the Father takes in hand to reverse these opinions, behold they are reversed; the sinner falls down and confesses his personal demerits, and when he rises, it is that he may be arrayed in the 'best robe.' After this he glories only in Christ, and in him crucified. In a moment of weakness—(for self-conceit rarely altogether departs)—he may be seen taking a look to the old rags he formerly wore, or to the works he once considered meritorious; but one sight is enough to turn his look upward again to the Saviour. From this brief weakness his abhorrence of *self* has acquired strength, and his grasp of the cross is firmer. Henceforth the burden of his song is, 'Not unto us, O Lord, not unto us; but unto thy name give glory, for thy mercy and thy truth's sake.'

(3.) Having given the order, and the order being obeyed, 'take away the filthy garments from him,' the next step in the process of a sinner's justification through the righteousness of Christ, is his becoming *personally interested* in that righteousness. Till he put off his own, Christ's could not be put on. The old raiment and the new could not assort well together; rags and silk cannot be adjusted; holiness and sin cannot herd together. No sooner, however, does God convince him of his spiritual destitution and nakedness, than he immediately performs his engagement—'*I will clothe thee with change of raiment;*' which, without figure, means that he will put down to his account the obedience and sufferings of his Surety, and forthwith deal with him as if Christ's life had been led, and as if Christ's death had been suffered by the sinner himself. This means, that when what Christ did as a mediator is reckoned to me, I am dealt with precisely as if I had done it all myself. I, a poor naked wretch, get the love, the approbation, the honour, and the blessing of the everlasting Father, just as substantially and surely as his own Son now gets them; and yet I am kept humble; for it is not *me*, the sinner, that God regards, but Jesus his anointed, or the righteousness of that Jesus which is now covering me. God 'beholds my shield, and looks upon the face of his anointed.' This helps to explain Paul's marvellous exclamation: 'I am crucified with Christ, nevertheless I live; *yet not I, but Christ liveth in me:* and the life which I now live in the flesh, I live by the faith of the Son of God, who loved me and gave himself for me.' Hence also the beautiful words of Justyn Martyr, in his epistle to Diognetus: 'God gave his Son a ransom for us; the Holy One for the transgressors, the innocent for the wicked, the righteous for the unrighteous, the incorruptible for the corruptible, the immortal for the mortal. For what else could *cover* our sins but his righteousness? In whom could we, transgressors and ungodly, be justified but only in the Son of God?

O sweet exchange!—O unsearchable contrivance! that the transgressions of *many* should be hidden in *one* righteous person, and the righteousness of *one* should justify *many* transgressors!' It thus appears that the pardoned sinner's '*change of raiment*' is just *Christ's righteousness* put upon him; or, in the strong but comprehensive language of the theologian, *imputed to him*. The doctrine of the imputation of mediatorial righteousness to the sinner, is an essential one. Many have crude, and not a few have no ideas at all upon the subject. Let us explain it:—

(4.) There are some passages of scripture which throw light upon what has been most properly called '*Christ's imputed righteousness.*' The first is in Psalm xxxii. 2 : 'Blesséd is the man to whom the Lord *imputeth* not iniquity.' The meaning of this is, that he only can be regarded the happy man whose sins are never to be charged against him, either in this or in the world to come; these sins are not put down against him—not reckoned to his account; for they are all '*blotted out*,' that is, forgiven. The apostle quotes this text in the third chapter of the Romans, in close connection with his argument that our salvation comes not from our own, but from the righteousness of Christ; hence we fairly infer, that the words of David, though forming a negative, are to be understood as containing an affirmative, viz., that the man is blessed whose sins are not imputed to, or charged against him, *because of the righteousness of Christ*, which is now imputed or placed to his account in the book of God's remembrance. 'The forgiveness of sins,' says one, 'is surely not a human fancy or a human action, in which a man says to himself, "I have forgiveness of my sins;" but a divine work, a living *word of God* spoken into the heart, which faith alone can appropriate. But the word and act of God is the most *positive* thing that we can conceive; it is *being* itself, on which account Luther most righteously terms the forgiveness of sins, "life and blessedness," for *it contains within itself the imputation of the righteousness of God.*'* Again, it is said by the apostle that this righteousness of God, which is by faith of Jesus Christ, is '*unto all, and upon all them that believe.*' Without adverting to the different readings of this expression, it may be used here as indicating *how* the sinner is held as righteous before God. God's own righteousness being '*upon*' him, that is, given away to him, and he to be regarded by divine law and justice as ever afterwards free from all their demands, if law meets him, and requests payment, it is now to regard him as solvent, because of the righteousness of God which it sees him wear and hears him plead; and if justice wax bold, and draw its sword, it is now to remember that he has suffered already all that is due in the person of his Surety. 'In these words, "unto all, and upon all,"' says

* Olshausen in loco.

Olshausen, 'we may observe not merely a heaping of synonymes, but a climax; the image of a flood of grace seems to be at the foundation of this expression; a flood which penetrates *to* all, and streams *over* all.' And again, when writing to Philemon concerning his runaway slave, the apostle says, 'If he hath wronged thee, or oweth thee aught, *put that on mine account;*' which means, 'the debt originally and really is that of Onesimus, but I charge myself with it, and bind myself to pay it; therefore, *impute* it to me—put it down to my account.' It is precisely in the same way that our Substitute says to God: 'The sins for which I obey, and suffer, and die, are not originally or really my sins, but I am willing to be treated as if they were such—impute them to me, or put them to my account.' And as it is strongly implied in Paul's language to Philemon that *his* payment of the slave's debt was to be reckoned to the slave as if he himself had settled it, so it is here the sinner is to be held as having done all that God required of him, solely on the ground of Christ having actually done so. There is here, therefore, a twofold imputation. Sin is imputed to Christ, and righteousness is imputed to the sinner; in neither case is the thing imputed the personal acquisition of the party; the *sin* is not Christ's own, and the righteousness is not the sinner's own; but the *exchange* made in the covenant of grace secures that the innocent Saviour be treated as guilty, and that the guilty sinner be treated as innocent.

We are now in the very midst of mystery; but though much darkness resteth upon these economic arrangements, a light—a clear and heartsome light—falls upon them from the scriptures quoted above. Is it not enough to re-assure us in the faithfulness and mercy of God, that the work of our Surety was so intrinsically and infinitely good, as that on its account the chief of sinners, in one moment, may be held and treated as the chief of saints? Yes, O inquirer after God, be satisfied upon this point—*imputation is now possible;* in truth, it is the *only thing* God can do with the righteousness of his beloved Son. If he do not impute it to others, it lies *useless* beside him; its acquirement on Christ's part was a piece of gratuitous and extravagant waste, and its injunction and acceptance on God's part was little else than a cruel ceremony. But away with these conjectures, almost bordering upon profanity! *It can be done!* God in all the beauties of his holiness can do it—and it delights him thus to dispense it to all who will take it. We can conceive of nothing so sublime as this resignation of his own righteousness by the Redeemer into the hands of his Father, unless it be that Father's free imputation or distribution of it amongst the guilty sons of men. How ecstatic the joy of the Son when he re-appeared before his Father's throne, carrying with him such a load of mediatorial excellence, for which personally he had no use, but which he had gathered together during a life of sorrow and suffering far away among the dismal and accursed regions of sin, in order that the yearnings of that Father's heart might flow outwards harmoniously with the purity and integrity of his character, to pardon the transgressors! The *fellow* of this joy must be understood to be that of the Father himself, in thus having it in his power to gratify his boundless, endless mercy, by saving lost sinners, and bringing them back to his bosom and his blessing, the travail of his Son's soul, and the emblems of his own unparalleled love.

(5.) *And who is it that thus imputes?* 'I will clothe thee,' saith God the Father. He is the Judge, and in that character he it is that either pardons or punishes: 'It is God that justifieth.' There is only one class of scriptures that seems to oppose this idea, and to trace justification to the sinner's *faith*. It is said of Abraham's faith, that it was 'counted (or imputed) to him for righteousness.' But this and parallel texts must be interpreted not by themselves, but in connection with others. It is elsewhere said that we 'are justified by faith;' but in this, and in the other, and in all similar passages, we are to view *faith* not as the thing *imputed*, but as the *way* or *means* to that thing which is the righteousness of God. Dr Chalmers puts this in his usual terse and forcible style: 'Beware of having any such view of faith as will lead you to annex to it the kind of merit, or of claim, or of glorying under the gospel which are annexed to works under the law. This, in fact, were just animating with a legal spirit the whole phraseology and doctrine of the gospel. It is God who justifies. He drew up the title-deed, and he bestowed the title-deed. It is ours simply to lay hold of it.' On God's part, this imputation is certainly an act of free grace. He may or he may not do it, for any claim the sinner can present. It only assumes the mysterious position of a *necessity*, when Christ himself prays the Father for it—that is to say, it is for Christ's sake alone that even the righteousness of God is put down to any sinner's account. No doubt this imputation is associated with faith; it is founded, in other words, in union to Christ himself. The branch has sap, and blossom, and fruit, because it is *in the tree.* The members of the body have life and action, because they are connected *with the head;* and sinners are quickened and pardoned, because they are in the Surety. But as branches in him, 'the vine,' they are grafted in by God, the '*husbandman.*' Thus, imputation is therefore ' the consequence of the legal relation which was established between him and them in the covenant of grace, by which he was constituted their Surety, and his acts in this character were made referable to them. His righteousness thus became imputable to them; and it is actually imputed when a real union is formed between them by the Spirit and by faith.'*

* Dr Dick.

(6.) *This important act is performed instantaneously with conversion.* It is easy to make a distinction between regeneration and justification; but to the simple investigator of truth, it will suffice to notice that, as it is when the infant is born that the first inspiration of the lungs is drawn, so it is when the sinner is born again that he is 'in Christ Jesus;' when in Christ Jesus 'there is no more condemnation;' and when there is no more condemnation, it must be because the act of pardon is passed; and that act is only passed when the righteousness of Christ is imputed. This imputation is coeval with regeneration. When we begin to live anew, we are justified; and when we are justified, we begin to live. Up to the moment of this union, then, even the saints to be, are under the wrath and curse of God. Hence we argue that one cannot be too soon at the work of faith and repentance; and in order to these, we cannot be one moment too soon before the tribunal of divine justice pleading the righteousness of Christ, as that alone which entitles the most abject sinner to the most precious blessings of heaven.

(7.) In one word, *the whole transaction,* of making men the better of what Christ did for them, is to be ascribed to the 'Holy Spirit of God.' This is indeed his peculiar work in the economy of grace. He descends with the *title* in his hand, and gives it to the sinner in the day in which he effectually calls him. He hears the will of the Father, 'Bring forth the best robe, and put it on him,' and instantly the robe is adjusted to the believer's person; in that moment he is forgiven, because in that moment the Holy Ghost 'covers him with the robe of righteousness.' All this being the doing of the Spirit, it is work that must stand. A garment woven by the life, and love, and blood, and death of the Son of God, and put on by the hands of Him who garnished the heavens, must be imperishable. The clothes of the Hebrews never wore done, while they wandered about in that waste howling wilderness; but they disappeared at length with them that wore them. The 'best robe' has another and higher destiny. It shall be worn for ever; for Christ's righteousness 'is an everlasting righteousness.' Angels lost their innocence, and were cast into hell. Adam lost his, and fell under the curse. But this is the 'best robe,' for it is imperishable. The possessor of it shall never again come under condemnation. It is alike his security for the past, the present, and the future; for the *past*, that his sins shall never rise up against him; for the *present*, that its peculiar temptations shall not have prevalence over him; and for the *future*, that he shall hold on his way rejoicing, and shall shine at length as the stars in the firmament for ever and ever.

CHAPTER VII.

JEHOVAH-TSIDKENU: THE LORD OUR RIGHTEOUSNESS.

PART III.

'Put ye on the Lord Jesus.'
ROM. xiii. 14.

IT now remains that we examine—

III. THE HUMAN ACTION UPON JUSTIFYING RIGHTEOUSNESS. Co-operation is a law in God's house. It is a gross abuse of the doctrine of free grace to infer from it, that because of ourselves we can do nothing in the way of meriting mercy, therefore we must be absolutely inactive in the whole process. This is that heresy, called Antinomianism, which strikes at the root of practical christianity, and turns 'the grace of God into lasciviousness;' or it is that fanatical delusion which has seized upon those who imagine that they are to lie passive in God's hands, and never put forth a single effort in the matter of their own salvation. Paul's argument in reference to both errors is unanswerable. In his epistle to the Romans, he clearly shows that the gospel *establishes*, but cannot *make void* the law; and in many passages of his writings, he indicates most distinctly that there is a very close connection between the divine and human agency in the sinner's salvation, and that so far from co-operation on his part being either absurd or impious, it is a most important, yea, a bounden duty, the neglect of which makes salvation impossible. The explanation as to how the whole process is a work of God, and yet that the sinner himself must in some way have action in it, we do not attempt, nor ought it ever to be attempted. This is certainly one of God's 'secret things' with which we ought not to intermeddle. The speculative christian has sustained very often serious damage to his comfort in religion, by seeking in this to be 'wise above what is written.' Betwixt divine sovereignty in conversion, and human consent thereto, 'there is a great gulf fixed,' so that they who would pass from the one to the other, cannot. It is enough for all the purposes of mercy, that we give to God himself the glory of originating and carrying forward a work of grace in the soul, and that, at the same time, we consider it to be our duty, 'whatsoever our hand findeth to do, to do it with our might;' yea, to 'strive to enter in at the strait gate;' to 'work out our own salvation with fear and trembling;' and to 'give diligence to make our calling and election sure.' In harmony with this view are all those scriptures which make it appear as if our salvation depended upon our own repentance, faith, and love: 'Unless ye repent, ye shall all likewise perish;' 'He that believeth shall be saved; he that believeth not shall be damned;' 'If any man love not the Lord Jesus Christ, let him be Anathema Maranatha.' There is another set of Bible proofs that throw the co-operation of the sinner into the form of *obedience* to a law: 'Turn ye, turn ye, why will ye die?' 'Look unto me;' 'This is his commandment, that we should believe on the name of his Son Jesus Christ;' 'Be ye therefore perfect, even as your Father who is in heaven is perfect;' 'Put ye on the Lord Jesus Christ;' 'Awake thou that sleepest, and arise from the dead, and Christ shall give thee light.' And there is a third class of texts in which sinful men are represented as claiming for themselves a share in the work of their restoration to the pardon and image of God: 'I will call upon the Lord, who is worthy to be praised, so shall I be saved from mine enemies;' 'I will wash mine hands in innocency;' 'I will go and return to my first husband; for then it was better with me than now;' 'Come, let us return unto the Lord;' 'I will arise, and go to my father, and will say unto him, Father, I have sinned against Heaven and before thee;' 'Ye see now how that by works a man is justified, and not by faith only.' A simple rule in biblical criticism harmonises these apparently contradictory passages, viz., that the Word of God must be interpreted in accordance with its own great first principles, and that whatever seemeth to differ from these must be explained as agreeing thereto. The application of this rule to the subject before our minds, brings it out clear of difficulties. It is a principle in christianity, that man cannot justify himself—that this cometh of 'the Lord our righteousness;' and it is a law of christianity, that he must accept of this righteousness, or believe in it, otherwise he hath no part or lot therein. In correspondence with this principle, scripture proclaims that God alone can 'forgive sins,' and that God alone can create within man a believing heart; and equally corresponding with this law, scripture contemplates man as under obligation to repent, believe, and obey, while no scripture whatever, that seems to give to this obedience, faith, and contrition, the credit of the pardon that accompanies them, can be literally, but must be subordinately explained. With regard to the human action upon the righteousness of Jesus Christ, this becomes both intelligible and interesting. In the preparation of that righteousness, we certainly had no part, neither can we take any credit in its being *imputed* to us by the Judge; and yet there is nothing more evident, than that if we are not actually using it for the purpose for which it was wrought out, we receive no advantage from it. In one view, God himself puts it on; and in another view, we must also 'put it on,' and when wearing it, must 'make mention of it, and of it only.' The meaning of this is plain. While believing that God is thus 'the author and finisher of our faith,' we must put into exercise our own minds upon the grand subject of the salvation purchased by Christ; that is, we must, as reasonable beings, assent to the plan of justification through the righteousness of another, and that other our divine Surety, as being the best, the only, the sufficient plan; and thus assenting, we must, as sinful beings, trust in that righteousness as our own, making it ever and exclusively the basis of all our intercourse with God, and of all our hopes of mercy and of life. Human action, then, in this direction, may assume one or other of the following forms:—

(1.) *A grateful appreciation of the merits of Christ's righteousness.* If we do not know its value, we will not use it; and if we do not use it, we perish. It was wrought out that we might offer it to God in lieu of our own, which we had lost, and as our only title to his forgiveness. But, if there be ignorance of its divine suitableness to our guilty and condemned state, and of its sole and perfect sufficiency to meet and satisfy all demands upon us, then we continue under the curse, and have no claim upon one particle of the divine clemency. It is far otherwise with him who 'puts it on.' He has had his eyes opened to see his own nakedness, together with the exquisite fitness of this 'best robe' to his whole person, of heart, soul, mind, and strength. The holiness of Christ's life is to him the 'perfection of beauty;' and the mysterious richness of Christ's death is to him 'the all and in all' of a finished atonement; hence his declaration, 'in the Lord alone I have righteousness.'

(2.) *A sincere depreciation of our own righteousness.* We must say of fancied personal merit as Job did of life, 'I loathe it.' It is neither natural nor reasonable for the sickly beggar to cherish his 'putrifying sores,' or boast of his 'filthy rags.' While hopeless of cure and of decent clothing, he may settle down with these in fatuous contentment; but give him the hope of the soothing draught and mollifying ointment, and let him only have within his offer and his reach a decent and comfortable dress, and he will manifest his interest by casting off his old raiment and appropriating the new; with these he will hie him with all possible speed to the nearest pool, where he may wash and make himself clean, and to the nearest friend, who may teach him the way to mix the anodyne and adjust the garments. And so it is with the serious penitent. Once he gloried in himself. He thought well of everything he did, and even considered that he laid God under obligations. He professed, as he thought, correct sentiments, and cultivated amiable dispositions. He abandoned certain sins in which he once loved to indulge, and began the practice of certain virtues, which he formerly disliked. He conformed in his religious connections to the ritual of the church; conducted himself with every regard to decency and honesty in his places in society, and went all proper lengths in charitable donations for the poor and the needy. He thus concluded, that upon these good works he had established a claim on the forbearance and mercy of the Almighty, and went about his secret and public devotions, making mention of his own righteousness, even of it only. Upon the enlightening of his eyes, however, by the Holy Ghost, all these things are seen in their true colours, and he immediately hastens to disrobe and cast away the garish livery of the Pharisee. He sees the filth of natural depravity in which all his imagined moral worth lies embedded, and the thorns and thistles of actual transgression, where he ever thought grew the roses and lilies of obedience. In his best emotions, he is conscious of selfishness; in his finest displays of a correct life, he marks their infinite distance from the high standard of the divine law; vanity and self-conceit he observes cowering down among the most winning and amiable of his affections, setting them on to beneficence, guiding them in the choice of objects, and receiving to themselves the complacent homage of the blessings of the destitute;—while, unbroken by a solitary exception, he can review the whole festivals of his piety as occasions rather for the gratification of his spiritual pride, than for the worship of God, or the good of his soul: 'Wherefore he abhors himself, and repents in dust and ashes.' By one act of self-depreciation he pulls down the fabric of a lifetime, scatters the hopes of all the past to the wind, and with his whole soul he regards the righteousness of his Surety as 'all his salvation, and all his desire.' There is now no resistance on his part to empty himself, that he may be filled with all the fulness that is in Christ; and no contending with the influence of heaven, to 'put off, concerning the former conversation, the old man which is corrupt, according to the deceitful lusts,' and to 'put on the new man, which after God is created in righteousness and true holiness.'

(3.) *A perpetual reference to Christ's righteousness as the procuring cause of every blessing.* It is not merely for the cancelling of his guilt at the first, nor for his title to 'eternal life' after death, that he values the worth of his Lord, but for every temporal and spiritual comfort in the meantime enjoyed. He is not ashamed to take even his cup of cold water, his morsel of bread, and his lowliest earthly benefit, on the ground of Christ's righteousness—which, indeed, is the true way of regarding all our mercies. Every breath we draw, every smile of love we enjoy, every domestic blessing, every farthing of property, every bound of a healthy constitution, and every tie of life that makes existence sweet, we ought to view as coming through the mediatorial sacrifice. IT IS ALL FOR CHRIST'S SAKE!—and this idea in the believer's mind throws a cheerful light on all the gifts and dispensations of God, and raises a spirit of gratitude within the bosom of every sanctified affection. The natural man may look with proud complacency on his gains, and boast of them as the reward of his own talents and enterprise; but still he feels that there is more of brag than truth in his protestations of satisfaction. To the believer, on the other hand, there is nothing half so sweet as the conviction, that all he has done and has received, he owes to his Redeemer's mediation. This with poverty, is to him wealth enough, and riches without this, would make him feel 'poor indeed.' In no point of view, perhaps, does christian Faith appear so beautiful and godlike as when she thus uses the righteousness of her Lord. To it, no doubt, she clings for pardon and acceptance; but to it, also, she leans for the mercy of every breath, of every sunshine, and of every hope. There is no difference between her plea for justification and that which she urges for daily nourishment; she calculates on the divine patience and forbearance upon no minor title to that which she presented when first rescued from the wrath of the Almighty; and ever as she fights her way and endures her trials, is she confident that her fervent prayers shall be heard only for Christ's sake. Whatever successes, indeed, attend the christian in the cultivation of spirituality, he never sets down any one of them to his own merits. On the contrary, the more of love, or hope, or heavenly-mindedness he can practise, the more does he feel his obligations to the grace of the Saviour. This reveals that otherwise mysterious feature of sanctified character—progress in piety and deepening humility going hand in hand, and never dwelling apart. He may say upon an occasion, 'I live;' but he immediately adds, 'yet, not I; Christ liveth in me.'

(4.) *The prompt and pious use of Christ's righteousness on special occasions.* Does the believer pray? He remembers, as he kneels, that it is a privilege, not a right. We should never presume to speak to God except when we have *Christ* clearly in our view. As there was a daily sacrifice under the law, so ought there to be under the gospel; not that Christ is to be every day sacrificed anew, but that in every devout approach to God, faith should first of all offer his sacrifice to the Holy One; and this is done by the inward persuasion that Christ died for us, and by the actual appeal for mercy being made on this account. It is this idea, when sincerely entertained, that gives efficacy to the clause with which most prayers conclude, '*for Christ's sake.*' Does the christian fall into sin? He remembers his Lord's righteousness, and while repenting of his conduct, he loses not his hope. He assures himself, that as his justification did not depend upon his personal condition, so neither can his sanctification be arrested, nor his safety endangered by his numerous infirmities. As he urged Christ upon the law when he sought its forgiveness, so he urges him still; and the plea that won the case at first, secures his best interests to the last. Does the christian fall into heavy trials? He remembers the righteousness of Christ, and consoles himself that none of these can be the expression of a vindictive purpose, seeing that God cannot be angry with him, now that he is 'hid with Christ,' and that therefore all of these must be the salutary discipline of an affectionate parent, who 'loves whom he chastens, and scourges every son and daughter whom he receives.' *Does the christian sustain the loss of all things?* He remembers the righteousness of Christ, and is contented. All earthly treasures may have fled, but this 'pearl of great price' remains; these would have gone at any rate, and have only left him a little sooner than he expected; but *this* is his dearest property, and with it he knows himself to be secure of all needed supplies, even to the hour of death; hence the losses and crosses of this life only work in him 'patience; and patience, experience; and experience, hope; and hope maketh not ashamed.' *Does the christian die?* He remembers the righteousness of Christ, and is *assured* that all is well. Even he would now be the victim of remorse, if he judged himself by his own godly life, or by any capacity of his own, adequately to make ready for the impending and awful future. His hopes could gather no strength from the memory of his privileges, his frames, his sacrifices, his experiences. If he looked back to his closet, he would be met by the ghosts of ten thousand callous prayers; if he revisited the sanctuary, he would be rebuked by the consciousness of innumerable imperfect services and unhallowed Sabbaths; if he reviewed his walk and conversation in the world, he would be silenced by the resurrection of many forgotten conformities to its spirit and its fashions; if he recounted his alms, and analysed his zeal, he would hide his head before the spectres of his vain and self-righteous motives; and if he finally resorted to his days and nights of bitter repentance, to his sweetest seasons of holy communion, and to any or to all of the gracious manifestations which were made to his soul, with every one of these would be associated the memory of wandering thoughts, fickle resolutions, and unfulfilled vows; and thus they would all fail to afford him consolation. No, no. His dying look is the very same with his living look—'unto Jesus;' his dying grasp is the same with his living one—the cross; his dying trust is the same with his living one—the finished work of Christ; and his dying cry is the same with his living testimony—'in the Lord alone I have righteousness.' Thus, living or dying, Christ and him crucified is all his confidence, and all his boast; hence he dies both happily and safely, saying, 'I know whom I have believed, and that he is able to keep that which I have committed to him against that day.' *Is the christian to rise again from the dead?* Then also he will remember the righteousness of Christ; and while others are calling upon the rocks and the mountains to 'fall on them, and hide them from the face of him that sitteth on the throne, and from the wrath of the Lamb; for the great day of his wrath is come, and who shall be able to stand?'—he will calmly approach the dread tribunal, and placing before the Judge *his own righteousness*, will confidently claim from him the promised crown of life. That claim will be honoured —that saint will be acquitted—that crown will be given. O wondrous righteousness, that thus in one moment celebrates the deliverance of the saint from the last consequence of sin, and his august coronation as one of God's kings and priests! *Is the christian to live for ever?* He will never forget the righteousness of Christ; that it is to it he owes his exaltation, and that still, and ever onward through endless ages, his obligations shall be the same. Hence the burden of the songs of eternity can never be changed, but must ever be, 'Thou art worthy to take the book, and to open the seals thereof: for thou wast slain, and hast redeemed us to God by thy blood out of every kindred, and tongue, and people, and nation: and hast made us unto our God kings and priests: and we shall reign on the earth.'

(5.) *The cheerful proclamation of Christ's righteousness before all the world.* 'I will make mention of thy righteousness, even of thine only.' This thing 'was not done in a corner,' neither is the christian's approbation of it silent or hidden. He goes up to the house-top with it; he goes into the highways and byways with it; he wears it in the palace, as well as in the cot, and testifies to its exclusive worth before the chair of the scorner, as well as in the assembly of the saints. 'It is the glory of God to conceal a thing,' but it is the glory of the christian to publish his confidence in the righteousness of Jesus. He cannot be ashamed of it, for he feels that he owes everything to it—priceless pardon, spotless purity, present peace, and the good hope of eternal life. Ashamed of himself and of his filthy rags he is; and if he were commanded to appear in them, he would seek some solitude of nature wherein to hide; but of Jesus he is not, and cannot be ashamed. Receiving the mercy of God through that Saviour, and rushing forthwith into the world a converted and forgiven man, he exclaims, 'God forbid that I should glory, save in the cross of our Lord Jesus Christ!' He feels that 'necessity is laid upon him,' and that he cannot 'but speak of the things he has seen and heard.' Men may laugh at him; friends may desert him; tyrants may denounce him; martyrdom may be before him; he heeds them not;—always and everywhere must he publish the matchless work of redeeming blood! It is under this sense of personal obligation, that he takes a deep interest in the spread of the gospel at home and abroad. Contemplating the race to which he belongs, as all equally guilty and condemned with himself; knowing that it was owing to no merit of his own that to him 'the word of this salvation was sent,' but purely owing to the free grace of God; and believing that the mediatorial sacrifice is as precious to mankind at large as it has been to him, and that all men are as welcome to an interest in it as he was, he lifts up his voice and weeps for 'the slain of the daughter of his people;' but all his zeal is not absorbed in sympathy—he takes action—he does all he can by personal example, and all he can to send and support others who are willing to go far hence among the Gentiles, to proclaim among them the 'unsearchable riches of Christ.'

And herein lies the secret of missionary zeal. No wonder that millions of professing christians do so little for the conversion of sinners. They are, after all, themselves destitute of personal interest in the justifying righteousness of the Redeemer. And no wonder that there are multitudes of genuine believers who are glad that the burden of bringing back a lost world to God devolves upon them; for they have tasted the joys of pardon, and they live in the exercise of hope. Christ is precious to them; and to the souls for whom he died they long to tell the story of his wondrous love, saying, 'Come hear, all ye that fear God, and I will declare what he hath done for my soul;' or, looking over the walls of Zion, and comprehending the world lying in wickedness, they shout with an exceeding loud voice, that the isles may hear, and that they that dwell in the uttermost parts of the earth may know, that 'God so loved the world, that he gave his only-begotten Son, that whosoever believeth in him should not perish, but have everlasting life.'

We cannot conclude this brief dissertation on the justifying righteousness of Christ, without an earnest and direct appeal to the reader who is still under the condemning sentence of the law. We ask him, why is it that you refuse to be pardoned? Why is it that you will not accept of this 'all-sufficient righteousness?' Why will you not come to Christ? Is it because of any fancied indifference on the Saviour's part, or of any severity exercised towards you which is not manifested towards others, or of any deficiency in the treasury of his righteousness, or of any imbecility in the spirit and power of his gracious invitations? Is it because he cannot, or, though able, will not save you? It cannot be; for none of these causes exist. The heart of Jehovah-Tsidkenu has never been indifferent to you, nor to any of the children of men. From eternity it glowed with love of unquenchable warmth. While on earth many waters could not quench it—not even the sorrows of hell, when they gat hold upon it. *Coldness* is an impossibility within that region of love 'which passeth knowledge.' His heart is as a fire of love; and at this moment it burns as intensely as ever, notwithstanding all your sins, and all your contemptuous opinions of it and of himself. Say not that this warmth is cherished only for saints, and that it is not, and cannot be felt for such as you, who continue his enemies. He 'came not to call the righteous, but sinners to repentance.' And, as you shall hear in the following chapters, his visits as a physician are not to 'the whole, but to the sick.' It was sinners that he loved from everlasting. Sinner! it is you that he loves still; over you he still yearns; over you—*you*, the doomed to destruction—he still weeps, as he wept over Jerusalem. *Coldness!*—coldness in the heart of the Saviour towards you! Perish the thought! The coldness you should complain of lies only about the region of your own heart. Yes; it is *winter* there—a wild and dreary winter too: the frost is keen, the ice is thick, the snow falls heavily, and every passage to your loyalty and your love is choked up with the gatherings of the long and severe storm of your most obstinate impenitence. O, torment not yourself with doubts anent the state of Jesus' heart towards you, but with thoughts anent the state of your own heart towards him! It is all right with his; would God it were all right with yours! But what a contrast between the two!—are you not ashamed, are you not confounded with it? *His* overflowing with love for you—yours charged with scorn for him; his panting after your salvation—yours loathing his heavenly grace; his yearning, yea, melting with pity for you—yours steeling itself against all his entreaties; his bleeding to the very core—yours hard as the adamant; his at length cold and motionless, because he died out of love for you—yours alive and active, but only that it may scout his mercy and sear itself against the eloquence and pathos of his unutterable sorrows. Reader, do you not perceive this contrast? What do you think of it? How will it do for a study on your death-bed? How will it look when it is exhibited in the judgment before an assembled world? How will it sound when its characteristics are read over in the hearing of the inflexible Judge? And how will you feel, when the assembled nations shall join in hissing you into your place, because you dared to despise the grace of its sovereign Lord? Ah, infatuated man! It will be his turn to grow cold then; and cold indeed must his heart be towards you. Not one single emotion of affection for you will then be found in that heart; no, not one. As the inexorable Judge, he will banish you for ever from it and from his presence. It will be your turn to grow warm then; to become awfully interested then in him, in yourself, in the future, and in eternity. But what will any warmth, any concern of yours, avail in such a position, and at such a crisis?. Nothing whatever. It is too late now; as you sowed in time, so now you shall reap; you 'sowed to the flesh,' and 'of the flesh you shall now reap corruption,' which is, misery and everlasting shame.

There is something oppressively awful in the conception of our Redeemer contemplating masses of mankind sinners, without one single emotion of pity for them or their fate in that day. One feels a difficulty in realising such a state of things in the heart of him who 'was made flesh and dwelt among us,' and 'who bore our griefs, and carried our sorrows;' yea, whose love was so strong that it carried him through the mysterious and agonising scenes of Gethsemane and Calvary; it does violence to our usual modes of judging about the meek and lowly Jesus, to think of him at all in the character of the stern and inflexible judge. When we read the inspired story of his wonderful forbearance, and of his pitiful care of the pilgrim-man; when we trace his providential vigilance, his amazing liberality, his singularly pathetic contrivances to win that pilgrim's heart, and to guide him into the paths that lead to heaven; when we muse on the revolutions of time, and on the vicissitudes of this mundane existence, taking into view the startling and momentous events of thousands of generations, and consider that all these are but parts of his ways for making everything work together for the good of his people; and when we reflect that he ascended to, and sits upon his present throne, for the express purpose of governing the universe, upon principles that should subjugate everything and every one to the magnificent economy of mercy over which he exclusively presides; when we dwell in thought on all this exquisitely-balanced system, and associate it all with his character as our attached and sympathising High Priest, it is indeed alike painful and bewildering to revolutionise the whole scene, and the whole character, and behold Jesus of Nazareth coming again to this world, but with a purpose, concerning millions of its inhabitants, the very opposite of that which moved him to come hither at the first. It may not be a pleasant, but it may be a profitable study, to read some of the gospel as it shall then be read. How think you, reader, shall it strike upon your ear, so familiar as it is at present with gospel sounds, to hear such passages as the following :—' The Son of man comes not to save sinners, but that sinners through him may be condemned.' 'He comes to seek, but not to save sinners.' ' This is a faithful saying, and worthy of all acceptation, that Jesus Christ comes into the world to turn the wicked into hell, and all the nations that have forgotten God.' 'As I live, saith the Lord, I have now no pleasure in your life, but rather that you should depart from me into everlasting fire.' 'Come unto me, all ye that labour and are heavy laden with your guilt, and I will give you eternal destruction.' ' Depart from me ; I never knew you.' Terrible and appalling as are these transpositions of well-known gospel texts, you may rest assured, O guilty reader! that if you appear at his bar impenitent and unbelieving, you must be thus addressed, and you must be thus punished. You now listen with indifference to the gracious version of the gospel ; but you shall not so listen to the judicial edition of the Saviour's words on that eventful day. You then shall hear, ay, and believe too; but your attention to, and faith in Christ then, can only issue in your inevitable condemnation.

And all this is true; it may be future, but it shall be all accomplished; it may be in your present mood of thought only the language of well-intentioned terrorism, but you will know it then to be the just and the irresistible deliverance of Him whose authority is only to be resisted now, that it may be yielded to then, without an iota of that mercy which is its sure and infallible concomitant, when in this life his kindness is appreciated, and his gospel is believed. Yes, he permits you to have it all your own way at present; but he will have it all his own way at last. You will then discover that Jesus on the judgment-seat is a very different person to deal with from Jesus on the cross. Toleration has had its day; redeeming patience has run to its limit; divine love has ceased to pity; and divine authority must and shall be completely honoured. Do you think that your contempt of such a God, of such a Saviour, with his atoning sacrifice and all-sufficient righteousness, and of such a steady, stately plan of mercy, is to be permitted to last for ever, or for ever to go uncondemned? You are in a deplorable mistake. It cannot be so, it ought not to be so—the honour of God, the glory of God's Son, the rights of God's people, the very safety of his throne, make it imperative that he shall arise and terribly avenge his insulted majesty and his despised salvation.

CHAPTER VIII.

JEHOVAH-ROPHI: THE LORD MY HEALER.

PART I.

> 'I am the Lord that healeth thee.'
> EXODUS xv. 26.

THE justification or pardon of a sinner is the *beginning*, but by no means the entire of what is called his salvation. Before God can have friendly communion with him, he certainly, first of all, secures man's reconciliation to divine law and justice by the death of his Son; but immediately on this, he proceeds with the believer's gradual sanctification. A sinner is both a guilty and an impure creature; and with a view to his living again with God, he must be more than forgiven—he must be made perfectly holy; and this result is certain. Remote though he be from it at the period of his conversion, he is certain to reach it, under the gracious training of the High Priest of his profession; 'for if, when we were enemies, we were reconciled to God by the death of his Son; much more, being reconciled, we shall be saved by his life.' In a word, whenever man is taken out of the cell in which, by law, he has been imprisoned, and where he has been the victim also of spiritual disease, he is conveyed into the hospital of gracious means, to be treated by the Physician there, and dismissed only when perfectly cured. *Sanctification* is thus the unfailing consequence of *justification*; so that if any man continues to live in, and love sin, he gives proof that he is not a pardoned sinner; but if he 'crucifies the flesh, with its affections and lusts,' and 'lives soberly, righteously, and godly in this present world,' he demonstrates that the act of pardon is past, and that he is rapidly meetening for a better world. Having already meditated on the source of the sinner's justification, and on the use to be made of Christ's righteousness when it has been imputed, we now, in natural order, proceed to view him under sanctification, or the spiritually restorative process. And as Jehovah-Jesus is ' our righteousness,' so we find him to be also 'our *healer*.' We shall therefore employ this metaphor as the basis of the following *illustrations* of the subject. We shall consider—

I. THE PATIENT AND HIS DISEASE. God is good, and 'his tender mercies are over all his works.' The inference from this is, that all his works must be good, and all his creatures happy; and it was so, till sin entered, and with it, 'death and all our woe.'

Familiar as we now are with misery, it is difficult to realise a period when the opposite was the condition of everything and of every one; when there was no groaning in creation, and sorrow and sighing had no existence; when conflict in the mind, vice in the heart, confusion in the moral faculty, and opposition in the will, were strangers in the human bosom; and when the serenity, sunshine, and fertility of nature were but the faint emblems of the delicious repose, and spiritual exuberance of the soul. We have ever been entire strangers to such primeval felicity, and have got so accustomed to associate, almost to identify, our very existence with internal collision with and opposition to the law of God, that we are in danger of concluding, that if this were not our original state, it is so now of necessity, and that therefore we are not in any way responsible for it, or for its consequences. Yes; men are found bold and wicked enough to reason thus, and even to go the length of holding that it was never otherwise; that all these phenomena are constitutional, the very laws of our nature, implying no moral change, and consequently involving no moral responsibility; they plead for what is termed 'the dignity of human nature;' they refuse to connect the diversified play of its passions and its power either with degeneracy or turpitude; and they fancy that if perfection in a higher degree of intelligence or of piety is to be associated with our history, it is to the future, and not to the past, that we must look as the epoch of its development. Now, can anything be said to justify such arrogant contradiction of God's word and human experience? There cannot. Certainly it is humiliating to contrast man as he is, with what God represents him to have been in innocence; and it is not easy, if it be possible, for us to conceive of a state of things wherein his soul must have been uninterruptedly absorbed in the love and service of God, and when, from its perfect harmony with the divine attributes, all its outgoings of feeling and desire embraced the entire brotherhood with a love of pure disinterestedness—a love which not only kept at a distance from, but lived in ignorance of that motley crowd of malignant dispositions which now degrade and curse the race. It is also somewhat natural to apologise for man as he is, on the conceited plea that just as he is, he ever was and must be, and that it is a libel upon him, and an insult to his Creator, to conclude that he has become degenerate. Born in sin, and habituated now to its service, he of course knows not any other condition of being. Habits become second nature, and to the unrenewed mind, nothing is so agreeable as to puff itself up with the conceit that, notwithstanding the strictures of theologians, it is, if only withdrawn from the contamination of evil example, still an upright and imposing specimen of the Creator's wisdom. 'What a piece of work is man! How noble in reason!—how infinite in faculties!—in form and moving, how express and admirable!—in action, how like an angel!—in apprehension, how like a god!' are appropriate expressions from proud and lying lips. Be it far from us to under-rate unjustly any creature of God. We admit that man is 'fearfully and wonderfully made;' that there is something sublime and stately even in his ruins—something that indicates in bygone ages a perfect edifice, yea, a temple where the Deity may have once resided. Let us not veil what proofs of divine skill remain, but neither let us hide the painful truth that the divine image has fled. In the serious view of the matter, now that God has retired from him, the glory is gone from man; we see it in the sin and misery that abound wherever he lives. In the beautiful, though mournful language of Howe: 'The lamps are extinct, the altar overturned, the light and love are now vanished, which did there, the one shine with so heavenly brightness, and the other beam with so pious fervour. The golden candlestick is displaced, and thrown away as a useless thing, to make room for the throne of the Prince of Darkness. The sacred incense, which sent rolling up in clouds its rich perfumes, is exchanged for a poisonous, hellish vapour, and here is, instead of a sweet savour, a stench. The comely order of this house is turned all into confusion, the beauties of holiness into noisome impurities. Behold the desolation! all things rude and waste, so that should there be any pretence to the divine presence, it might be said, If God be here, why is it thus? The faded glory, the darkness, the disorder, the impurity, the decayed state in all respects of this temple, too plainly show the great Inhabitant is gone.'

But to keep to the figure of the text; man is now the victim of a spiritual disease. Such is the invariable testimony of the Bible. When he sinned, he lost his health; into every vein was transfused the fatal poison, and not only was health lost—life itself was lost; for what is the existence of a rational being totally destitute of holiness, but *death?* To drink in sin, is to suck in death, for 'the wages of sin is death.' Imbibing this idea, holy men of old were accustomed to speak of sin as their sickness: 'The whole head is sick, and the whole heart faint,' said Isaiah. '*Heal* me, O Lord,' said the Psalmist, 'for my bones are vexed;' '*heal* my soul, for I have sinned against thee;' '*heal* me, O Lord, and I shall be healed.' God himself, to encourage such cries, says, 'If my people pray and seek my face, and turn from their wicked ways, then will I hear from heaven, and forgive their sin, and will *heal* their bond.' When Gratitude for this mercy lifts up her voice, it is thus she sings: 'Bless the Lord, O my soul, who *healeth* all thy diseases;' 'praise ye the Lord, for he *healeth* the broken in heart.' When the prophet would lay emphasis on the preciousness of Christ's sacrifice, he says, 'By his stripes we are *healed,*'— a fine and cheering thought, re-echoed centuries afterwards by an apostle. In a word, when the Hebrew bard winds up the Old Testament scriptures, he waxes poetical, and unveils the rising of the Sun of Righteousness, 'with *healing* under his wings.' And when the hoary-headed John, who puts the conclusion to the sacred canon, would enrapture the soul with the beauties and blessings of Paradise, he strikes his harp in praise of the tree of life, whose 'leaves were for the *healing* of the nations.'

When there is such a body of scripture bearing upon man as thus needing some *healing* measures, we are more than warranted, we are obliged to contemplate him as a patient suffering under some direful moral malady, and that it is upon this account that God now communicates with him. If it be not so, then the Bible is not intended for man. If he be not 'sick unto death,' then the sacrifice of Christ is not provided for him—to him no divine Healer is sent. But the references are all to him. The appalling description every way suits him, while the nature assumed by his kind Physician, as well as the character and design of his mediatorial work, confirm it. Jesus said, 'I came not to call the righteous, but sinners to repentance;' and to the sneering Pharisees he declared, when intimating the object of his mission, 'they that be whole need not a physician, but they that are sick.' Let us, then, briefly consider the pathology of this spiritual malady.

1. *It is moral and not physical.* It is sin and its

effects. Physical disease is no doubt to be traced to sin, but the connection between them is a mystery. The seat of this malady is in the soul, every faculty of which is deeply affected with it—more especially its judgment, its heart, and its will. The *judgment* is deranged; it actually 'does not like to retain God in its knowledge;' rather than do so, it takes up with other gods—opposes the one only and true God—insults Jehovah, laughs at him, dares him, would have everything different from what he has ordained, and, in the crisis of its delirious strength, imagines that it has hurled him from his throne. The result is, according to the law of moral declension, that the disease increases more and more, till the very knowledge of God goes out of the judgment altogether, and 'the fool saith in his heart, There is no God.' The *heart* also is sick; it sympathises with the judgment, and renounces God. Its nature is to love him most fervently and supremely, but now it hates him most intensely. It calls in the world and its trifles, the flesh and its lusts, the devil and his principalities, and entertains them with the music and the wine of its homage. Whatever is holy it loathes—whatever is heavenly it hates—whatever is divine it madly defies. It is a hard, a stony, a rotten heart, hence it has no attachments to the generous and the good; it is sordid and impure, hence it prostitutes itself to the lusts of every unclean thing. As for the *will*, the disease of sin has made fearful havoc with it. In relation to God, indeed, man has no will at all. To every good thing in his law, it is reprobate; it is perverse and obstinate in the extreme, and never indicates this so powerfully, as in doggedly refusing even his pardoning mercy; hence these words, 'Ye *will* not come unto me, that ye may have life.'

2. *It is universal.* There is not one exception. Sin is the disease, not of one, but of every age—not of one, but of 'all people that on earth do dwell;' for 'all have sinned and come short of the glory of God.' Of all that have been born of woman, Jesus Christ alone has been uninfected with sin. It is coeval with our existence; for 'we were shapen in iniquity, and in sin did our mothers conceive us.' New islands and continents have been and may be discovered, where languages hitherto unknown are spoken, and where singular habitudes obtain; but whatever other elements exist, the people are all found to be dying of this moral plague—singular proof, however the dispersion and the dissimilitude may be accounted for, that we are all descended from one common parentage.

3. *It is loathsome.* It must be something very bad, when even the eye of the God of pity cannot look upon it,—something especially nauseous, when benevolent angels fled from the region of infection,—something indisputably disgusting, when the very patients themselves become disaffected to each other on account of its 'wounds, and bruises, and putrifying sores;'

but above all, it must be revolting in the highest degree, when even He who undertook to cure it, shrunk back for a moment from the cup of its mixtures which he came to drink, that the dying might live, and exclaimed, 'Father, if it be possible, let this cup pass from me.' A putrid corpse is a ghastly sight, but it is fair to look upon compared with a putrid soul.

4. *Its progress is rapid.* How soon did it blacken the entire face of nature! How quickly it did its work on holy Adam! Instantly on being infected, he began to skulk and lie, and ere long a murderer grew up in his family. By and by, the whole world became corrupt; and 'God saw that the wickedness of man was great in the earth, and that every imagination of the thoughts of his heart was only evil continually.' It is only when it meets with the salutary checks of the gospel that its progress is retarded; but apart from all remedies, it has been ever found that sin makes quick work in the utter ruin of the soul—fearfully quick work in the entire destruction of holy and virtuous motives, and in the unutterable wretchedness which it entails on its victims.

5. *It is incurable.* By human skill it certainly is. We may say of it as the prophet said to the Assyrian, 'There is no healing of thy bruise; thy wound is grievous;' and with Jeremiah we may complain: 'Why is my pain perpetual, and my wound incurable, which refuseth to be healed?' Prescriptions innumerable have been given, and experiments of all kinds

tried, from the vaunting proposals of philosophy and the amiable efforts of benevolence, down to the ridiculous quackery of the empiric, and the profane orgies of superstition. But all have been in vain; and to each may be addressed the charge, 'Thou hast no healing medicines.' Sin has spread itself alike ragingly among the comparatively sound retreats of wisdom, as among the lowest purlieus of ignorance—into cities of the highest renown, and cabins of deepest degradation. It is as rampant in Europe as in Africa, and bids equal defiance to the lights of the nineteenth century, and the darkest of the mediæval ages. It spares none. It resists effectually all attempts to subdue or eradicate its virus. Hence have miserably failed all the efforts of unenlightened reason, in every period and in every part of the world, to cure man of this hereditary distemper.

6. *It is fatal.* 'The soul that sinneth, it shall die.' No man has ever yet seen a fatal case; for this implies the state of the lost—the irretrievably lost soul, in the region of torments. Unless we could pay a visit to the dead-house of the wicked, we cannot describe the appearance of a soul to which sin has proved fatal. But from scripture accounts, we may conceive of its horrible condition; and from what can be seen of its progress in those instances where no cure had ever taken the least effect, we may imagine somewhat of the appalling reality. It ought to be enough for us to know, that where no remedy is applied, a fatal

termination is certain. Left to run its course, reaction or convalescence is equally impossible with the upward flow of the mountain cataract, or the joyous agility of the lifeless body. It takes the very body to pieces, and reduces it to dust. It attacks the vitals of the mental part; and though it cannot annihilate its existence, it entirely and for ever separates it from God, and hope, and peace; for 'there is no peace, saith my God, to the wicked;' and 'the wicked shall be turned into hell, and all the nations that forget God.' There 'their worm dieth not, and the fire is not quenched;' there 'the smoke of their torment ascendeth up for ever and ever;' and there they shall be the victims of unutterable, intolerable, and everlasting woe. Such is the fatal termination of sin. But let us now turn to—

II. THE PHYSICIAN AND HIS REMEDY. Scripture tells us that there was once a council held in heaven, and that the subject of deliberation was a suitable remedy for the disease of sin. We are further told of the result—and a memorable one it was for our world. A physician equal to the task was found in the person of the only-begotten Son of God himself; and the remedy proposed was nothing less than the 'shed blood' of his Son, as 'our passover, sacrificed for us.' None of the angels had skill enough, and nothing but 'the blood of God' had virtue sufficient to cure the malady. The gospel tells the marvellous tale—how that in due time the promised Healer appeared on earth, 'made of a woman, and made under the law;' having descended to this infected region, in order that he might take the disease upon himself, and by reason of his divine strength exhaust its virus, and thus deprive it of its power to kill. Strictly speaking, he could not really be the subject of sin; and indeed it was necessary that our Surety should be, and he was, 'without sin;' but though not inherently, he was by *imputation* connected with it: 'The Lord hath laid on him the iniquity of us all;' 'Surely he hath borne our griefs and carried our sorrows.' We read in history of a warlike monarch who was wounded in battle by a poisoned arrow. Death was inevitable, unless some one with courage and love enough would suck out the poison. Such an one appeared in his own wife, who extracted it with her lips. The life of her husband was preserved. But what was this, or any other authenticated case of disinterested suffering, compared with the sacrifices of our Lord Jesus, in order that sin-stricken souls might look upon his cross and live for ever?

1. Let us reflect on his *personal dignity*. He who did this was the equal of the Father. Creation came forth at his fiat, and before him the hierarchy of heaven 'veil their faces with their wings.' He was the favourite of all the celestial inhabitants; and beyond all, when the Lord 'gave to the sea his decree that

the waters should not pass his commandment: when he appointed the foundations of the earth: then *He* was by him as one brought up with him, and he was daily his delight.' He was 'the Angel of the Covenant,' who appeared and spake unto the patriarchs; the shekinah that dwelt between the cherubims; the 'man of war,' who fought and won all the battles of his people; the God of the prophets, who 'spake as they were moved by his Spirit;' the spotless son of Mary; the worker of miracles; the wisest of preachers; the most warm-hearted of friends; the most compassionate of benefactors; and at length, the triumphant conqueror of hell, of death, and of the grave!

2. Let us reflect, especially, on his *mediatorial services*—on the obedience, the suffering, and the death to which, as in the former chapter we have seen, he cheerfully submitted, so that a justifying righteousness might be procured for the guilty. While sojourning among men, he cured miraculously all manner of bodily diseases, his most prominent public character being that of a *physician*. We cannot fail to notice in this, his intention to signify the spiritual object of his mission, which was to open the eyes of the blind understanding, the ears of the deaf spirit, and the heart of the loveless ingrate. All kinds of patients came to him, and all were cured of whatsoever disease they had. And so all sinners are equally welcome to apply his healing virtue to every moral sore and spiritual sickness. He will cure every one of them,

from the trembling paralytic to the wild demoniac; from the earliest symptoms of the disease in smiling childhood to the unmentionable debaucheries of a full-grown vice. He can, and sometimes does effect his cure at once, as in the case of the thief who died at his side; and even where the use of means is prescribed, and a length of time elapses before perfect holiness is attained, the progress of convalescence is sure and steady. In his hands there never was and never can be a relapse. In the course of the treatment there may be sometimes varieties both of pulse and pith, of cordial attachment to divine things, and of religious strength in attempting divine duty; but *progression* is the law which the convalescent soul obeys. And how is all this effected? In the case of his miracles, he did all by the simple exercise of his almighty will; 'the power of the Lord was present to heal them.' It is far different, however, in his cure of souls. He cannot do this by a mere word. He cannot simply will it. By power alone he might call into being orbs of day for the firmament, or orbs of light for the eyeballs of the blind. But more, infinitely more than his sovereign word is required here. His own blood must flow—his own soul must be 'sorrowful even unto death;' he himself must 'give up the ghost,' and for a time be the tenant of the dust, to which the sinner was sentenced to return.

3. *This leads us to inspect the remedy.* There are two ways of speaking about it; either as 'the blood

of Christ,' which is the procuring cause of spiritual life, or as 'the gospel of Christ,' which publishes and offers that blood to the diseased and dying soul, and which, when believed, begins and completes its recovery. Substantially these things are the same; for *the gospel* cannot be believed, except by the sinner's appropriation of that blood of atonement which it reveals; and that atonement cannot be received except as it is represented and offered in that gospel. Thus the *message* describing the remedy is often, by a metonymy, put for the remedy itself; so that he who believes the 'word of God' is in reality using the blood of the Saviour. In this view, after all, even the cure of the soul is effected by a word—*the* word of God; but in that word is lodged not the mere power that bids the thunder roll or the lightning flash,—in its sacred volume reposes the omnipotence of *mercy!* and forth from its oracles stream the light and life of a finished redemption. Truth, then—not any truth, or all truth—but *the* truth '*as it is in Jesus*,' is the grand moral cure for the most terrible of human ills. This truth was the music of that angels' song which aroused the drowsy shepherds from their midnight watch, and led them adoringly to the infant Saviour. Nor have its notes been ever silenced. The hills of Judea took them up from the plains of Bethlehem; the sea of Galilee wafted them from these hills to the river Jordan; and ever since, Jordan has overflowed with them all its banks, and transmitted the delicious harmony over centuries of time, and continents of people. The beloved disciple thus winds up his gospel: 'And there are also many other things which Jesus did, the which, if they should be written every one, I suppose that even the world itself could not contain the books that should be written.' If this be true of the benevolent deeds of Christ in the days of his flesh, what language is adequate to do justice to the cures which he has been effecting ever since in the souls of millions upon millions of the vilest and most inveterate cases, and which are all at this moment the glorified trophies of his gospel in the kingdom of heaven! That gospel cannot be long heard without producing some effect, and it cannot be believed for one single instant without deciding the cure. Before the wonderful record of his love, the melting eloquence of his tears, the bloody sweat of the garden, the heart-rending tragedy of the cross, the power of his glorious resurrection, the doctrine of his holy word, and the law of his persuasive mouth, the rocks of human depravity have been rent in twain, the tempests of fierce passions have been stilled, the fury of raging lusts has been subdued, and every kind and degree of spiritual loathsomeness has been changed into the beauties of holiness and the handmaids of piety.

4. *And this gospel, believed on, is the only remedy.* Jehovah-Rophi has devised no other; no other is needed; none other is therefore ever applied. The

soul has lost its *hope,* and it is the gospel that replaces it. It has the deadly power of sin in every faculty, and it is the gospel that neutralises the vile influence, abolishes the death, and restores to life. If sin has the sting of death, the gospel extracts it. If the strength of sin be the law, the gospel overcomes it. The soul has lost its *light,* and it is the gospel that shines into it. It has lost its *peace,* and it is the gospel that tranquillises it. It has lost its *purity,* and it is the gospel that sanctifies it. It has lost its *love,* and it is the gospel that re-inflames it. Sin has twisted its *will* and tortured it into every evil bias, and it is the gospel that reduces its dislocations, and makes it pliant as the tender twig. The gospel has done all this, and the gospel alone can do it. Education has done much for the intellect; science and art have done much for civilisation; benevolence has done much for humanity; and all combined have succeeded in mightily improving our social character and condition. But not one of these agencies ever cured man of his spiritual disease. They do not attack the seat of it; and after exhausting their vigour upon his outward state, they leave him still 'dead in trespasses and in sins.' The uttermost of these remedies is, therefore, infinitely short of his greatest needs. Nay, even though they may boast of having amputated some morbid limb, or raised up some feeble hand, or effaced many blots, and filled up many scars, and imparted a hue of health, it has amounted to a mere topical or superficial amendment. The patient has not lost one of the bad symptoms; he is still sick at heart—still nauseates wholesome food; some festering sore breaks out every now and then, and by and by the artificial stimulants and soothing emollients lose power, and he droops, and falls, and dies. In other words, his nature has never been changed—he has not been converted—his sins remain unforgiven, and his conscience unpurged of dead works; hence he dies as he lived, 'without God,' and without title to eternal life. What miserable illustrations of this have we in the flickering lives and despairing deaths of the world's moral heroes! They betook themselves to tonics of their own decoction, and only discovered their inefficacy when the death-gurgle was in their throats. The gospel remedy alone never fails. All who have tried it have found it to be an exceedingly *simple* one, neither complicated in its own nature, nor disagreeable for use; an exceedingly *easy* one, not requiring waste of means or exertion of strength on their part, but intrinsically powerful on the very first application; an exceedingly *pleasant* one, alike sweet to the taste and joyous in the after consequences —offensive it may be to the carnal and conceited, but good and grateful to the believing soul; an exceedingly *cheap* one—yea, 'without money and without price.' It cannot be purchased; the wealth of worlds, the universe itself were inadequate; therefore blessed be God that bankrupt man has no conditions of sale annexed to it. If he be foolish or profane enough to offer to this *Healer* any price for his medicine, any remuneration for his skill, the remedy in that moment loses its power.

Be persuaded, then, diseased and dying reader, to visit Jehovah-Rophi, and try his precious cure. Is he not such an one as you can trust? He knows what is man, and what man needs, and he is best able and willing to administer. O employ him without delay! You will find his visits always seasonable, and he never prescribes in the dark, or operates on a venture. His attentions are all disinterested, and never fag or fail. He is uniformly successful; for 'of all whom the Father hath given to him, not one is lost.' Come, then, to the blood of his cross, and wash in it, and be cleansed from all your filthiness and all your uncleanness. 'Though you have been among the pots, yet shall ye be as the wings of a dove covered with silver, and her feathers with yellow gold.' Come to the consolations of his gospel, and have every tumult lulled. Come to his rich grace, which is sufficient for every phase and every turn of the malady, upholding, strengthening, soothing, and rejoicing the soul. Come to the influences of his Holy Spirit, which are certain to make the remedy effectual for even the worst and most hopeless—for the opening of the eyes, of the ears, and of the mouth, and for the confirmation of the feeblest. What a physician! What a remedy! While of all mere pretenders we may say, 'They have healed the hurt of the daughter of my people slightly,' of Rophi we may affirm, he has come 'to heal the broken-hearted,' and he has healed all who have had the sense to apply to him. If any remain uncured who have this gospel preached unto them, they are perishing of their own accord, and to them these solemn words are addressed: 'For the hurt of the daughter of my people am I hurt; I am black; astonishment hath taken hold on me. Is there no balm in Gilead? is there no physician there? why then is not the health of the daughter of my people recovered?'

III. THE CURE AND ITS EFFECTS. 'What are these which are arrayed in white robes, and whence came they? These are they who came out of great tribulation, and have washed their robes, and made them white in the blood of the Lamb.' This beautiful scripture presents to our view the perfection of Christ's cure. There they are at length in his Father's house, all clothed and in their right minds, employing their restored vigour and transparent purity in the high services of celestial adoration; nothing now shall ever harm or expose them to infection, for 'they shall sin no more.' It were, indeed, a delightful theme to expatiate on the blessedness of such spiritual and bounding health as theirs, and of the glorious and honourable use they make of it; but who is sufficient for such a theme? 'eye hath not seen, nor ear heard, neither have entered into the heart of man the things which God hath prepared for them that love him.' It may be less sublime, but equally useful to go round the *lower wards,* and see the cure progressing among the convalescent patients; all of them came to Jesus to be healed; one with an impenitent heart; another with a godless creed; a third with a sordid soul; a fourth with a self-righteous spirit; a fifth with libidinous desires; a sixth with a lying and profane tongue; a seventh with hands imbrued in a brother's blood; an eighth with an evil eye; a ninth with a calumnious mouth; and, indeed, multitudes with the malady in all its stages, and of every modification, gathered together from every region of the habitable earth. What wretched beings they were till they came here! how happy looking they all are now! some, of course, more or less sickly still, as all advance not with equal rapidity. But inquire at each as you pass along, and the unanimous testimony will be, We were *once* 'fornicators, or idolaters, or adulterers, or effeminate, or abusers of ourselves with mankind, or thieves, or covetous, or drunkards, or revilers, or extortioners;' but we are now 'washed, we are sanctified, we are justified, in the name of the Lord Jesus, and by the Spirit of our God.' Yes; here every wounded heart has the 'oil of joy' poured into it, and every wounded spirit is mollified with the ointment of grace. They are all sensibly and visibly getting better, and will soon be able to say with the dying saint, 'Ere long we shall be quite well.' But who is this that walks these wards with such heavenly benignity and noiseless foot? Mark him well; he has a word and a smile for every one: here he drops some balm, and there he administers the wine of consolation; yonder he wipes away a tear, and further on you see him clothing the heavy spirit with the 'garments of praise.' If there be, at any stage of his perambulation, an indication of special interest—a waxing more earnest in manner, or a stooping more condescendingly in position—you will find out that the cause of it all is the desperate case of some chief sinner, who has just been received. Who can this be? Who, but Jehovah-Rophi, the divine and merciful Saviour! Attend his footsteps daily, as he pursues his work of curing souls, and you will not hesitate to ascribe him all the praise of every cure, from beginning to end.

1. *You will praise him as beginning the cure.* None but he could. To *heal* is his exclusive prerogative. 'See now,' he says, 'that I, even I, am he, and there is no God with me; I kill and I make alive; I wound and I heal;' and, again, 'When Israel was a child then I loved him, and called my son out of Egypt; I taught Ephraim also to go, taking them by their arms, but they knew not that I healed them.' Ask any of his patients, and they will re-echo these exquisitely tender words. David will tell you that he is 'the health of his countenance,' that he 'cried

unto the Lord,' and that he had healed him. Isaiah will tell you, 'with his stripes we are healed.' Jeremiah will tell you that he 'will restore health unto thee and heal thee;' and Paul, and every apostle, will substantially add their testimony, by declaring that 'there is salvation in none other,' and that 'without the shedding of blood there is no remission of sins.' And how can it be otherwise, when you look at the virulent nature of the complaint? Sin stupifies the sufferer, and almost suffocates his respiration. When bodily disease waxes extreme, the patient soon becomes miserable. He then cares and asks for no cure. He is, therefore, completely dependent on others; and so it is with sickly, dying man. It was when the distemper was raging in his vitals, and when he raved deliriously, that Jesus passed by and touched him. In that touch, virtue went out of the Physician and cured the patient. It was when we were 'without strength' that he died for the ungodly. It was when we had ruined our constitution in riotous living, and when we had spent our all upon other physicians, that he stooped to breathe over our spirits the healing breath of his pity and his grace. And terrible, indeed, must the disease be, when to no voice will it yield but to his whose voice is 'powerful and full of majesty,' and when no remedy takes effect upon it but the precious blood that flows warm from his own heart.

2. *You will praise him as carrying forward the cure.* It for the most part happens, that the patient

remains in the hospital a long time before he is dismissed cured. Meanwhile he receives constant attention and kindness from the medical officers and careful nurses. So it is here. After the act of justification, the work of sanctification goes forward; the means of grace are used, the providences of God are blessed, and the Spirit of God is given, and all for the purpose of progressing the holiness or health of sinners. The crisis of a fever is often accompanied with great prostration of strength, but this crisis once over, vigour gradually returns, under judicious care and nourishing diet. It is often, too, when he is at the weakest that the ebbing tide of life suddenly turns, and flows steadily on to its height. And thus there is sometimes a moment in spiritual sickness when the pulse cannot be felt; but this, also, is a moment of hope; for it is not till man becomes *nothing* that Christ is made anything to him. 'When I am weak,' said Paul, 'then am I strong.' Yea, it has happened that, as one would say, death has already taken place; and so it has; but, then, this is that death to sin which all die who afterwards ' live to righteousness.' Now, it is from this spiritual death-bed that Jesus raises the sinner, and then kindly nurses him till he is able to leave the sick-room, and bear the climate and work the work of the better land. He gives him pastors and teachers, and Sabbaths and sacraments. He gives him books to read—the holy scriptures, which are a complete pharmacopeia for religious improvement; 'he sent his holy word,' says the Psalmist, ' and healed them'—even ' the sincere milk of the word, that he might grow thereby,' together with his portion of meat in due season, as he was able to bear it. In a word, by order and prudence, and the blessing of the Holy Spirit on both, he secures the patient's steady and stately elevation to that perfection which must be the grand issue of the whole.

3. *You will praise him, therefore, for also consummating the cure.* This he does when he removes them from the church below to the church above. Then the cure is so complete, that when presented to his Father, they are all 'without spot, or wrinkle, or any such thing;' so complete, indeed, that it could never be discovered that the leprosy of sin had smitten them. It was a law in the house of Moses, that if one man smote his fellow to his hurt, he was to see to his cure; the commandment was, ' he shall cause him to be thoroughly healed;' and such also is the law in the house of God: each sinner must be '*thoroughly healed*' before the Saviour can introduce him to the Father; and thoroughly healed now he certainly is. Look into that glorified soul; its *understanding* now is a perfect globe of light, transparent as light itself; its *judgment* now is entirely surrendered to the mind of God, and gives command to all around it to do him reverence; its *affections* now are all enthroned by occupying their original positions,—created Love, devoid of all selfish cravings, nestles in the

bosom of the Uncreated; Faith waits no longer at the door, but enters and takes possession of all the promises; Joy is now perfect at her music, sings no more on minor keys, and keeps no willow in her garden, because she has no need to hang any harp thereon; and Hope is full: she has no use for her anchor now—herself is within the veil, and is possessor of all she surveys. But to crown all, even the *will*, that perverse tyrant, cheerfully submits itself to God; it is, indeed, unconscious of its own existence, so thoroughly absorbed is it in doing his holy pleasure. Man, therefore, is at last himself again, and all that has been falsely sung in praise of his present condition must be discarded as falling now infinitely short of the truth. To all this must be added, the restoration to him of his very body which was laid in the grave. His divine Physician, by his mighty power, reproduces it in a state and form suitable to a soul made perfect in holiness. So shall it be found in the morning of resurrection: 'It is sown in corruption, it is raised in incorruption: it is sown in dishonour, it is raised in glory: it is sown in weakness, it is raised in power: it is sown a natural body, it is raised a spiritual body.'

CHAPTER IX.

JEHOVAH-ROPHI: THE LORD MY HEALER.

PART II.

'Is there no balm in Gilead? is there no physician there?'
JEREMIAH viii. 22.

GILEAD lay to the east of Jordan, towards Arabia. The 'balm' or balsam tree which grew there, and there only, was supposed to be an exotic—a transplant from Arabia, and one of the gifts of the Queen of Sheba to Solomon. It was regarded the most peculiar of the vegetable productions of Palestine. To all balsamic substances special virtues were ascribed; but from being more scarce, and, at the same time, highly medicinal, the plant of Gilead was had in peculiar estimation; many sought after it, and physicians went to the spot where it grew to collect, prepare, and apply it. In the beginning of April, cuts were made in the branches of the tree, from which the drops of balm dropped into vessels placed underneath for the purpose of receiving it. One of these cuts yielded only three or four drops in the day, or one drachm's weight; and the most prolific tree, during a whole season, did not give more than fifteen drachms in whole. A few drops, medicinally applied, were found in a short time to cure any wound, especially if inflammation had commenced. In the time of Alexander, its price was twice its own weight in silver. It is to this balm, then, that the prophet so touchingly alludes in the verse above quoted. His allusion, however, must be *spiritually* understood. He had been bewailing the deplorable condition of Israel in their captivity, and naturally had his thoughts turned to their sins, which he conceives to be their disease; and then, sympathising with them in the pains which it occasioned, and especially in its fatal tendency, he appeals to the mercy and grace of Jehovah, which could heal them and give them life, under the figure of the balm in Gilead, and the physician there, expressing his surprise that any should be unhealed or unpardoned when such abundant and suitable remedies were at their door. In like manner, may we not ask the sinner perishing under the gospel dispensation, 'Why is it so?' Is there no blood in Calvary? and is there no Saviour there? It must be from not properly appreciating either the skill of the Physician, or the intrinsic worth of his remedy. Let us, therefore, dedicate what remains to the practical application of the whole subject, by showing what is requisite to the proper appreciation of 'the Lord our Healer.'

I. THERE MUST BE THE PAINFUL CONSCIOUSNESS OF THE DISEASE. If we admit no need of, we shall discern no merit in Jesus Christ. Now, we have seen already that, whether avowed or not, disease of a very dangerous character does exist, vitiating and deranging every faculty of the soul. Some scriptures call this disease by the most extreme name that can be employed, '*death*.' It may therefore be asked, how can the *dead* be conscious? how can a corpse feel? how can these dry bones live? While held as dead in one sense, however, God treats and speaks to us as *alive* in another sense, and that so important as to make us accountable for rejecting the offered remedy. How is this to be explained? The free-thinker says it cannot be reconciled with truth, and hence he discards the doctrine. Let us humbly consider the matter. We see man utterly careless about God and the soul, about Jesus Christ and his salvation. If this be not spiritual death, what is it? for these are the very things about which, as a reasonable and immortal being, he ought to be most concerned. At the same time, we see him all alive to worldly things, quick to feel reverses or resent injuries, and forward to take advantage of more fortunate times. Nay, even with regard to religion, we see him sometimes slightly affected, reason slipping in a whisper that all is not right, and conscience partially awakened. When this is accompanied with some heavy trial, we see also a sort of languid and clumsy attempt at spiritual action, which, however, ends in a mournful relapse into still deeper indifference. To all this extent, then, of resisting conscience, stifling inquiry, and trifling with gospel warnings, may the sinner be said, though still dead, to be so far alive as to make him responsible for not carrying out and acting upon his convictions. There is certainly, in this state of things, proof that he has some *natural* capacity left, by which he ought to improve these intimations of disease, and seek after a proper remedy. At the same time, these are nothing more than *natural* fears. They lack religious or spiritual vitality. Still, man is responsible for the use to which he turns them. Existing in the conscience of a heathen, we know that they shall aggravate his guilt: 'For when the Gentiles, which have not the law, do by nature the things contained in the law, these, having not the law, are a law unto themselves.' If it be so with the Gentile that has not heard the gospel, it must be so with the gospel-hearer on a greater scale of responsibility. In resisting even such natural fears, he resists a greater amount of light, and incurs more guilt; for though these fears do not in themselves lead to Christ, yet the Spirit of God does use them for this end, and by means of them often quickens the soul into spiritual being. The two consciences that cried out, the one, 'Lord, save me; I perish,' and the other, 'Sirs, what must I do to be saved?' yielded to these fears, and found pardon. It is most manifestly, therefore, the duty of all under such influences, to place them before God, and ask him to impart to them the divine element, which would attract them at once to the cross. This, after all, just resolves the argument into our absolute need of the Spirit of God to produce within us such a sense of Christ's suitableness, as shall teach us to appreciate and apply his blood. It is unnatural for man to acknowledge himself spiritually unclean; he is ashamed of this, denies it, and finally imposes upon himself that he is not such a victim. Hence the idea of disease leaves him, and with the idea, the wish for its cure. Matters, of course, wax worse and worse; and left to himself, the end is fatal. There has never been a case when, unaided from above, the Physician has been sent for or the remedy used: 'It is the Spirit that quickeneth.' There may be a sort of consciousness that there is sickness which we ourselves cannot cure; but till the Spirit of God impregnates this consciousness with his own influence, it is never successful; which without figure means, that conscience may and does accuse man of sin, but until God sprinkles it with the peace-speaking blood of Christ, 'there is no soundness in it.'

Another question occurs: Can man be made responsible for not doing that which it is declared the Spirit of God alone can do? No man, certainly, is accountable for the non-production in himself of that sense of spiritual need which is inseparable from the spiritual cure. But there is an awful amount of

JEHOVAH-ROPHI. 171

responsibility, notwithstanding. Why, for instance, is he in such a condition that he cannot do his duty? Why has he thus incapacitated himself? Why has he so disinclined his mind as that, though he has the natural conviction of something being far wrong within him, he has no will, no heart whatever to the work of penitence or to the grace of pardon? This is not the doing of God; for he is not and cannot be the author of evil. This is altogether the curse and the guilt of the sinner. But in addition to this, he is certainly accountable for the use of those means of grace which the Spirit has promised to bless, for using these sincerely, prayerfully, hopefully, and perseveringly, and for his stubborn resistance to those thoughts which the use of such means originates, and which ought to lead him at once to Jesus Christ. When we say, therefore, that in order to appreciate the Saviour, we must first feel our need of him, we mean, that until we have used all the means in our power, and that in the spirit of mind clamantly demanded by the necessities of the case, to persuade ourselves that we are in a dying state, we will never spend one right thought on him who came to heal us. The simplest illustration of this is found in the figurative language of scripture, which describes sin as disease, and Christ as its healer. Now, a person may have the seeds of incurable disease, and not know it. Others see the symptoms, pity the doomed one, and predict his early death. Friendship may venture to hint it to him; but the uneasiness occasioned is momentary, for the inward evil has not yet gone so far as to inflict pain. Hence there is no precaution used, no physician consulted, and no cure wished for. But let organic disease pass from the chronic to the acute, then alarm is taken, and every available mean is earnestly sought after. Let us not despise this simple mode of illustrating a mysterious subject. The Lord Jesus himself has set the example. Its use, therefore, must be a powerful help to spiritual persuasion, when such a Master in Israel condescended to it for such an end. How, then, stands the matter with you? You have the disease of sin; it is working in your vitals; it is blanching your spiritual aspect, enfeebling your spiritual energies, covering with blotches your spiritual form, and giving evidence to all around you that you are fast sinking, and must soon die. Your friends hint it to you—your pastors affirm it—your Bibles prove it—your earthly afflictions corroborate it—and perhaps every now and then you are actually made to stand still and to think, Can this be true? But you do not follow it up—you forget—you permit Satan, the world, and the flesh, to deceive you into the idea that it is all a delusion, or that, if not perfectly well, you are but slightly ailing, and that, by a little care, you must soon recover; and thus it is that your souls die. We would earnestly beseech you that peruse these lines to pause and ponder. O labour—we say, *labour* to convince yourselves of your need of Christ, that before the Father would send such a Son, and before the Son would die such a death, there must have existed a tremendous necessity! Labour, then to get your hard hearts broken; for while they resist the Father—while they receive blow upon blow from the hammer of God's word, and yet remain insensate—hard as the granite they must be. Labour to bring down the judgment to all the conclusions of scripture, and to fill all the passions with the most intense and unquenchable desires after spiritual convalescence. We say, *labour* for all this; because idleness is fatal here to hope as well as to health. You must be resolutely, prayerfully, and constantly at the work; and if you be so, it is certain that, ere long, the awful sense of need shall come, the burning fever shall be felt, the stench of the putrifying sores shall be intolerable, and the agonising terrors of appalling dissolution shall then fling you down prostrate under despair, transfixing you with the arrows of compunctuous visitations!

Indeed! you respond; and is this the reward you promise to such laborious efforts? You would have us work our minds out of what you call a false security; but still we enjoy somewhat of the sense of it, false and deceiving though it be;—you would have us hurry our thoughts out of what you call the region of meteor glare; but still we enjoy that which, if it be not absolute light, is not absolute darkness;—you would have us relinquish our hold of what you call a broken reed; but still we enjoy the grasp of something tangible, which, if it prevent not, at least breaks the fall;—you would have us dissolve our carousals, empty our wine-cups, silence our timbrels, cease our dancing, and call a halt to all our gay and gleesome life, which you describe as altogether vanity, but which to us makes lagging time speed merrily by, and drowns the dissonance of life's cries and cares;—and you would persuade us, that whatever be our worldly state, bodily health, or intellectual greatness, we are, after all, poor, miserable, blind, and naked—that we are the most contemptible creatures in existence, and are hastening on, with terrific rapidity, to the region of lost souls! Yes; you have expressed it so far truthfully; such are the very conclusions to which we would have you to labour to come, and that for this plain but weighty reason—all this is indispensable to your appreciation of Jesus the physician, and to the instant application of his all-availing remedy. How, think you, is it that up to this day you have never been in earnest about your own salvation? It is just because you have been taking it for granted that you have been well enough, and have never believed that with you all is lost. Had you been so persuaded, you would have fled to the Cross long ere this; for 'to know ourselves diseased is half our cure.' Nothing will hinder you then. The terrors of the Lord will give the speed of lightning to your motion, and your passion for cure will wax so strong, that no hinderance will be felt in your way; nothing will be accounted a sacrifice; everything that helps you forward to Christ will be hailed as an accessory, in order that you may be surely and entirely in and with him who is the Physician in Gilead, and applies the balm that is there for the cure of the wounded and the peace of the dying.

II. THERE MUST BE AN INTELLIGENT ACQUAINTANCE WITH THE PHYSICIAN. His consummate skill must with us not be matter of hearsay merely—we must *discern* such qualities in him, and know assuredly that he is perfectly qualified. We have seen that till men are consciously ill, they care not for medical interference, but that then they seek one in whom, from repute or their own experience, they have confidence. In the spiritual case, however, the patient has no previous experience to guide him, and in lieu of this, the same Spirit that made him *feel* his malady lets him see the Healer, even Jesus. This is the gracious result of a believing examination of the Bible, where the Saviour's healing powers are fully delineated and divinely accredited, where multitudes of successful cures are duly registered, and where the most powerful persuasives urge on the weakliest and the most despairing, to ask his advice and use his prescriptions. But it ought to be especially noticed, that no man has any right to expect such an insight into the Saviour's worth, apart from a very diligent searching of the scriptures. His testimonials must be read and studied that we may clearly perceive *why* he ever came to sustain such a relationship to us, and *how* it is that his divine righteousness is sufficient to justify. In addition, to acquire such a knowledge of Christ, as will dispose us to put ourselves entirely into his hands, we must come to the decided conviction, that sin can be forgiven in no other way than through the blood of his cross sprinkled upon us; that in this way its guilt is absolutely certain to be cancelled; and that so far as our own individual case goes, he is just as willing as he is competent to deal with and cure it. If any man doubt either the one or the other of these propositions, he rejects the remedy, and dies. If Christ did not die for that man, then that man must die for himself; but Christ's death has, beyond all controversy, removed every legal obstacle out of every sinner's road, and therefore, in that sense, he is the propitiation for 'the sins of the whole world.' To be assured of this adaptation of the atonement to one's own case, is to use the remedy which gives eternal life to the soul. Every sinner that has so used it, has recovered; and they who quibble about its suitableness, or the Physician's intentions to make it available for them, perish in the meantime. Studying the cross under these impressions fills the mind with light, clears the heart of fears, and 'purges the conscience from dead works.' No other kind of study serves any good purpose. Mere dreamy notions of his character will not do; mere fragmentary intelligence caught up from books, catechisms, liturgies, confessions, and conversations, will not do; mere solemn thoughts, floating like clouds before the mind, or occasionally supplied with new matter from pulpit prelections, will not do; mere superficial and superstitious acknowledgments of our needs and of his appropriate qualities will not do; above all, mere hypocritical or nominal christianity will not do. None of these exercises ever lead to the object at which we look—the unreserved surrender of our precious souls into his hands to be healed.

JESUS CHRIST AND HIM CRUCIFIED IS A STUDY—is the greatest of all intellectual and moral studies—not a toy to be sported with or a tale to be told—not an ephemeral lesson to be got to-day and forgotten to-morrow—not a mere branch of education to qualify for some humble sphere; but a mighty volume of earnest thinking—a theme of awful solemnity and majestic proportions—the root, and trunk, and branch of the tree of life—A STUDY FOR ETERNITY. We would be far from *limiting* the restorative power of his saving truth, or of defining to a point what is the exact space over which the human mind must travel, in order actually to reach and touch him. Still we would strenuously insist upon a change to the better in the habits of many in these things. O for more severe and thoroughly earnest investigation into the 'great mystery of godliness!' Most professing christians trifle with it. *Superficial thinking* on Christ is the sin, the disgrace, the ruin of the age we live in. It is this which makes and keeps his church a dwarf. The depths of his healing power are not sounded, the length and breadth of his pity for our souls are not scanned, and his admirable suitableness as the Physician of souls is not revealed, by superficial thinking. Such thinking may send us into the membership of the church, and become the deceptive aliment on which we feed our false hopes up to death; but it never saved a sinner, it never cured a soul. To expect that confidence is to be established in him otherwise than by constant meditation, reading, and praying, is presumption of no common order, which would not be tolerated in the affairs of the world, and would be laughed at even among fools. And yet, there are tens of thousands of whom it were worse than ridiculous to affirm, that they have profoundly studied the love and life, the sufferings and death of the incarnate Son of God. David of old made God's word his study both day and night, and came very near in his practice of the divine testimonies to what was required of Israel: 'Thou shalt teach them diligently unto thy children, and shalt talk of them when thou sittest in thine house, and when thou walkest by the way, and when thou sittest down, and when thou risest up.' How few, alas! treat the gospel in this fashion! On the contrary, do not most men, while proving their intellectual vigour by mastering earthly sciences, give to the *weightier matters* of 'the wisdom of God' feeble reflection, and devote a lifetime's intensity to that wisdom which is 'earthly, sensual, and devilish?' Let the reader be impressed with the importance of this subject, by carefully considering the evils that flow from such tampering with divine truth. For example—

1. *Multitudes, in consequence, never appreciate Christ at all.* They never reach the conviction that they need him, and hence they do not apply to him. Not having examined his credentials, they never argue from these that they must be diseased and dying. It is the sincere and believing study of Christ alone that leads men to his atonement. For the miserable victims of this fatal negligence we are not only to look to the outcasts of society, or to that swarm of heathenism which is huddled together in the dingy and loathsome back parts of crowded cities, but to that throng also of baptised and professing religionists who, from habit or fashion, connect themselves with the church. These are they who pay out a sum of money, and, as it were, matriculate for the sake of the external rites of christianity, but who give themselves as little to the study of their religion as many who enrol themselves members of a university, and yet give no heed to the lectures delivered, nor to the sciences for which lectures were endowed, books published, and expensive apparatus provided. Neither party acquire as much genuine learning as would

qualify them for keeping a door in their respective seminaries. The fact is, there is no study in the matter. A mere smattering of religion is thought to be enough to pass them respectably through life. What an insult to the truth of God! what a depreciation of the philosophy of salvation! what a contempt of the skill and power of Jehovah-Rophi! Not only do souls perish, but an appalling amount of the precious means of saving souls is thus wasted and lost. The temple builds her altars, kindles her fires, and lights up her lamps in vain. The pulpit reads, and thinks, and pleads in vain. The avenues to the throne of grace are opened up in vain. The Sabbath bell rings its inviting peals in vain. The religious press pours forth its contributions in vain; nay, and worse than all, up to this point, God has loved, Christ has died, and the Holy Spirit has warned in vain. There is balm in Gilead, but they will not place their pitchers underneath to catch one healing drop; there is a Physician there, but they despise his offered help.

2. *A second evil is the deceit which many practise upon themselves, that they do, when in reality they do not appreciate Christ.* A certain amount is often mistaken for the requisite amount of religious knowledge. On obtaining this small portion, books are laid aside, and systematic application is no longer felt to be necessary. When such is the case, we are but tyros in the school of Christ—we are only at the alphabet; and if we do not immediately form loftier

ideas of his 'excellent knowledge,' we shall never get the length of first principles. No man can rightly study the christianity of Christ without feeling every day the overwhelming truth, that it is an illimitable and unfathomable theme. No man can begin in a serious frame to scan its dimensions, and penetrate into its awful interior, without the solemn conviction, that it is a wanton insult to treat the story of redeeming love, the delineations of its plan, and the very secrets of its Author's heart, as if they could be spanned by the intellect of a child, or mastered by the glance of a holiday attention. Would God that the doctrines of the Bible were attended to with one tithe of the earnest mind we give to the things of this world!—then would the communicant rolls of British churches be rapidly thinned; then would men of their own accord neither touch, taste, nor handle the holy and divine elements of the temple; then would they hasten from the altar lest its fires should spring upon and consume them—lest that awful sword that has just struck the bleeding Lamb, return not to its scabbard till it has mingled their blood with their profanity. So long, however, as such low and unworthy opinions exist of what constitutes the true excellence of the Saviour, multitudes must contrive to deceive themselves and others with the idea, that to them it has been given to know as they should be known, the 'mysteries of the kingdom.'

3. *A third evil is the unworthy ideas which even the*

genuine disciples of Christ entertain of his unparalleled excellence. This is not so disastrous an evil as the two former, but it is much to be deplored. No doubt, through all eternity, Christ shall never be appreciated as he deserves; still it is within the limits of possibility, that his people here might form a far higher estimate of his peculiar fitness as their Mediator, and become more experimentally acquainted with the richness of his grace, and, consequently, make more decided approaches to that pattern of piety which he exemplified and enforces, if they would only raise the standard of religious attainments, and exact from, and expect in one another, a greater breadth of christian learning, as well as a larger amount of christian conduct. The truth is, that while every believer has as much knowledge of Christ as ensures the commencement of his spiritual cure, there are yet many who may be ashamed of their deficiencies in this respect—deficiencies to which we must trace the comparatively comfortless opinions which they entertain of the virtue of atoning blood. The fact is, the disciples of christianity are too soon taken from the school—too soon treated as full grown—too soon examined for membership—pass that examination too easily, and are too soon (as they themselves may think) on 'the foundation.' The church is, in consequence, only a half-learned church; and though we do not here apply the proverb, that 'no learning is better than half-learning,' for any learning of Christ is certainly better than none at all, yet would we exceedingly deplore the desultory application of God's people, in general, to their holiest studies. Their occasional falls into sin, their proneness to carnality, their frequent conformities to this world, their spiritual barrenness, their complaints of coldness and instability in religion, their poor thoughts of Jesus Christ, and their paltry sacrifices, and feeble efforts on his behalf, are but too intelligible symptoms of their educational defects, their intellectual poverty, their scriptural stintedness, and their entire christian disproportions. Ours, indeed, is all the poorer and darker a world from this slim and slurring system. Even as it is, christians must be regarded 'the salt of the earth,' and 'the lights of the world;' but O, if they would only discipline their minds more sturdily in their lessons; if they would only fill their lamps more purely from the vessels of the sanctuary; if they would only whet their appetites by more devotedness to the Bible; if they would only study more on their knees and in their closets; and if they would take their stand more frequently beside that 'ACCURSED TREE,' and wait till the hum and stir of the world's day were past, till the veiled sun had sunk to rest behind Judean hills, till the passions of men are momentarily quieted in the hours of sleep, till the very demons of darkness have retired from the spot where they imagine victory to be theirs, and until with these shades and solitudes of meditative eve, they have drawn around themselves the august spirits of patriarchs, prophets, and apostles, who all spoke as they were moved by the Holy Ghost; and if they would only, night after night, plunge their minds into the deep stream of love and truth that flows down from that fountain of life; if they would only then and there think and muse, and muse and think again, how great would they become! what mighty men in the scriptures! what constellations to the church! what luminaries to the world! May our Lord hasten the time when, by a larger outpouring of the Spirit of all grace, his people shall make Christ, who is 'the wisdom of God and the power of God unto salvation,' their most profound and constant study, so that, as his 'living epistles,' more and more of his skill and power to heal 'all manner of diseases' may be read by the dying on every side! Nor has the church, in any age, lacked provocations to this good work, and this high condition of christian attainment. What is it that causes the people of God to differ from one another? Some are of weak faith, contracted minds, and sordid dispositions; they seem to live only for themselves, so that if they were to die and be buried to-morrow, nobody in the church or in the world could discern that the grave had closed over them. Others are manifestly of a different cast; they are refined and sensitive in temperament, feel strongly the claims of Christ upon them, are ever found at the post of danger or of duty, ever scheming for the good of precious souls, ever ready, active, zealous towards all good works; the cause of God lies heavy upon their minds; the good of souls is ever uppermost in their heart, and the glory of Jesus is the crown upon the whole of their plans and actions. While they live they make themselves felt and heard, and when they die their tombs are visited by mourners, who grieve, not so much for themselves, as for the loss which the church and the world have sustained. The difference is all to be traced to the degree in which Christ and him crucified have been studied, and to the estimates formed of the essentiality to their well-being of his 'healing stripes.' Appreciation and study always go together, the one being the reward of the other. More advanced believers have made, and are still making, religion their 'study all the day;' and, ever as they gaze and muse, the sublime dimensions of redeeming love are gradually opened up. In the one we see the stupidity and indifference of defective scholarship; in the other the high attainments that ever wait upon the glorious marchings of the human mind over the cultivated field of truth, together with its flights of thought and contemplation among those lustrous orbs, which draw light from that Sun which riseth 'with healing in his wings.'

III. THERE MUST BE THE APPLICATION OF THE REMEDY. It is of no use merely to call a physician and get his prescriptions. To be the better of both, the medicine must be taken and the remedy applied. In like manner, the Holy Spirit, in employing this figurative language to describe the spiritual remedy, certainly intends us to take up the idea, that to be cured by Christ we must actually apply it. The sore could not be healed simply by the odour of the ointment, nor the fever allayed by the sight of the physician. We must submit ourselves to him, that he may do what is considered best in the circumstances. The patient must have no mind of his own in the matter, except to give his consent to the specified treatment. The physician's skill on the one hand, and the patient's acquiescence on the other, may bring about the desired cure. And it is thus that we must use Christ and his precious blood. We must believe him to be an infallible authority, and proceed at once to act upon his opinion. We must take the cups of medicine he offers, every one of them, and in the order and at the times he specifies—the cup of salvation first, the cup of affliction next, and all the other mixtures of a gracious and providential character which contribute to recovery. To the festering wound we must apply his mollifying ointment, and to the blind orb his healing eye-salve. We must abandon the use of all quack remedies, and peremptorily dismiss all former attendants. To drop his justifying blood on our guilt, to sprinkle it on our impurities, and ever afterwards to use it for strength, for comfort, and for confirmation, is actually to apply Christ to the diseased soul, and to certify its cure. In simple language, this just means that we cannot be saved unless, with our understandings enlightened and our hearts affected, we believe that Jesus lived and died for us—that all he did was in our stead—that what he did was perfectly sufficient—that neither law nor justice did or could demand any more—that he is at this moment and at every moment willing to receive, and pardon, and accept us, and that in the very moment in which we thus believe, our cure is begun and our life is saved. Is there not then but a step between every sinner and eternal salvation? And why is it that this step is not taken? The Physician is able and willing; the remedy is in his hands ready to be applied, and the patient confronts both—his consent alone being necessary to the instant commencement of a process which is certain to deliver him from the curse of the law, and to make him an heir of everlasting life. Why is it that this consent is withheld? On the understanding that the sickness is *felt* and that the Physician's art is *appreciated*, O why is it that there should be any reluctance at once to proceed to do as he wishes? This question is capable of solution only by abandoning the supposition on which it rests. The sickness of sin cannot be felt, and the work of Christ cannot be known in any case where he is not instantly believed in. No man believing that a fatal poison has been unwittingly swallowed by him, and under the terror of a speedy and painful death, will refuse the antidote. No sinner whose enlightened conscience accuses him of guilt, and who is under the fear of the impending wrath of God, will hesitate to hide himself in Christ, where such wrath cannot reach him, and where he finds that all his legal debts are discharged in full and for ever. The sinner dies if he does not thus appropriate Christ; and whoever he be, he has not one vestige of excuse for remaining unforgiven, after Christ has been preached to him. He has none, for instance, in the *offensiveness of the cross* to his natural pride. Naaman the Syrian could not brook the idea of washing in the Jordan when Abana and Pharpar, rivers in Damascus, were still flowing; but he had to yield to the prophet's terms before his leprosy was healed. And so must the leprous soul do with the blood that flows from the cross; there is only this difference, Naaman dipped seven times in Jordan before his flesh returned to him—the sinner has only to do it once in the stream from Calvary, and all is well. He has no excuse in *the holiness of the law* or in the dignity of the Lawgiver, both of which we have seen are perfectly satisfied by Jehovah-Tsidkenu, 'the Lord our righteousness.' He has none from the *character or age of his sins*, for 'Christ is able to save to the uttermost all that come unto God by him;' and no living sinner is *beyond* this uttermost, neither has any poor wretch ever perished who has ventured his all upon that ability. He has none from the *numerous failures* of his past attempts, for, if sincere in his wishes, God has already accepted his 'day of small things,' and can neither 'break the bruised reed nor quench the smoking flax.' These efforts must not be discontinued; they are the strugglings of a newly-born heart, which, by the administration of a little more of God's sufficient grace, are certain to issue in the desired consummation. He has none *in his absolute poverty*, in any or in every respect, for the more entirely he denudes himself of his fancied merits, the more welcome he is; yea, till he strips himself completely naked, and falls prostrate before the cross, to be washed in the blood and clothed with the seamless vesture of the righteousness of Jesus, he is not regarded. The poor woman in the gospel was just in the very condition that recommended her to the Saviour, when she came to him after she had 'spent her all' upon other physicians, who did not succeed in curing her. He was her last resort, but her best; nor did her choice of him only when all others had failed, in the least degree disincline him towards her. He has none from any *past and positive rejection* of Christ and his mercy; for Jesus allows no consideration whatever to influence him when the supplant is fairly at his feet, and when his healing art is appealed to. He is quick to avail himself of the opportunity of saving all who avail themselves of the simple condition of taking what he offers. He has none from the *general nature of the gospel invita-*

tions; for the idea of mere *numbers* does not enter into it otherwise than to assure the whole world that in him there is enough and to spare for all. The minor must be included in the major proposition; and if the pardon of sin be offered to all without exception, then thou art included, O man, whosoever thou art that readest. He has no excuse, in short, from any consideration whatever; for it is irrespective of all that possibly can be comprehended within the extremes of human guilt, that Jesus stands upon our globe and cries, 'If any man thirst, let him come to me and drink.' Heaven's high arches receive and re-echo that cry; for thus saith the Eternal One, 'Come NOW and let us reason together: though your sins be as scarlet, they shall be white as snow: though they be red like crimson, they shall be as wool;' and with the same glorious assurance the church's revelation on earth is sublimely wound up, 'The Spirit and the bride say, Come. And let him that heareth say, Come. And *whosoever will,* let him take of the water of life freely.'

IV. THERE MUST BE, FINALLY, THE CONSEQUENT PROOF OF THE CURE, IN THE MANIFESTATIONS OF HOLINESS. This closing remark may be thought out of place, inasmuch as if the cure be actually begun, then Christ must have been appreciated already. This is so far true; appreciated, certainly, he must have been, to a certain extent, but not appreciated, even yet, as he ought to be. In the first flush of returning health, after long disease, the patient thinks he is duly grateful to his attentive physician; but after he is permitted to leave the sick chamber, and especially after, with thorough invigoration, he goes out and again breathes the fresh air, witnesses the green fields, associates with dear friends, and applies himself to his proper engagements, it is then that he more correctly estimates the skill to which, under God, he is indebted, and the value of the health itself to which he has been restored. In like manner, having believed, we ought to go about doing good; we ought to take plenty of exercise in every walk of christian and benevolent enterprise. We are now better, and ought to appear in the society of the godly; we are now strong, and ought to exert ourselves in the proper business of life, even the glory of God. Thus, the more able we feel for our duties, and the more pleasure we take in them, the more grateful we will be to the Lord, who 'healeth all our diseases;' that is, the more and better we will appreciate the inestimable benefit he has conferred upon us. Let us, then, who profess to be cured, test our new health in the activities of practical piety. This is unquestionably our duty. It is not only the best way to know Christ experimentally for ourselves, but to recommend him to others. We never more effectually sound forth his praise, than when we exemplify or embody his religion in our life. By this, others, poor and diseased as we once were, are astonished to see our agility, our usefulness, and our happiness, and they are induced to apply to him who *thought out* our case, and to use for themselves that *remedy* which with us has been so successful. Thus, by the eminent holiness and the undimmed lustre of the children of light, the whole world shall, in due time, be provoked to try Christ's healing virtue, and every one that tries shall partake of similar blessings.

CHAPTER X.

JEHOVAH-SHALOM: THE LORD OUR PEACE.

PART I.

'Then Gideon built an altar there unto the Lord, and called it Jehovah-Shalom.'

JUDGES vi. 24.

FAMILIAR as we now are with the idea of the pardon of sin, it is not natural to us, and could never have been mooted by human reason. We see this in the case of the fallen angels. They never knew anything but despair; and Satan's efforts to ruin man went upon the hope, that if he could only get him to sin, he should succeed beyond the possibility of failure. Hence, also, our first parents had no such thought after the fall; they only trembled and waited for death—having not the slightest hope, till God himself spake *peace*, and thus dropped the embryo promise of a Saviour into their minds. The idea was then born, and was the earliest note in the song which afterwards burst in full harmony upon a wondering world—the first wave of that flag of truce, which, streaming from all the towers of Zion, is yet to rally and lead back mankind to God. But was there not peace between God and man before sin? Yes; only it was of an entirely different character from that which was subsequently proclaimed from the cross. The former was the result of the creature's innocence, and of God's manifested friendship; and, indeed, was rather joyful or blissful existence than peace. Strictly speaking, peace in relation to God and the sinner is an economic term, implying the previous existence of *dispeace* or war; just as when you speak of a coming calm, you fancy a previous storm; or of restored health, you fancy disease; or of repaired fortunes you fancy losses. That calm to be appreciated, implies that you have confronted the fury of the elements; that convalescence, to be understood, implies that you have undergone severe pain; and that property, to be valued, implies that you have suffered in adversity. In like manner, when we aim at a correct apprehension of peace from and with God, we must know and feel that by nature we are at variance with him, and that it can only be by grace that hostilities are suspended and peace restored. Having then, in the former chapters, shown God's anxious desires to subdue the war that is carried on among men against his law, and also the glorious provision he has made to give pardon on the ground of Christ's imputed righteousness, and to restore purity to our nature by the work of the Spirit through the truth; that is, having seen the guilty sinner justified and sanctified, let us now contemplate the necessary consequence of all this in the *peace* which he now enjoys, or the grand result of the imputation of Christ's righteousness on the one hand, and the believing acceptance of it on the other. To do this great subject justice, we must submit the following propositions :—

I. BETWEEN GOD AND THE UNRENEWED SOUL THERE IS DISPEACE. Whence does this arise?

1. *From contrariety of nature.* Though of the same nature as to holiness when created, (for 'in the image of God created he him,') there is and must be opposition when the one continues holy and the other becomes sinful. While they were alike, all was harmony; but when sin entered, all became disparity and antithesis. And who would have it otherwise? Our depraved hearts now feel God's law to be a grievous burden, and our alienated minds now cleave to the dust whence our bodies sprung, rather than to the heaven from whence came our deathless souls; but does even reason assent to it, that God should be pleased with such a melancholy reversal of his original will? It does not. We can conceive of nothing more terrific in its results upon the whole intelligent creation, than that there should be harmony between rebellion and the Holy One. If the creature will sin, let not God consent; if he will pollute himself,

O let the Deity remove far from him; and if he must be miserable, let not the God of peace approve. Thus, that law which separates God from man, and which at first seems to be so harsh and cruel, is the law of kindness to the universe—is the just and righteous reason why, from contrariety of nature, there cannot be peace between them. If there were, he could neither be the God of love, nor of purity, nor of goodness. In fact, the supposition borders upon blasphemy, and conjures up the dark and dread idea of a demon.

2. *From opposite wills.* This is a corollary from the former. Contrariety in nature leads to opposition in will. God's will is and ever must be to the keeping of the law, or obedience to its very letter. Man's will is now, and while unrenewed, ever must be, to the breaking of the law, or to disobedience. These two things can never meet. Two rivers can never amalgamate while the one runs from the other 'as far as the east is from the west.' There cannot be, at one and the same time, supreme love and supreme dislike to the law. Two such antagonist principles never were conjoined in any one intelligent being. There may be, as we think it probable there is, an *intellectual* conviction in the breasts of devils, that the will of the Almighty, howsoever expressed, is essentially excellent, but they do not on that account *love* it—they the more cordially hate it, because of its purity and integrity. It is often so with man. He perceives that

whatsoever the Creator commands must be good, but he feels notwithstanding an antipathy to the spirituality of every divine precept. This is most painfully exhibited in his opposition even to 'the will of God in Christ concerning him.' The gospel is just another *decalogue* suited to a guilty world; and its commandments are all expressive of God's earnest wish that all men should repent, believe, and be saved through his Son. Here, as one would think, there should be agreement at once. But there is not. There is just as much dispeace as ever. Men *will* not be saved any more than they will be holy. It is indeed humbling to think of it; their will is to perish, while God's will is to pardon. Can there be harmony here? O who would have it so? We reply, let dispeace on this account ever last; for God forbid that our will, and not his, should be done.

3. *From different designs.* God's design is to prevent the spread of rebellion. He therefore manifests his hatred of sin by avowing his difference with the sinner on that account. To do otherwise might promote among his subjects the spirit of perilous disaffection. But God must ever be the supreme and only potentate, therefore between him and disloyalty there must be set up an unmistakeable token of his inflexible purpose to put an end to its increase, if not to its existence. He will have all his creatures everywhere to know that 'he is God,' and that 'besides him there is none else.' Now, it is

man's design to spread rebellion. This was the object of Satan when he tempted him, and he is of the spirit of the tempter. He takes of him; and hence, if left entirely to himself, he would become in his turn the tempter of Innocence, if he could find her upon the earth. The sinner wishes to be his own master; there is nothing he so much relishes as the sense of freedom from the divine restraints; he therefore, in this respect, finds it his interest to resist God, and encourage within himself, and all whom he can influence, *godless living*. But specially it is God's design in redemption to bring men back again to himself and his service, and therefore he will have no peace with man so long as he desires not the knowledge of God's ways.

4. *From unequal forces.* God is omnipotent. He has determined not only to stigmatise, but to exterminate sin, and he will do it. 'Is anything too hard for the Lord?' 'Who hath hardened himself against him and prospered?' 'Who would set the briars and thorns against me in battle? I would go through them; I would burn them together.' Yielding on God's part to the plots or wishes of sinful men cannot be expected; as soon could he surrender his throne. In such a case, what can be the issue but distance between them? Man may not yield, but he shall never succeed. He is a weak creature even in innocence compared with Jehovah; he is weakness itself in his fallen estate. All his opposition must

therefore be abortive. It never sets aside the plans and processes of the divine government, and re-acts only upon the rebel in the way of sending him farther down into degeneracy and farther off from God. True, in the lowest depths he may still oppose God, but 'he that sitteth in the heavens shall laugh.' This cheerless exile, if mercy prevent not, must be perpetuated for ever; for God cannot give way, and the sinner will not.

5. *From unalienable decrees.* God has said it, 'There is no peace to the wicked.' While the sinner, then, remains obstinate, he shall find God inflexible. Hence the actual misery and the awful conflict in the human soul. Unbelieving man is ever under a cloud—a curse is ever resting upon him. He is reported to and known in heaven as an enemy of the Most High, and behold all godly agencies make common cause against him as a common foe. It is a fearful condition; God frowns upon him always in his rebellion, yea, the curse not causeless falleth ever like a blight upon his 'basket and his store,' so that all he does shall prosper ill. Conscience frowns upon him. Despite of himself, he is ill at ease; the monitor within vexes him in the world, haunts him in sleep, frightens him in trouble, and appals him in death; for being the vicegerent of God, conscience is ever on God's side. Angels frown upon him. They are holy, and must repudiate sin wherever they find it. They are God's armies, and must and do fight to

suppress rebellion whenever they are so commissioned. The very world whom he worships frowns upon him. Yes, singular enough, though he is its willing slave, he takes its contempt and its scowl for wages, and mistakes its cheats and its strokes for honour. It certainly promises fair, but is ever false; no word it gives is kept, and all its elements only tantalise, if they do not destroy his soul.

In these circumstances, how can there exist anything but distance between God and the unrenewed sinner? He is a solitary Ishmaelite; every holy hand is against him, and he is against every holy one. The war of rebellion is everlasting. Under a terrible law, the rebel is driven by an infatuation to perpetuate the fight even in the midst of endless defeats. O truly 'there is no peace to the wicked.' There may be a lull, as sometimes in the thick of a bloody battle, night sets in, the roar of the cannon is silenced, and the shouting of the warrior is not heard; but the morning dawns, and the furies of war are again at work. Let the sinner then remember that what he now mistakes for peace is only the stillness and inaction of some midnight hour. When the trumpet sounds in the morning of resurrection, there shall be an awful re-awakening of God upon his conscience, of conscience upon himself, of angels upon his sin, and of every heavenly interest against his head. But lest some may think that by certain well-managed devices they may yet pacify all these, and thus be also at peace with God, let us sift such a thought and expose its vanity.

II. THIS DISPEACE REMAINS, AND IS AGGRAVATED BY EVERY HUMAN EXPEDIENT TO REMOVE IT. Whatever vain man may say, he feels that there is deep-rooted alienation between God and him. He may forget this in the tumult of a worldly life, but whenever a pause comes, say in some night of sore trouble, he hears again what after all was never silenced—only the din of the conflict drowned its still small voice—he hears conscience, and then fears exceedingly lest God should arise and tear him in pieces. This accounts, in part, for his resort to certain devices for the bringing about of peace. It is indeed marvellous, that depraved as human nature is everywhere, it is always discovered at some device for propitiating the favour of Deity. You will see the heathen at it in his sacrifices to idols—the mahommedan at it in his prayers within the mosque—the papist at it in his beads, ave-marias, and haircloth—the protestant at it in his external conformity to christian institutes—the pharisee at it in his fastings, long prayers, and broad phylacteries—the worldling at it in his obeisance to public decency—the sensualist at it in his weak attempt to justify the gratification of what he calls natural appetites—the deist at it in his pitiful plaudits of the greatness and benevolence of God—the dying at it in their latter flights to a gospel altar they have ever sneered at—and all at it in their innumerable varieties of appeal to Heaven for mercy now and hereafter.

Not one of them all succeeds. The Creator has endowed conscience with a faculty of discovering the utter worthlessness of all human expedients for its pacification. The consequence is, that by man's devices matters are only made worse. The more that is spent upon the work of self-righteousness, the more havoc is made upon those feelings and hopes which were living upon the idea of a confirmed peace. A river may be arrested in its course by the throwing up of some huge barricade; a furious fire may be partially quenched by the letting in of water; a final onset of the remnant of a great army may for a moment turn the tide of success; but there is delusion in the idea that a pause must be a peace: not only is it not so, but in a little the pent-up stream, the smothered fire, the stunned brigade, all gather up their innate strength, and by reason of concentrated force, rush forward to deal out terrible vengeance against opposing expedients. And so it is with the sinner in his efforts to roll back the tides, or quench the flames, or overthrow the charges of his own conscience. The waters of self-accusation shall burst forth, and, in heedless speed, lay prostrate his Babel towers—a moral flood, they re-enact the horrors of a spiritual deluge; the fires of infernal lusts must again rage, and take vengeance on themselves for the self-denial of an hour; the onslaught of all holy powers shall come down like the Assyrian with death on its wings, and what fire and water have left standing, the thunderbolts of an angry law and an incensed justice shall completely destroy. All this has been already proved in the epitome given in a former chapter, to prove the impossibility of a fallen nature giving to holy law either a perfect obedience or a sufficient atonement.*

III. PEACE IS RESTORED BY THE APPREHENSION OF THE MERCY OF GOD IN CHRIST. If we minutely analyse the dispeace, we shall find, among its other causes, these two different but powerful elements— the idea of God's anger, and the hopelessness of the case. The idea of the divine indignation disposes to the fear and hatred of God, and the hopelessness of the case intensifies that hatred to an appalling degree. To have such dispeace removed, it is evident that these two elements must be taken out of the sinner's mind. But can these undergo any change? Can God ever cease to be angry at sin, and can the sinner ever hope for mercy from such a God? At once and emphatically we reply to both questions, *No*. It is therefore evident that the *results* or *effects* of this stern immutability must be taken away, otherwise this dispeace must be perpetuated. One of the effects of God's displeasure at sin is his banishment of the

* See Part I. of 'Jehovah-Tsidkenu.'

sinner from his presence, and the infliction upon him of the sentence of death. Now, till this sentence be repealed, and this exile be brought back, there cannot be harmony between them. But the sentence is repealed, and the sinner is recalled, and that in a way perfectly consistent with the sovereignty and holiness of God; a divine substitute, as we have seen, has borne the sentence, proclaimed the pardon, and re-opened the door of friendly communion. In former chapters we contemplated the proofs of God's anger at sin by his laying upon Jesus Christ 'the iniquities of us all,' and we have also beheld, through the process of sanctification or healing, the hope of mercy restored to the human breast. No doubt, had the matter been left in the sinner's own hands, he would have been hopeless for ever. Looking within himself, he sees all in confusion—all his conceptions of God are comfortless, yea fountains of terror. Looking without him to his own life, he sees everything he has done and is doing daringly defiant of his Creator. Looking to Sinai, he hears the thunder, and sees the lightnings of the Lawgiver's holiness; and looking to God, he sees no smile of approbation, and hears no accent of love. How, then, can it be otherwise with him, than that he should be the victim of despair, so long as he has nothing else to look to, or will contemplate nothing else but himself and his own works? Still, despair ought not now to curse any son of man. Why? Because not only is it his privilege, it is his duty to look away from himself to the grace of God in Christ; and whenever he does so, he finds peace. God in Christ smiles upon him, speaks peaceably to him, offers him pardon, and invites him to fellowship. God in Christ explains to him that all this can be, and is done consistently with his truth and integrity; and so soon as the sinner sees that it is done through the obedience and death of Christ, the hope that fled in the fall, returns in the faith of man. A faith's view of the bleeding Lamb of God taking away not only the sins of the world, but his own sins, and casting them all 'into the depths of the sea,' is the only sight that gives resurrection to the confidence of a guilty sinner in the willingness of God to pardon him. By this he makes the discovery that God is not his personal enemy—on the contrary, that God is his best friend, and has done for him what none but God could accomplish. How can such a view of God beget anything but love in his heart? and where love presides peace dwells. Yes, nothing but this conviction, that God loves us, and has so loved us as to send his only-begotten Son to die for us, can tranquillise the sin-stricken conscience. Nor is it a mere recognition of God's love of benevolence that pacifies it: such could never bring peace; it is the clear apprehension of mercy flowing out of God to him through the righteousness of his Surety, that causes him to rejoice in God. Though still conscious of sin, he sees that an adequate satisfaction has been rendered, and that for him to fear either law or justice, now that he is 'hid in Christ,' is to be gratuitously tormented. His thoughts of God now undergo a complete change. He believes that he is no longer angry with him, but that his 'anger is turned away.' His conscience speaks kindly to him, for the blood of Christ has purged it from the dead works that cried out against his life. The angels whisper love to him, and tell him that they are charged to minister to him as an heir of salvation, till they convey him home to his Father's house. And even the world no longer scowls; he is at peace with it, and he permits not its cares or trifles to torture him any more. He desires it not, he fears it not; he is crucified unto it and it unto him. All those faces upon which formerly sat the look of indignation, the believer now sees luxuriant in smiles; and hence he fears no more; fearing no more, he fights no more, and fighting no more, he is at peace; his weapons of war are laid aside, God's cause is espoused, and the rest of heaven begins. He glories now in the Peacemaker, Jesus Christ the righteous.

Ponder well, reader, the infinite importance of cherishing those kindly thoughts of God of which we have already spoken. So long as you entertain harsh thoughts of him, of his law, of his yoke, or of his Son Christ, you will war against him; but whenever you believe that 'God is love,' and that in Christ he is 'reconciling the world unto himself;' so soon as your heart has melted under the matchless pathos of that scripture, 'Like as a father pitieth his children, so the Lord pitieth them that fear him; for he knoweth our frame; he remembereth that we are dust;' yea, so soon as you open your whole mind to the transcendent fascinations of that love which bled on Calvary, and which now pleads in heaven on your behalf, condescending daily to your low estate, forbearing hourly with you in your constant shortcomings, and dispensing constantly to you the riches of his grace; the shyness of diffidence, the hesitation of doubt, and the terror of despair all flee away, and peace with God reigns paramount. Why then is it that any sinner of mankind continues to war against his compassionate Father—that any can sit and listen to the melting overtures of his mercy, and yet cherish dislike to or hatred of him—that all who hear the good tidings do not leap at one joyous bound into the arms of everlasting love? O, if there be one greater mystery to the angels than another, it is, that even one foe to God can be found among the children of men! This, however, suggests a topic deserving of the most serious attention, as it lays us under still greater obligations to our Creator, and makes us still more guilty if we despise or neglect them. Foreseeing the hardening effects of sin, and the certainty that even his love in redemption would be resisted by sinful men, God made suitable provision to meet the emergency

IV. Peace with God is restored through the agency of the Holy Ghost. An apostle enumerates the fruits of the Spirit to be 'love, joy, peace, long-suffering, gentleness, goodness, faith, meekness, temperance.' Here we see that 'peace' is one of these fruits. Let us then take great care not to 'grieve the Holy Spirit of God,' by overlooking his love in the matter of our salvation. He is God equally with the Son and the Father, and his share in our redemption must be understood to be equal with theirs. It was a great thing for the Father to devise the plan and consent to its execution in the person of his only-begotten Son. It was a great thing for the Son to consent to take our nature, and in it to bear the curse due to our sins; but surely it was not less great in the Spirit to give his consent to the pardon of the guilty, which, had it been withheld (I speak as a man), must have been fatal to the proposal. He is the Author of the Bible; for 'holy men of old spake as they were moved by the Holy Ghost.' He is the Creator of our Lord's humanity; for it is written, 'that which is conceived in her (Mary) is of the Holy Ghost.' He abides still with man on the earth, striving with him by word, and ordinance, and providence, 'convincing him of sin, and righteousness, and judgment,' carrying forward his sanctification, and making him triumphant over all his spiritual enemies, till he completes his holiness, and then conducts him into the very presence of God. All this the Spirit has to do down to the day of judgment; for with the church he must remain till the last member of the family has been born again unto God. Thus we come to the conclusion, that in mercifully providing such a heavenly teacher, quickener, comforter, and guide, in the person of the blessed Spirit, we are indebted to his operations for our comfort in religion, that is, for our peace with God. No doubt Jesus himself is in a very peculiar sense alone 'our peace;' but this is not enough. He has laid the foundations of amicable relations between God and the sinner in his sacrifice of atonement; but the actual formation and enjoyment of these relations proceed from the Spirit. 'It is the Spirit that quickeneth.' 'No man can say that Jesus is the Christ but by the Holy Ghost.' Yes, Jesus is the 'Peacemaker,' inasmuch as by his cross he slays the enmity of the sinner's heart; but humbling as it must be to our proud nature, there must be something more than this for the enjoyment of peace with God, just as we cannot be the better for the righteousness of Christ simply because he wrought it out for us; to be the better of it, God must impute it, and we must submit to it, and by faith wear it, and continually make mention thereof. Even so, to enjoy this peace we must with all docility submit to the teaching of the Spirit upon the subject, and, passive in his hands, allow him to mould our will and affections entirely into the likeness of

God. It is the Spirit alone that knows where Christ is to be found, and he leads the sinner to him, otherwise he should lose himself in the darkness of his own stupid imaginations. It is the Spirit that moves above the chaos of our ruined natures, and calls up all that is there to be renewed and re-established under his plastic hand. He is the harmoniser of all our thoughts with God's thoughts, and of all our ways with God's ways. He is the breaker up of the fallow ground, the sower of the seed, the giver of the dew unto Israel, and the divine influence that breathes upon all, and makes all contribute to the work of reconciling love. Finding two great conditions in the covenant of grace (besides those which Christ himself has ratified by his blood), namely, God's pardon and man's faith, he is the grand consummator of both; he gives faith to man, and gets for him pardon from God through Christ; and all this he does through the medium of his truth. He gives to that truth this high honour, that no peace is ever found except when it is known and believed. It is while reading there that he 'takes of the things that are Christ's and shows them to us.' As we look, he impresses, enlightens, and interests the mind; and while the process on our side goes on of searching, thinking, and trusting, lovely, gentle, celestial peace takes possession. Lo! it is there, there fresh from heaven, there fixed in the pardoned soul, there for ever.

V. WHEN PEACE WITH GOD IS MADE, TRUE PROSPERITY BEGINS. There were troublous times to Israel when the angel appeared to Gideon. The Midianites were at war with them, and hence much confusion, unhappiness, and disaster. But a time of peace was foretold, and with it a period of prosperity; everything was to return to its proper channel; trade, agriculture, and religion were to thrive, and all the relative interests of the commonwealth. Some indeed think that one of the primary references in the name given by Gideon to his altar— Jehovah-Shalom—was to this. It has ever been, that war destroys the arts which flourish in the time of peace, and that while it is waged, there is no addition made to intellectual, scientific, or religious wealth. How impressively true is all this of the welfare of the human soul from the day of its revolt from God! On the very commencement of hostilities everything went to ruin. Not only was the very soil cut up and made unprolific, and the fruits thereof blasted—not only were the elements of nature thrown into confusion—not only were the lower animals transformed into beasts and birds of prey, but human nature itself degenerated into something little short of fiendish—the immortal part flourished no more; it lost its best knowledge, its purity, its peace; and instead of making advances towards perfection, was rapidly going down to the image of Satan. Was the soul a field upon which grew, in all their beauty and fragrance, the flowers of original innocence? Did the river of God's pleasure run through that field, and water and fertilise it? Did the ray of the divine favour gently rest upon and maintain their perennial exuberance? Did the angel of God joyfully visit and cull from its lovely pastures the sweet-scented herbs, and carry them to heaven as proofs of the Creator's diligence and love? Yes, it was indeed so. But when the hot and suffocating sirocco of sin blew over it, all this beauty withered away, and all the incense that arose from it became nauseous. The field was converted into a desert, where thorns and thistles grew rankly and fully. And was the soul of man a temple which reared its noble turrets to the skies, which in ingenuity was exquisite, in capacities powerful, and in adaptation to its design complete? Was its interior always lighted up with the glory of God, and did the high festivals of adoring piety distinguish all its services? Did God himself say of it, 'This is my rest; here I will stay, for I do like it?' Yes: it was indeed so. But when the tocsin of war sounded, the Deity fled, and lo! the windows were darkened, the service of the day was closed, the altar fell down, the worshipping priest rushed forth to blaspheme, and amid the roar of heaven's artillery and the fires of its indignation, the high towers thereof fell, and the stately edifice was a ruin.

While sin continues unchecked, confusion and misery riot; and had not the Lord of peace interfered, the suicidal conflict might have exterminated our race. But a truce was proclaimed. The parties met, and by breathing the hope of pardon, the process of, and the tendency to rebellion, were suddenly arrested. Man was melted into penitence, and embraced anew the God he had defied. And thus it is, that, inspired now with the hope of salvation, the soul begins again to cultivate her freedom. The peaceful husbandman labours where the demon of war ravaged—the 'swords are beat into ploughshares, and the spears into pruning-hooks.' The wells of life again spring up in the desert—the Sun of Righteousness again rises—God himself again walks among the sweet-smelling meadows, and the whisper of the Angel of the Covenant is heard among the trees of the garden: 'Rise up, my love, my fair one, and come away. For lo, the winter is past, the rain is over and gone; the flowers appear on the earth; the time of the singing of birds is come, and the voice of the turtle is heard in our land; the fig-tree putteth forth her green figs, and the vines with the tender grape give a good smell. Arise, my love, my fair one, and come away.' Hearing this peaceful song, all the faculties of the soul live anew, and all the affections of the heart bound upwards to enfold their first love. Demon-like, these faculties had in apostacy despaired of reconciliation, and set themselves against their Creator, while these affections, conscious of a foul adultery, twined themselves more firmly about the loathsome body of sin. But, behold what a wonderful power lies in the æolian cadences of hope! what almightiness slumbers in the warm breath of love! Instantly, when it is believed that 'there is forgiveness with God that he may be feared,' the dogged rebel succumbs, and as snow in summer, opposition melts away. Yes, in the very day when peace is proclaimed, the temple of the soul rises from its ruins—the Divine Architect re-builds—the Deity takes up again his abode—the altar is raised—the fires again burn—the incense again smokes—music again fills the spacious arches, which ring with ancient hallelujahs. Busy, busy all the day, and busy, busy all the night, the ministers of the sanctuary ply their hands, till the whole edifice is re-constructed. The cope-stone is brought out and put on, and then hosannas roll like solemn thunder up to the ear of God. To drop all figure; wherever a sinner is justified, adopted and sanctified, he is reconciled to God, and continues so till death. The interval is a time of peace—a blessed little millennium to his soul, during which he is growing in grace. There may be now and then skirmishes from remaining corruptions, but he fights against them, not against God. His war now is against his enemies, and as he is ever made more than a conqueror through him that loved him, so is war to a certain extent favourable to his prosperity. Such is the necessary consequence of his present imperfect state, and surrounded as he is with so much of what is hostile to his spirituality. But an end to this strife is certain, and is at hand. Death ends it. The death of Christ put an end to his humiliation, and secured his reign as the Prince of Peace. And so the death of Christ puts an extinguisher upon all the believer's corruptions, and secures his seat on the same throne. And if on earth, and in this tabernacle, such rapid strides are made in the useful arts by peaceful christians, with what inconceivable velocity must they progress in heaven, where no opposition is met, but where they are ever fascinated and invigorated by the presence of God, of angels, and of perfected spirits! Heaven is the temple of peace, and eternal life is the enjoyment of perfect peace! Surely, then, the inhabitants therefore must not only be perfectly happy, but be for ever going forward to the perfection of the great and blessed God.

CHAPTER XI.

JEHOVAH-SHALOM: THE LORD OUR PEACE.

PART II.

'Let the peace of God rule in your hearts.'
COLOSSIANS iii. 15.

IT now remains that we inquire into the special influence which 'peace with God' wields over the heart, or into the great practical purposes which its residence there is intended and calculated to promote. These words of the apostle, 'Let the peace of God rule in your hearts,' emphatically instruct us here. Let us, first of all, ascertain their meaning.

1. '*The peace of God.*' These words describe the happiness of the believer. He is at rest, because his conscience tells him he is pardoned for Christ's sake, and that his title to eternal life is made out for, and made over to him. God is now his friend—not that he was ever his enemy—but the believer now knows it—he knows that in the atonement God is pacified towards him, and he is pacified towards God. This

knowledge he has by the Spirit's teaching; and hence the satisfaction it contributes to him is called 'the peace of God.' The words have by some been rendered—'the peace of Christ,' because he is said to be 'our peace,' or peacemaker, by the sacrifice he made of himself for our sins. There is no essential difference between the two. Indeed, to the whole of the persons of the Godhead, they may be very properly applied, inasmuch as the Father devised, the Son accomplished, and the Holy Spirit applies this peace. On these accounts, and simply because it can be obtained in no other way, and enjoyed by no man unless he receive it into his heart by faith, is it described by the apostle to be 'the peace of God that passeth all understanding.' It is, and ever must be incomprehensible, how such a being as God should ever have thought so kindly of us, and how such as we should ever come to be upon such endearing and intimate terms of friendship with him. Being, however, God's peace, and not man's, we see how it is secured to us, and how it reaches at length perfection. Had it been an earth-born peace, and dependent on human works and aspects, it should have soon yielded to the solicitations of the world, and been shifting as the sands of the sea, or ebbing and flowing as its tides. Dwelling, however, in God himself, guarded by his holy word, and fed by the Spirit of peace, it can never either be removed or diminished. The peace of God, then, is just the sweet consciousness of his forgiving love, and the happy tranquillity which is thereby maintained in the believing soul, together with the cheerful submission of all the intellectual, moral, and religious powers to his will and rule.

2. '*Let the peace of God rule.*' This word *rule* was originally used to designate the official duties of the umpire or president of the Olympic games. He was sole judge or ruler among the wrestlers. He was, therefore, a kind of centre of influence; and the consciousness that his eye was ever upon them, and that his word was to be the law of adjudication, was a motive to energetic contention, and indeed the governing idea in their minds throughout. In fact, it became to them, while in the games, a superior power to suppress indolent dispositions, and prevent careless action. On the other hand, the eye of the umpire ever surveyed the arena, and his judgment decided the prizes. The apostle, then, may be understood as here giving a kind of personification to 'the peace of God,' or rather to the believing consciousness of its existence in his own heart. He represents this consciousness as an umpire or ruler, enthroned in the christian's heart, giving laws to all within it for the suppression of whatever threatens to disturb this divine peace. His exhortation is just tantamount to this—as he who overcomes all the other gladiators keeps a steady eye on the umpire, and ever realises the prize to be given, so be it your concern to submit all that remains of evil, as well as all that has been produced by grace, to the fair and legitimate influence of the peace you enjoy, just that

you may conquer to the end, and at the end get the crown of life. In this interesting view of the passage, the spiritual blessing of peace is put by metonymy for the Author of that blessing. So that it is not the Prince of Peace himself, but the peace he produces, that we are taught to obey. The sense of this peace is to be the reigning power, and to it we must yield all due homage.

3. '*In the heart.*' The heart is to be both the seat and the subject of this government of peace. The heart has been described to be 'the centre of personality, and the depository of the feelings,'* and, as such, it is the most appropriate place for the throne and the executive of the 'peace of God.' In many scriptures the heart is put for the whole inner man, and as that inner man is a rebellious kingdom, it seems fitting to all the ends of mercy, that in its very centre the antagonistic and pacifying sentiment of friendship with God should be established in full authority. It is in that very heart that sin has erected its dark throne, that deceitfulness ranges the entire region of sentient being, that 'the lusts which war against the soul' continue their conflict, and where, if they could, they would even yet displace God and re-seat themselves in power. The heart, therefore, is just the place where a spiritual administration of sufficient strength ought to be fixed for the suppression of these loitering and harassing foes; for the working out of an irresistible counter-agency to sin; for a terror to all incipient

* Olshausen.

insubordinations, and for the encouragement of all friendly allies who are ready and able to love God and 'follow after holiness.'

4. 'In *your hearts*'—that is, in the hearts of christians, or in renewed hearts. God's peace is not in the old heart, and, consequently, does not rule there. But in every one justified by faith that peace is found. In the old heart all is rebellion. When God is for peace, it is for war, because it does not know him. If it knew him as the God of mercy in Christ, it would hate him not a moment longer, and instead of loving what he hates, and hating what he loves, it would take pleasure only in that by which he was glorified. It is not peace, then, but war, that rules in the hearts of the wicked—they are conscious of having incurred God's indignation, and are in consequence the victims of terror—they are miserable; and this sense of misery is so powerful that it governs them. They are its slaves, and under its influence are contending against God and his righteousness.

Let all, then, who believe in Christ, and enjoy this peace, contemplate from this passage who and what is the king of their inner man, to what kind of government they are to surrender themselves, and what amount of homage they are to give to the happy sense of being at peace with God, which they now enjoy. We shall, in pursuance of this most interesting and practical view of the subject, submit the following important propositions.

I. THE PEACE OF GOD RULES, WHEN IT IS MADE THE CENTRE AROUND WHICH ALL THE THOUGHTS OF THE HEART REVOLVE. A centre of influence is a common expression, referring sometimes to the point of diffusion, and at others to that of attraction. It is the point of diffusing influence, in the case of the sun, from which light issues; or in the case of the throne, from which government proceeds; and it is the point of attraction when, as a centre, the sun draws towards itself those heavenly bodies that revolve around it, or when the wisdom and clemency of the throne engage and fix the affections as well as the submission of the subjects. Hence astronomers speak of a centrifugal and centripetal power in the heavenly bodies—the power, namely, by which they either recede from, or are attracted to a common centre. It is then rather to the attractive or centripetal influence of the sense of God's friendship that we refer, when we speak of it as the centre to the thoughts of our hearts. The consciousness of this friendship is as a sun within the soul, not only illuminating all its powers, but drawing them all to that orbit which keeps them constantly under its rays, and therefore always in their proper places. Away from such a peace, the understanding is darkened, but when brought into it, all there is light; every faculty is attracted to its perihelium, and blazes with solar effulgence. Who can associate with the absence of this peace anything but the grossest ignorance of God as a God of love and mercy, wicked opposition to his law, contemptuous rejection of his gospel, and the death, in short, of all the spiritual powers of man? But how changed does man become when he reads, thinks, reflects in the midst of the persuasion of God's merciful designs and doings! When he sits down in this position, he is instantly 'clothed, and in his right mind.' Here he feels his way confidently back to the bosom of divine love; here he is gently fascinated into the conviction that, notwithstanding all he has done against God, there is nothing in God against his pardon and acceptance; here he comes to be made more and more willing, in the day of God's power, to do all and to be all that God would have him to be and to do: and here he lives and moves under those gracious experiences which raise him upwards to the enjoyment of still purer and happier existence. It is, therefore, clearly the duty and interest of all believers to abide near to the centre of attractive knowledge, authority and life.

It is admitted that in the christian life there are difficulties. The best of men have natural repugnancies to God and holiness; and as for unbelieving men, they cannot lead such a life at all, just because they live entirely away from this peaceful centre. Hence they are driven to and fro by the merciless winds, and describe the wayward and wild track of the meteor rather than the steady revolutions of the planet. But let not even the friend of God be presumptuous or over-confident. Such was Abraham, and yet he could lie; such was David, and he could heinously sin; such was Peter, and he could deny his Master. At such times they must have been off their axis—away from the centre of influence; therefore, they fell, and when they rose again, it was by the returning sense of God's loving-kindness, or by the attractions of the peace of the cross. The christian has much to do with his heart. He has to keep it 'with all diligence' in the fear and love of God, and in zealous activity for the service of God. But none of these things can be done except within the circle of believing sentiments and desires. Let him, therefore, in all circumstances, keep fast hold of his conviction that God is his best friend, and then he will find Christ's 'yoke to be easy and his burden to be light.' It is precisely from this point that the mystery of godliness discloses to his view its manifold beauties, which, in their turn, charm him with the discovery of the 'secret of the Lord.' It is by erecting his christian telescope from this platform, and commencing his studies here, that he never hesitates as to the quarter into which he should send his affections and his trust; or, in general, as to the path in which he ought to walk. Procession follows persuasion here. Having taken such sublime observations of God, he at once moves forward, and has already gone far on his way; while those who have started from other points of thought and inquiry, stumble, and loiter, and never attain. All religion in the abstract has its beginning in God, and all concrete religion, or religion operative in man, takes its rise from the apprehension of mercy in Christ. It is utterly in vain for the soul to attempt getting near to God otherwise than from this peace as the centre of attraction. Is success in reading possible so long as the alphabet is unlearned, or the summing up of a lesson in arithmetic likely, before numerals have been mastered? Can the barbarian comprehend the revolutions of the planets in ignorance of the laws of gravitation? Can the unphilosophic ploughboy discourse on the natural history of the mountain daisy, or of the different grasses that clothe the field, while the principles of botany are to him a dead letter? Common sense says no to these queries; and so it does also to this—can any sinner become or continue a christian who knows not or forgets the God of salvation, or who goes out to the practice of the great ethics of the gospel from any other centre than the 'peace of God' in his heart?

And here you have the explanation of two things that appear to some rather dark: the melancholy failures of those who appear to be in earnest in their efforts after vital christianity, and the no less sad inconsistencies of many who are in reality the disciples of Christ. Every one of the former class fail, because they have not the peace of God; they set out, but not from a centre—not from the conviction that God's friendship is the alpha of living religion, and that until they have it, they only stultify and stupify themselves, finding no comfort in the doctrines of the cross, and doing no good for him who died on it. On the other hand, the genuine believer may trace all contrasts in his life between profession and practice, belief and experience, to not precisely the same cause, but to one of a similar character. He goes wrong, when in the exercise of any sentiment or desire he sets out away from the immediate conviction that God has reconciled him to himself. Other centres have been chosen, to the attractions of which he has yielded—the centres, it may be, of selfishness, vanity, presumption, routine, the force of example, the sense of shame, the fear of exposure, or the love of approbation. Hence every step he takes under such influence puts him in a still falser position, and draws him towards error. Before he regains his proper position, he must retrace every step, he must unbind and cast from him every such control, and set himself down again amid his enjoyments of 'peace with God.' O how easy we should all feel the work of God to be, if we would only look at it, and go to it, and work in it from this happy sense of his friendship! What an amount of useless labour, what a world of confusion and perplexity it would save us; what a heap of precious time it would redeem; from what mortifications and heart-sickening failures it would defend us; and to what advanced stages of christian piety it would infallibly conduct us! Let us see then that in this respect we give to '*the peace of God*' the rule in our hearts, by commissioning all the thoughts thereof to go out from under its meridian light. This is to begin at the beginning; this is to transcribe the very letters of his love into every lesson of holy wisdom; this is to put the elements of his religion into every working of the affections; this is to open up the fountain of his own power upon the earliest outgoings of the inner man, and to secure for them all, whithersoever they may be going, the strength that is in the Almighty arm. It is impossible to over-estimate the moral mightiness that is in this christian principle, that all we think, do, and say, should, in the very embryos of every thought, deed, and word, be placed under the attractions of this ruling power, seeing that thereby the germs of spiritual life are implanted in every one of them, that the incorruptible seed of God's word impregnates every one of them, and that therefrom they receive that centripetal power which regulates their onward movements, until they are found rejoicing in the very bosom of the Father of lights.

II. THE PEACE OF GOD RULES WHEN IT IS MADE THE THRONE FROM WHICH THE HEART RECEIVES ALL ITS LAWS. In the figurative language of the Bible, the throne of God is said to be 'in heaven,' from which proceed the laws by which he governs the universe, superintending and controlling all creatures and all their actions. Nature, says the philosopher, is under the influence of certain fixed principles, the meaning of which must be, that the Creator allots every element in nature to its proper object, and fixes them in their proper place. The angels have their position around the throne of God. Him alone they serve; that is, they are strangers to any influence except that which reaches them directly from God. They are so holy that it is impossible for them to feel any other authority. If they leave that position, it is to go on errands of love; and so soon as their commission is executed, they are back again and in his presence. When violence is done to any of these laws, there is a convulsion and devastation; and when any of the angels acknowledge another power, they become devils. Now, so it is with the heart of the christian. Laws are framed for its regulation, and the power that administers them is this 'peace of God.' If the christian wish to continue a loyal subject, he must allow his happy sense of this peace to *rule* him. From this, as from a throne, he must take his impulses, and the directions by which his whole conduct, inner and outer, must be regulated. He is forbidden to 'consult with flesh and blood,' because this world unchristianises him, and expels him from the throne to which his loyalty is pledged. But to consult alone with the spiritual Ruler in his heart, he succeeds in every work to which he is devoted. From no other throne descends the influence that preserves him in the love and fear of God. Take it away; remove his belief in

God's friendship, and a reign of terror begins, which issues in all manner of evil. War against God and his own soul is again proclaimed. When there is no hope in God, there is no authority from God. We do not obey what we hate, but that which we love and trust in we willingly serve. To be at peace with God, then, is the throne of power to the believing soul—it is irresistible, and issues laws which will be obeyed, and exercises vigilance which cannot be deceived. Apply this great truth, and you will find it by experience to be true.

Have you inward fears? Place them before this throne, and they disappear; for how can they remain at one and the same time with a persuasion of God's loving-kindness? Fear always obeys orders from such a quarter. A man cannot both tremble and rejoice in the Lord; he cannot both love and hate—the one must displace the other. Surely fears only reside in an unpurged conscience.

Have you inward lusts? You have; but subjecting them to the sense of this peace crucifies them. For what believer can tolerate the motions of sin, who is continually under the impression that God hates sin, and loves holiness? God, he says, is the God of peace, and I have the peace of God within me; therefore, far from me be that 'abominable thing which he hates.' When Paul thought of inward corruption, he was wretched, but when he dragged it up to the throne, to the recollection of mercy, he exclaimed, 'I thank

God, who giveth me the victory through our Lord Jesus Christ.' Thus, in every case, the believing recollection of God's wonderful love has sufficient power to 'crucify the flesh with its affections and lusts;' and this solves the mystery of the growing purity of frail man, 'whose days are as grass.'

Have you unstable affections towards God? Call them up, every one of them, to the very footstool of mercy, and they will receive such a commandment as will establish and fix them upon the Lord. To love God is the first and the great commandment; but to know and believe the love of God, for us is the only way now by which we can keep it. It is love that begets love. It was the love of God that originated the plan of reconciliation, and it is our approach by this love that constrains us to love him in return 'with pure hearts fervently.' Why then, O christian, do you complain of the coldness of your heart towards him? You may have this coldness expelled, this ice within you broken up, and dissolved in the twinkling of an eye. Carry your frozen natures to the light and heat that stream from the assurance of God's being at peace with you. Meditate over again on all the steps of the mediatorial service, and specially recognise that 'love of Christ which passeth knowledge,' and you will soon experience an augmentation of gratitude which will win from you the exclamation, 'I will extol thee, my God, O King, and I will bless thy name for ever and ever;' 'for in the day when I cried thou answeredst me, and strengthenedst me with strength in my soul.'

> 'All thoughts, all passions, all delights,
> Whatever stirs this mortal frame,
> All are the ministers of this love,
> And own its sacred flame.'

It was the thought of this love that converted thee at the first, penetrated all the depths of thy depravity, permeated all the recesses of thy deceit, swayed all thy master powers. Thy frozen heart no kindness could reach, but before this love it speedily became a living stream. Thou wert high and haughty, but it clothed thee with meekness; thou wert avaricious, and it made thee munificent; thou wert a miser, and it made thee rise rich in liberality—rich, and it made thee sit down poor in spirit; thou wert a debauchee, and it made thee hunger and thirst after righteousness; thou wert an infidel, and it made thee a lowly and docile disciple of Jesus of Nazareth. If this love did this for thee when thou wert in thy sins, surely its power must be tenfold greater now that thou hast drunk so deeply out of its cup.

Have you little zeal for God? Your zeal has been cooling, just because it has wandered for a little from before the throne. Recall and replace it beneath the sense of divine mercy, and you will be ready to say with the good man of old, 'My heart is hot within me; while I was musing the fire burned;' or with Christ himself in the agonies of atonement, 'The zeal of thine house hath eaten me up.' Here, perhaps, we have the explanation of the dislike of many to sacrifice for Christ. Their zeal is small, because 'the peace of God' does not rule in their hearts. If they would only give it the power, they would not remain another day inactive; if they would only thus think, 'He loved me, and gave himself for me,' zeal would be enkindled, and offerings would be multiplied. It is not alone in the Lord's Supper that we are to remember Christ—we can do all his will in everything by always keeping him before our minds; for this remembrance of him is just another mode of describing the *throne* that is erected in every believing soul, even 'the peace of God;' and where such peace rules, their zeal for the Lord of hosts becomes great.

Have you trials to bear? Analyse them in his presence, and you will not murmur; for if he has endured so much on your account, you will feel that it is but a small thing for you to suffer on his. Read them by the light of this *peace*, and you will learn that they are blessings in disguise. Contemplate from this point the direction in which they carry you, and you will see that it is to a 'more exceeding and an eternal weight of glory.'

And have you duties to perform? Have you daily to 'grow in grace'—to please God, in everything—to love all men, 'specially they that are of the household of faith'—to resist all manner of temptations—to prepare for death and judgment, and to be 'made meet for the inheritance of the saints in light?' then ever and strongly cherish within you the apostle's persuasion, that God 'is able to keep that which you have committed to him against that day,' and that till then his 'grace is sufficient for thee, and his strength will be made perfect in weakness.' Banish far and for ever from you all doubt as to your personal interest in new covenant love; yea, just obey the scripture: 'Let the peace of God rule in your hearts;' and then, whatever be the pressing duty, you will do it; whatever the temptation, you will overcome it; whatever the sacrifice, you will make it; and whatever be the amount or degree of all your obligations, you will honour them all, and God will be glorified in them all.

III. THE PEACE OF GOD RULES, WHEN IT IS MADE THE SOURCE FROM WHICH THE HEART DRAWS ALL ITS SUPPLIES. The peace of God is a great fountain of supply, from which come down many good and perfect gifts. As to their conversion, christians confess that they owe it to the work of the Holy Spirit, while their subsequent spiritual life is supported and made fruitful in holiness equally by his grace. By the grace of God they are what they are, and by the grace of God they continue to be what grace made them. Now, the christian life has many hinderances to its purity and strength, its comfort and productiveness. Divine aid alone can cast up and remove these. In the Bible we are taught that the Spirit of God works in this direction, and works successfully; and that the grace of Christ is ever made so sufficient, as that a free course is at length opened up for every genuine soul going Zionward. We are taught, moreover, that God's perfections and promises are all engaged in this work of sanctification, and continue to ensure the christian in successive victories over all his foes. In what, then, does the idea suggested by the above proposition, that 'the peace of God' is this source of supply, differ from this plain and well-understood doctrine, that it is 'not by might, nor by power, but by my Spirit, saith the Lord?' There is in fact no essential difference between them. In the one case we say that 'grace,' in the other that peace,' is the source of supply. This second view is figurative or allegorical, tracing divine influence to a mode of thinking about God as the friend of the sinner, or to that peace with him and with conscience which follows such a conviction. Having been inwrought by the Spirit, this conviction remains a source of spiritual strength, and when all other considerations fail to move the christian, this one, when properly handled, invariably succeeds. There is, indeed, no conceivable vicissitude in the life of faith for which this happy persuasion does not provide suitable supply. Take, for example, that which is perhaps the christian's most anxious concern, *his progressive purity of mind and heart.* It is already a settled point with him that he must bear a far more striking resemblance to the likeness of his Father in heaven. He not only hears the call, 'Be ye holy, for I am holy,' but he is determined to comply with it. He has no idea of enjoying the friendship of God apart from such holy effort; and he has no idea of being able for such effort apart from the persuasion, that 'the indignation of the Almighty' has passed away from him. To get quit, then, of his impurities, he must bring them to this fountain of living water; and as one thought after another rushes into his mind of God's most merciful provision for, and gracious complacency in him, these impurities are sunk under a sense of shame; they are covered with confusion; they flee away from the region of the heart, and, for the time, lofty and sanctifying contemplations of divine love exert a sublime ascendancy. How can the heart of a believer indulge in carnal delights, in unchaste thoughts, at the very time that it draws water with joy out of this well of salvation? Impossible! This stream is living and pure, carries away in its flow all uncleanness, 'washes throughly,' and makes white the interior of the new man. If, then, *purity* be (and purity is) the very strength of the christian, as well as his most beautiful ornament, it is evident he can have no source from which to feed and increase it, like to the consciousness of being at peace with God through the blood of Jesus Christ.

For a second illustration, take the solicitude of the christian about *the growth of his faith.* He is sometimes the victim of spiritual disquietude, and is so frequently overtaken by his enemies as to lose for a season his sight and sense of the gracious ruler in his heart—'the peace of God.' The voice of that ruler is not heard as it once was; the touch of his pacifying sceptre is not felt; and the influence of the charmer is weakened, if not withheld. Then it is that he is heard lifting up his voice, weeping, 'O my God, my soul is cast down within me!' In such a season, night overtakes him, his spiritual adversaries gain upon him, the weapons of his warfare are wrenched from him, and his hope of mercy well nigh disappears. But though wrestling, he is not defeated; and though comfortless, he is not despairing. In a happy moment for him, the memory of the past, like the faint echo of soft music, comes stealing over his spirit; he remembers God, God in Christ; he recollects the Lamb of God—the blood of that Lamb—the infinite efficacy of that blood, and the pledge divine that makes this efficacy sure for his pardon and acceptance. To such reminiscences his fainting faith clings, and gradually raises itself up again to former power. In the confusion of some spiritual combat, he had just turned his eye from the umpire, and consequently the influence that descends from the smiles and encouragements of that high authority, was lost. He had just for a small moment let slip from his mind that he was a child of God, and suddenly the old carnal confidence made a plunge to regain lost honour, and spiritual weakness was the result. But, in a blissful instant, his look rested anew upon the tribunal of the Judge—even upon the mercy-seat—from thence he inhaled new vigour; then, springing to his feet, he seizes again 'the whole armour of God,' and puts his foes to rout.

The delightful assurance, indeed, that God is at peace with him, and that he is at peace with God, carries the christian triumphantly to the end of his course on earth. There is not a weakness which it cannot strengthen; not a temptation which it cannot disenchant; not a sorrow which it cannot heal; not a difficulty of any kind which it cannot solve; not an enemy which it cannot defeat or slay; and not a well-founded hope, whether as to this or another world, which it cannot realise. Herein lies the secret of all eminent piety. It is just in proportion as God's people keep the atmosphere clear around this bright orb of christian experience, that they 'quench the violence of fire, escape the edge of the sword, out of weakness are made strong, wax valiant in fight, and turn to flight the armies of the aliens.' Hence, if you walk much in the paths of the just, you will find that they who are weak in their convictions of this peace, are comparatively sordid and useless believers: often rather a damper than an accession to the church of which they are members; having a greater resemblance to cumberers of the ground than to faithful husbandmen; and daily in imminent danger of bringing disgrace upon their religion and ruin upon themselves. It is in the day, and under the reign of conscious peace, that christians themselves live and reign. If you wish, then, greatly to prosper, place yourselves under the sceptre of the King of Salem. This ruler in the new heart will take care that all things will contribute to your piety and your joy. You yourselves would often faint and fail, but he cannot permit any adverse interest to resist or gainsay his authority. His word is law; his look is power; and his despatches are decisive, for he is alone the judge. While, then, he gives the crown to christians, and maintains in their hearts the assurance that it is so, the remainder of the struggle on the grand arena of faith is prosecuted with increasing vigour, and constantly supplied with clearer convictions that in the end complete victory awaits them. And thus it is that 'the peace of God rules in their hearts.'

IV. THE PEACE OF GOD RULES, WHEN IT IS MADE THE PATTERN AFTER WHICH THE HEART IS CONFORMED. We are called upon to be 'followers of God as dear children,' and also to 'let the same mind be in us that was also in Christ Jesus.' Such injunctions are no doubt very comprehensive. They take in the wide range of all that is lovely in the divine character, and imitable in Christ's. Applied to the present subject, we are at liberty to think of them in connection with that influence which God, as the God of peace, exerts upon our tempers and dispositions towards our fellow-christians and fellow-creatures. The injunction of the apostle, indeed, stands in this connection: 'Put on,' he exhorts, 'as the elect of God, holy and beloved, bowels of mercies, kindness, humbleness of mind, meekness and long-suffering, forbearing one another, and forgiving one another.' This beautiful exhortation is then wound up with an appeal 'to the peace of God' as that which ought to rule and govern us in the cultivation of such christian virtues, or as the great example according to which, in their practice, they should be conformed.

Now, a peaceful temper is placed high in the Bible catalogue of christian attainments. The peacemakers are said to be blessed, and they are called 'the children of God.' To be consistent, then, with their filial relationship to God, as the God of love and peace, they must be the children of peace; cherishing towards each other the kind, forbearing, and forgiving temper which God has manifested towards them. Tempers of an opposite character cannot dwell in justified and pacified bosoms—cannot rule where the God of peace reigns. Occasionally, when under the influence of sudden irritation, temper may get the better of them; rash and threatening words may escape, and even revengeful deeds may be done; but these are the infirmities that prove them to be as yet fallible creatures—infirmities of which they have no sooner been guilty than they repent and make reparation. No child of God can remain long in sullen passion, or keep up a system of vile suspiciousness or annoyance against others. Yea, rather, when they are for war, he is for peace. Being at peace with himself, and especially with God, his natural propensities undergo perpetual chastening and discipline from the meek and lowly Jesus. To be of a bad and quarrelsome temper is still to be under the dominion of sin : to be uncharitable, cruel, selfish, unforgiving, and revengeful, is to be the child of passion and the slave of the devil. Hence these things cannot give any permanent character to christians who are all more or less under that charity which 'suffereth long and is kind, which envieth not, vaunteth not itself, and is not puffed up; which doth not behave itself unseemly, seeketh not her own, is not easily provoked, thinketh no evil, rejoiceth not in iniquity, but rejoiceth in the truth; which beareth all things, believeth all things, hopeth all things, endureth all things.' All this is true in reference to the christian's ordinary bearing towards his fellow-creatures, but emphatically true when directed to his brethren in the Lord. 'Behold how good and how pleasant it is for brethren to dwell together in unity,' was the testimony of godliness under the old dispensation; and 'Behold how these christians love one another,' exclaimed they of the 'fulness of the times.' And is it not most befitting that all they of the household of faith should be also of the family of peace and love—that every one of them should be beautiful and characteristic illustrations of the Saviour's school of kindness, so that when reviled, they revile not again; when smitten on the one cheek, they turn the other also; when compelled to go one mile, to go two; when sued for their coat, to give their cloak also? Yes, it is true; the children of this peace love their enemies, 'bless them that curse, do good to them that hate, and pray for them that despitefully use and persecute them.' It is their high distinction to forgive their brethren who offend them, not for seven times, but 'until seventy times seven;' and it is their precious privilege thus to pray, 'forgive us our debts as we forgive our debtors.'

It is a wonder to many, how christians manage to keep their hearts and minds in such an equable, tranquil, and charitable condition, with such an infirm nature and in such a tormenting and provoking world as this. Let the wonder cease in contemplating the *rule* of their faith and the *pattern* of their manners. None were so vile as they themselves once were, and yet even God has forgiven them. This is a conviction that has power with them, and prevails to tame the fiercest spirit. Even yet they must be borne with every moment; and however easily provoked before, they become more and more meek, yea, dumb under every discovery of such condescension. They have been enriched solely out of God's long-suffering, and are therefore increasingly filled with admiration of his munificent love. They have been so gently dealt with all over and all along, that however obstinate and hardened once, they now know the glad transition from darkness to light, from hate to love, from being the veriest slaves of vice into the beatitudes of saintship, and from the lowest depths of moral madness to the comely high places of right-minded and heavenly-minded men. The happy consciousness of all this exerts such a mighty authority over them, that they pant after conformity, in their entire social temperament, to the character and conduct of God. Yes, what can it be but this delicious sense of God's mercy to them that transforms them into his likeness? They make his treatment of them the pattern of their treatment of others, and their growing appreciation of his unparalleled pity, silently but surely helps on the process of assimilation. If, then, you would taste the sweetness of a placid temper, of a gentle spirit, of a benign disposition, if, in one word, you would be like the great and blessed God, be reconciled to him in the first instance; let the war betwixt you cease, and determine to believe that, for Christ's sake, all your abominable sins have been freely pardoned; convince your conscience that all spiritual blessings are now to flow towards it, that its guilt is cancelled and its pollution washed out in atoning blood; yea, settle the whole matter between God and you, and settle it amicably on the ground of Christ's righteousness; and after you have done all this, you will feel the irritable element ousing out of your nature, a holy calm breathed through your soul; or, in a word, that 'the peace of God rules in your hearts.' It is variance with God that certifies quarrels among men. While not reconciled to him, they will not be reconciled to one another; but when they accept of his mercy, they are both disposed and qualified to show it to others. For, whatever other prescriptions moral physicians may give your vile tempers, this is the only one that is effectual. Be at peace with God first, and peace with all men follows. The gentle and forgiving spirit is just a copy of redeeming love. Let us then pray that 'the God of peace, who brought again from the dead our Lord Jesus, that great Shepherd of the sheep, through the blood of the everlasting covenant, may make us perfect in every good work to do his will, working in us that which is well-pleasing in his sight, through Jesus Christ; to whom be glory for ever and ever. Amen.'

One important observation remains. In making 'the peace of God' their pattern, christians feel themselves under powerful obligations to publish the tidings of salvation to the whole world. What *they* have felt to be so precious, *all* men need; and what has been bestowed upon them so freely, they will freely give. God loved the world—so will and do they; God *so* loved the world as to give his only-begotten Son to die for its sins, and they so love the world that they engage in every proper enterprise for the diffusion of the glorious intelligence. God made no distinction of tribes and tongues, neither do they; they preach the gospel 'to every creature.' God's pity was for the very chief of sinners, and theirs goes down as far and extends as wide. What God has done in finding a Saviour for man, they cannot do; but they can and they do offer that Saviour to all the ends of the earth. Their love to the lost of their race is quickened and enriched by their own delightful experience of their heavenly Father's mercy; and what they have found to be so sweet, they desire to share with all the rest of the family. Thus though they do not in the strict sense of the word become saviours, yet do they continually carry about the Saviour with them, and thereby shed the blessings of his redemption on every hand. And why? Because they wish to *please* God. To please him is their highest attainment, and they know that the surest way to do this, is to carry out his merciful designs on our fallen world. They are absolutely certain to please him by falling in with his redemption plans, and strenuously and sincerely working them out along with him. In this they are making his mind their mind, his love their love, his mercifulness their mercifulness, and his glory their life; so that, not only is he their *pattern*, but they actually become partakers of the divine nature by profound sympathy with God in the salvation of precious souls. But they also wish to *satisfy* Christ. To satisfy his soul is an attainment equal in grandeur and importance to the pleasing of God; and they are convinced that they must succeed in this, if they only persuade men, by the riches of his love and the preciousness of his blood, to embrace him as their all-sufficient Saviour. They are as sure of satisfying that soul; and O how they long after it!—that soul which was once agonised with mysterious spiritual travail—when they thus drink into his spirit, as if they were already casting their own crowns at his feet in the sanctuary above. And in all this they are making his mediatorial power their own, not by rightful possession, but by merciful application; his blood is their blood, his righteousness their righteousness, his interest in the perishing their interest, and his joy in their return their own chief good; so that not only is he too the *pattern* after which they are fashioned, but they really become absorbed in him, and lose their identity in his mighty enterprise of reconciliation and eternal life.

CHAPTER XII.

JEHOVAH-NISSI: THE LORD MY BANNER.

PART I.

'And Moses built an altar, and called the name of it Jehovah-Nissi.'
EXOD. xvii. 15.

THE occasion on which Moses built the altar which he named 'Jehovah-Nissi' is memorable in the history of the Israelitish wars. The battle was with Amalek in the vale of Rephidim. While it raged, Moses was upon the top of the adjacent hill. He held in his hand the rod by which he had done so many wonderful things in the land of Egypt. In this he acted as standard-bearer to the army; for when he raised his arm, Israel prevailed, and when he let it fall, Amalek. At the going down of the sun, the hosts of Jehovah gained the victory, to celebrate which, the altar 'Jehovah-Nissi,' or 'the Lord my Banner,' was reared. Though applied to the altar, however, its strict reference is to Jehovah himself, and signifies that not to Joshua or his soldiers, and not even to

Moses and his intercession, is the victory to be ascribed, but to God alone—he, and he only is the *banner* of his people; which means, that he is the 'Captain of their salvation,' not only, as we have seen, at their first entrance into the armies of the living God, and in the gracious discipline and training to which they are subjected, but to the very end of their warfare. He fights for them all their battles, and he wins for them all their victories. He has the credit of beginning it, and he will have the glory of ending it. The salvation of the soul is Christ's work throughout. He digs it out of the pit, and he sets it down upon the throne. He clothes it at first with the best robe, and at the last with life and immortality. He is the banner before which all their enemies flee away, and underneath which they contend in safety and with success. Thus, the first idea suggested by this title is, that *divine protection*, or grace, is given to those who have been first justified, then healed, and then reconciled. Having begun the good work in them, he will *perfect* it. And he does perfect it. None are ever 'plucked out' of his hands. But for his being on their side, every weapon formed against them should prosper, and every engagement should be a lost one, for, saith the prophet, 'When the enemy shall come in like a flood, the Spirit of the Lord shall lift up a standard (a banner) against him;' and again, 'The Assyrian shall pass over to his stronghold for fear, and his princes shall be afraid of the ensign (the banner), saith the Lord, whose fire is in Zion, and his furnace in Jerusalem.' The altar 'Jehovah-Nissi' was thus an emphatic exponent of the presiding idea of that sublime psalm beginning, 'God is our refuge and our strength;' and Solomon poetically places the same thought before the mind when he says, 'he brought me to the banqueting-house, and his banner over me was love.' Upon other banners might be seen devices unsightly or ferocious; on this, a Saviour's love—a love which is omnipotent against all our enemies, and justifies the argument of the apostle, 'If God be for us, who can be against us?' It is of great importance to christians to have this doctrine wrought into their minds. It fills them with courage, and they need it; it animates them with hope, and they pant for it; it blesses them with victory, and they celebrate it for ever. Having, therefore, in the former chapters, seen the strong foundations laid, above which all believing sinners are raised to pardon, purity, and peace, let us follow up the discussion by cheering them onward in what remains of their life of faith. No higher source of encouragement can be presented to them than this, 'Jehovah-Nissi' is their banner— their shield—their high tower; 'the Lord of hosts is on their side.' In a word, everything God is, and everything God does, are made to float over them and their interests, while fighting in this Rephidim, as so many ensigns which cheer, and rally, and embolden them, until their warfare has been accomplished. Let us illustrate this idea—

I. THE ATTRIBUTES OF GOD ARE BANNERS TO HIS PEOPLE. It is indeed a splendid thought that the church has a banner in each one of the divine perfections. These perfections were all offended with man in the fall of the first Adam, but they are all reconciled in the rise of the second. Christ's death ranked them again on our side. Therein we see them vieing with each other to secure our happiness and life. O it were an high honour, an unassailable security, to have the friendship of even one of God's wonderful perfections; but how much more high that honour, and how much more unassailable that security, when we know that they are all pledged to our interests! No doubt the Redeemer is our great advocate with the Father, but it derogates not from this honour to say, that through his advocacy every perfection of the Godhead becomes a willing intercessor for the liberty and life of believers. Now, when we think of the greatness and purity of these divine attributes, in contrast with our unworthiness and meanness, it appears not at all probable that they should be thus engaged. But though not probable, God be praised it is true.

Divine wisdom is our banner. Thrilling consideration! The same perfection which garnished these beautiful heavens, and which hung up and arranged in order all the shining lamps of the firmament—

which gave being to the universe—'adjusted all its parts—constituted its systematic relations, and curiously wrought its diversified wonders'—is now friendly to man! Let them doubt it who have not heard of the scheme of salvation, and of all the means of grace by which this God, who is our God, opposes the subtlest wiles of our enemies—by which he counsels us in every extremity—leads and instructs us in the way we should go—sets life and immortality before our eyes, and causes us to know experimentally 'what is the hope of his calling, and what the riches of the glory of his inheritance in the saints, and what is the exceeding greatness of his power towards them who believe.'

Divine justice is our banner! a truth not only calculated to rejoice our hearts but to call forth our amazement. Is not justice that attribute which is termed inflexible—which abates nothing of its claims—and is the stern and inexorable advocate of the divine honour and sovereignty? yet we see even it stepping forth to plead for sinners—for those who, by bold and unholy aggressions, had dared its indignation, and laughed at the sheen of its sword. Yes, this is also true—this same attribute which could not pardon sin without an atonement, cannot now refuse to vindicate our cause; for all its claims against us have, by the propitiation of Jesus, been fully and honourably settled. This indeed is comforting, but it requires great faith. Let your faith then rest on this, that the same perfection which gave Christ a bitter cup, and abated not to him one drop of the wrath which it contained, which attended him closely to the cross, and laid him as its victim on that mysterious altar, and which did not quit him for one moment till it saw the pale ensigns of death spread over his cheek, and heard his expiring voice exclaim in agony, 'It is finished'—that this same perfection will see to it, that the believer shall not want one of the blessings of the covenant, and that amid all the conflicts and fires of this militant scene, not one hair of his head shall be touched. Hear it, O Israel, the sword that smote the shepherd was for the sheep.

Divine holiness is our banner. To nature this is scarcely credible. God cannot look upon sin, much less have communion with the guilty; and still is it true that the High and Holy One, who inhabiteth the praises of eternity, dwells with the contrite and the humble. As wisdom discovered a fountain, and as justice struck it with its sword, and gave vent to its cleansing waters, so it is the part of holiness to carry its people to these waters, that they may be washed from all their uncleanness. This perfection is for us, not to countenance or take part in our sins, but to deliver us from them; to make us white as snow, though our sins be as scarlet; to make them as wool, though they be as crimson. Holiness knows that, in the day of the Lord, she has to present his people to him without spot or blemish; and also to introduce them into a temple filled with the divine purity, into which nothing that is unclean can enter; hence is she continually diligent to 'wash their robes, and make them white in the blood of the Lamb,' that they may be all ready to go into his marriage supper.

Divine power is our banner. Here indeed is a 'hiding place,' wherein neither broken law nor insulted justice can find us; or, if they should seek and find us here, it could only be to forgive and bless us. Yea, herein hid, we need not fear 'though the earth be removed, and though the mountains be carried into the midst of the sea; though the waters thereof roar and be troubled, and though the mountains shake with the swelling thereof: God is our refuge and our strength.' The power which upholds worlds without number, which confines suns, and moons, and stars to their orbits, which equalises the distance, and prevents the collision of the heavenly bodies—which rules in the armies of heaven, and binds rebel angels with the chains of darkness—which overwhelmed the old world in the flood, and destroyed the cities of the plain with fire—even that same power is our defence; it is exerted on our side to subdue our enemies, and advance all our interests: hence we sing, 'They that trust in the Lord shall be as mount Zion, which cannot be removed, but abideth for ever; as the mountains are round about Jerusalem, so the Lord is round about his people, from henceforth, even for ever.'

In a word, *divine mercy is our banner.* And can it indeed be, the gentle reader asks, that this God, whom I have so heinously offended, will be merciful to such a worm—to such an ingrate as I am? Blessed be his merciful name that we are permitted to reply, 'The Lord is a God full of compassion, and gracious, long-suffering, and plenteous in mercy.' If we may use the language, there are none of the divine perfections upon which so much is drawn— none which has so uninterruptedly to be in exercise on our behalf. If Mercy were but for a moment to hide her lovely countenance, or to hush her pleading voice, that would be a fatal moment to us all; for then Justice would let fall her sword. What a blessing, therefore, that we, who are so full of infirmities, should have to deal with a God who is so full of mercies! All praise be to the mercy of Jehovah; to mercy, our availing and incessant advocate in the Godhead! Lift up your eyes to the heaven of heavens, and behold this beauteous seraph at her work. Are we every instant dishonouring the majesty of God? See, she reconciles us and secures our pardon. Does Justice frown? Mercy points her to the Lamb on the throne, and Justice smiles. Is Holiness offended? Mercy points her to the blood of atonement and Holiness is appeased. Does Power shake his sceptre in indignation? Mercy points him to the victory of the cross, and Power recalls his anger. Does the law cry for an honoured and perfect obedience?

Mercy points to the sufficient righteousness of Christ, and the law smiles over the bright and shining robe which so gentle a hand hath thrown over the offender. Does Mercy herself become displeased? Does she turn? does she repent? and is she about to forsake? No, God be thanked. She herself looks once more at the cross, and once more cries out to her people, 'In a little wrath I hid my face from thee for a moment, but with everlasting kindness will I have mercy on thee!' For all our sins mercy obtains pardon, 'for mercy reaches unto the clouds;' for all our shortcomings mercy obtains forgiveness, 'for mercy endureth for ever;' for all our sorrows mercy finds a balm, for 'his mercy is over all his works.'

II. THE PROVIDENCES OF GOD ARE BANNERS TO HIS PEOPLE. The providence of God is both *special* and *general;* but to whichever class they belong, all his providences are on his people's side.

This is true of the special providences of God. No doubt his people, in reference to their worldly circumstances, are often poor and unhappy. Of many of them the uttermost that can be said is, that their bread and their water are sure; but of what are deemed the comforts and luxuries of life, they know nothing. They are generally also an afflicted people; tears run down their cheeks, and the voice of their lamentation ascends, 'Many are the afflictions of the righteous.' But shall we suppose that these arrangements are against them? By no means. If their lot in the world be tribulation, we are assured that it will work, and does 'work out for them a more exceeding, and an eternal weight of glory.' Their trials and privations are all manifestations of God's parental regard; hence in every event of their life a blessing is lodged—some precious pearl is secreted. It is certainly highly honourable to them, that however much disregarded they may be by the great and the mighty of the earth, over their short but simple annals Jehovah himself is ever watchful—that whether by night or by day, his eye is over them—whether they are asleep or awake—in the house, or in the field, the Shepherd of Israel preserves them from evil; that while enthroned monarchs lie down encompassed by walls of security, and ministered to by thousands, they are far more secure; for the Lord sustains them, and they need not be afraid though ten thousands of people set themselves against them round about. It is also most dignifying to their character, and blissful to their condition, that no event of their lives, however comparatively trifling, is absolutely without its beneficial influence. Circumstances that pass unnoticed, and that are, in reference to worldly men, unworthy of notice, start into importance when they occur in the lot of the righteous, inasmuch as they are freighted with some little good to their souls. This must be so, else our Lord's account of the 'fall of the sparrow,' and the 'numbering of the hairs of our heads,' loses much of its force. You have seen the acorn drop, as if by accident, from its parent branch; you have seen it raised and carried by the whirlwind into some adjacent streamlet; you have seen it now playing on the surface of the water, now hiding in the crevices of the bank; you have seen it sucked into and hurried over the cataract, then lodged in the dark cavern, or mid the foaming surge; anon, you have seen it emerge from the boiling cauldron, and dashed with the spray on some adjoining field—there it is embedded in the soil, and after many years it becomes a lofty oak, whose branches 'stretch their longing arms afar.' In like manner, it not unfrequently happens that, many years afterwards, an event which was almost unnoticed when it occurred, is remembered by God's people as seen in the light of other events, and then perceived to have been either the beginning to a train of effects of great importance, or the connecting link of others from which it must have been injurious to their best interests to have been dissociated. How strikingly is all this illustrated in the history of Joseph, Moses, and David, and indeed of all the people of God, of whatever age or land, if their history were but written!

But the *general* as well as the special providences of God are banners to his people. Not only in the smaller circle of their domestic affairs, and in the more extended one of their domestic relations, but as members of society at large, everything is systematised for and directly bears upon their welfare. A propitious influence is carried to their interests, both from the comparatively trivial occurrence that is no sooner done than forgotten, and from that more momentous event which shakes society to its centre, which convulses the continents of the earth, which is written in the chronicles of nations, and remembered by mankind in every age. The thought, indeed, is sublime, and almost overwhelming, that the vast system of superintendence which Jehovah exercises over the whole globe has a pointed reference to the good of his chosen children. The edicts of kings, and the acts of potentates—the wisdom alike and the tyranny of their laws—the rise equally with the ruin of their empires—are all overruled for their good; so that it is all one to them whether thrones and principalities are shaken to their foundations, or more firmly secured. If, as subjects, they rejoice under a mild and forbearing administration, and are in possession of every civil privilege; if, as christians, they are blessed with religious as well as civil liberty—they owe it all to that Providence who has the hearts of the kings and senators of the earth in his hand. If, on the other hand, they are persecuted and hunted like the partridge on the mountains; if the sun shine not on them, and darkness becloud their prospects: if opposition from men, if temptations and suggestions from Satan, if wants and weaknesses, if internal conflicts and griefs, and the long, long train of worldly tribulations, pour out upon them their stores of tempest, and fill their souls with dismay—still even these providences must be confessed to be for their good. 'We dare not say that even in these there is any superfluous severity, that in this constitution of things there is any needless or uncalled for trouble. Adversities never befal them without a cause, nor are sent but on a proper errand. These storms are never allowed to rise, but in order to dispel some noxious vapours, or restore the salubrity of the moral atmosphere.

But, in fine, he takes a narrow and unbecoming view of providence, who supposes that its dispensations act independently of, or in separate detachments from, one another. This undervalues also the high honour and privilege of believers. For their good, all the events of providence act in unison—they co-operate. This is mysterious; but it is true that the whole of these events, far and near, great and small, are acting in concert for their good. It has been beautifully said, 'Taken separately or individually, it may be impossible to see that they are connected, but they must be viewed in their consequences and effects, in their dependencies and connections, as component parts of one gigantic system—as links hanging together of one extensive chain. For, it is by adjusting into one consistent whole the various events that fill up human life—it is by arranging in the happiest succession all the occurrences of that complicated scene, and it is by bending to his own purpose, things which appear most opposite and contrary, that Jehovah accomplishes his harmonious schemes for the good of his own. As in a physical composition, made up of many ingredients of different qualities, these ingredients, if taken singly, would do no good, or perhaps do injury, but if mixed together by a skilful hand, may be productive of much benefit, so here it is not one part of providence that works out the spiritual good, but the whole of them together being mutually connected, influenced, and assisted. Or, as all the rivers on the face of the globe, however circuitous they may be in their progress, and however opposite in their course, meet at length in the fathomless abyss of the ocean, and there contribute to increase the mass of waters, so all the seemingly discordant events in the life of a good man are made to preserve, upon the whole, an unerring tendency to his good, and to conspire for promoting it to the last moments of his life.' 'The Lord reigneth; let the earth rejoice.' Such, O believer, is that great edifice of encouragement and hope which the gospel hath reared up for those whom God loves, and on whose side his purposes and perfections are engaged.

III. THE GRACE OF GOD IS A BANNER TO HIS PEOPLE. Do we look back into the ages of eternity? we see grace proposing the plan of mercy, and accepting of the offer of the eternal Son to be the surety of sinners. Do we review the former dispensation? grace was their banner during its different periods downwards. God then kept them as the apple of his eye, and established his covenant with them, 'even the sure mercies of David;' and when the fulness of the times was come, Grace was gloriously displayed in the mission of the Son into our world. For the sake of his people, God spared him not, but delivered him up for them all. For their sakes, God 'bruised him and put him to grief.' And why was so dear a Son brought to such a low estate? Why was he tempted in the wilderness? Why was he agonised in Gethsemane, buffetted in the hall, nailed to a cross, and laid in a grave? In all this you see God's grace working out the salvation of his people; and the same grace that suggested and accomplished the amazing scheme, was exerted on the morning of the appointed day, to give attestation to its being perfect in the resurrection of the Lord from the dead. Grace for his people! was the voice which burst from Joseph's sepulchre, when the angel rolled away the stone, and the risen Saviour stood triumphant over death and the grave. Grace for his people! was the shout with which he ascended up on high, 'leading captivity captive, and receiving gifts for men.' Grace for his people! was the loudest hosannah of heaven, when its gates of glory were opened, and the King of glory entered. Grace for his people! were the joyful words that fell from his lips, as he took his seat on the august throne which had been prepared for him from the foundation of the world. Grace for his people! is engraved in letters of love around the mediatorial crown; and grace for his people! is the voice which is continually heard issuing from the glorious Shechinah in the innumerable gifts and blessings which are showered down upon them. Yea, for their sakes Jehovah has constituted his throne a throne of grace, his sceptre a sceptre of grace, and his government an administration of grace. In the temple above there is now erected an altar of grace; standing before it there is a Priest of grace, who continually intercedes for them, that they receive grace upon grace. O had we the power, but for a moment, willingly should we draw aside the vail of the inner sanctuary, and show you that all heaven, though full of glory, is but one fountain of grace to believers, the streams of which descend to make glad the city of our God. But why need we enlarge, for are not all the people of God just the monuments of his grace? By that grace they are what they are. It found them in the deep pit, and raised them from it. It found them bleeding in the open field, and pitied and bound up their wounds. It found them in the power and under the chain of Satan, and it gave them liberty. It found them weak—it made them strong. It found them polluted—it made them holy. It opened their eyes, and ears, and mouths—it made them leap like the hart, and rejoice like the strong man to run a race. It clothed them in the comeliest garments—the righteousness of Jesus. It conformed their souls to the loveliest image—'the image of the invisible God.' It adopted them into the family of God. It put within them the hope of eternal life; and at this moment it is nourishing all their virtues, fighting all their battles, subduing all their enemies, and carrying them all forward to glory. Nor shall the work and friendship of grace be suspended until, having passed through this valley of Baca, and having finished their course, they shall close their earthly career in peace. At that blessed moment, *grace* for them shall pass into *glory*, and all the purposes of God in instituting the system under which they have been tutored, shall be finally and completely accomplished. Glory to his people! will be the rapturous welcome which shall meet them at the gates of Paradise, and glory, glory, glory, will be the matter of their joy, and the theme of their song through all eternity!

But, apart from its manifestations in the mediatorial work of Christ, we see that God's grace is for his people in all the ordinances of his appointment. To that grace they are indebted for *the preaching of the gospel*, which converts their souls and prepares them for judgment. Think you, if God had not been for us, he would have caused the Sun of Righteousness to rise upon our world—dissipated the darkness of our natural minds, and raised our hopes of an inheritance above? If he had not been for us, would he have preserved a seed to serve him, and to transmit from age to age the records of his mercy? If he had not been for us, would he have put the gospel trumpet into the hands of the gospel heralds, and made them proclaim aloud and afar, 'Peace on earth, and goodwill to men?' No. We have the best evidence that God is on our side, when we look at the mercy and wisdom of this magnificent moral apparatus by which Christ and him crucified are held up to the view and faith of all generations. Again, are we not indebted *to the grace of God for the Bible?* And surely he never would have sent us such a revelation, but with the intention of conferring upon us the blessings which it promises. Why did he give us poor sinners this infallible directory of a way to escape, if he had not wished to guide our steps into the paths of life? And why did he hang up the burning and shining lamp above us, if he had not desired to guide our shattered bark across the stormy sea of life, and 'to the hills of God—the everlasting hills—to point the sinner's eye?' Again, if his grace be not for us, why has he instituted the ordinance of *prayer*—prayer, the door by which we enter his presence to find grace—our retreat in the hour of conscious guilt to ask aid, for Christ's sake, to find forgiveness—our hiding place when beset with temptations, and our trumpet wherewith we alarm Heaven to come to our aid in every time of need? In fine, is not the *institution of our holy sacraments* decided evidence that the grace of God is for his people? To baptism they are indebted for their early dedication by their parents to God, and for admission into the church visible, ere yet they are able to appreciate its blessings. To many of them the external sign is accompanied by 'the washing of regeneration, and the renewing of the Holy Ghost;' and to all of them afterwards are secured every blessing signified by the solemn rite. And where would mankind have been but for the institution of the Lord's Supper? What would have been the consequence if grace had neglected to erect this memorial of Jesus' atonement? By this time, and long before this, the world would have forgotten the story of Jesus of Nazareth—Bethlehem and its manger—Mary and her babe—Galilee and its fishermen—Judea and its benefactor—Calvary and its cross. Joseph's sepulchre and its tenant would have been clean gone from the memory of men, perhaps from the records of history; and how fearful must have been the consequences to a world lying in guilt! 'There is no other name under heaven given among men whereby we can be saved but the name of Jesus.' Had men, therefore, lost sight of this name, they must have perished. But God be thanked that his grace was for us here! We still have the institution of the Supper—an institution which not only perpetuates from age to age the glorious truth that Christ died for sin, but which, to them that by faith observe it, is the medium of joyful fellowship with God, and the channel through which his abundant grace is ever made sufficient for them.

Say not that the discussion of this subject is useless. As the people of God, you need to be cheered and encouraged in this scene of conflict and trial. Be cheered then and encouraged by the considerations to which your attention has been called. The Lord of hosts is with you—he is on your side. May we not then ask with the apostle, 'If God be for you, who can be against you?' No doubt there are many against you—many who plot and long for your destruction, but not so against you as seriously to injure you. We are told that there are even some who plot against the Lord and his Anointed, but that he laughs at them, and dashes them in pieces like a potter's vessel. Equally disastrous to your enemies will be the wrath of God, who, in wondrous condescension, makes common cause with you. Your enemies are his enemies. Which of you then shall doubt the issue of the warfare? Let none doubt it. You shall, you must triumph. You have Jehovah-Nissi, who is 'strong and mighty in battle,' on your side. You have Jesus Christ, who triumphed over the powers of hell, on your side. You have the Holy Spirit, who moved upon the face of the waters, on your side. You have the angels, 'who excel in strength,' on your side. You fight beneath the standard of heaven—you fight against the foes of heaven—you fight for the glory of the God of heaven—you fight for the possession of heaven—fight on, and fight bravely, soldiers of the cross, and victory shall be yours. How can you doubt it? For whether shall the Most High be most interested in your efforts, which are all for his glory, or in the efforts of the powers of darkness, which are all to hurl him from his throne? This, then, is your encouragement, though there be some *against* you, they never can succeed. They can never be so against you as to destroy you. They may trouble you with their hostility, and perhaps now and then make some little inroads on your peace; but the waves of their opposition, like the waves of the sea, have their appointed limits; to the one as to the other God says, 'Hitherto shalt thou come and no farther.' They can never be so against you as to exclude you from heaven; of that inheritance you are as sure as if you were already before God. You may doubt about it—your fellow-christians may doubt about it—and it may be Satan, that arch-deceiver, may sometimes have a flickering ray of hope that he may cheat you out of it, but all is secure; as joint-heirs with Christ, you shall yet see God, and live. Why, then, should you ever be harassed with fears? Is there one created being, think you, in the wide universe of God—and if you will, let him be stronger than the angels, than the mightiest of the angels; yea, let him have strength above the concentrated power both of angels and of men—is there such an one against you? Fear him not; God is with you. Sooner could this morning's babe move the mountain from its seat—sooner could your feeble voices arrest the sun in its course—sooner could the puny arm of mortal rend asunder the veil between time and eternity—sooner could these impossible things be done, than that any of you should be plucked out of his hands who has ' given you eternal life.'

'The hosts of God encamp around
   The dwellings of the just;
Protection He affords to all
   Who make his name their trust.

'O! make but trial of his love;
   Experience will decide
How blest they are, and only they,
   Who in his truth confide.

'Fear Him, ye saints, and you will then
   Have nothing else to fear;
Make *you* his service your delight,
   Your wants HE'll make his care.'

CHAPTER XIII.

JEHOVAH-NISSI: THE LORD MY BANNER.

PART II.

'In the name of our God we will set up our banners.'
PSALM xx. 5.

THE Lord is on our side. We owe all our religion and our hopes to his grace and love. This is the *first* idea connected with the title, Jehovah-Nissi. The second is like unto it, viz., that we are on the Lord's side; his cause we espouse, and devote to it all we are by his grace and enjoy from his pardon. We proceed to the illustration.

The figure employed, 'a banner,' is borrowed from a military signal. It is frequently to be met with in scripture, and seems to be used indiscriminately with the words *standard* and *ensign*. The four grand divisions of the army of Israel had each a banner of different colours, for the sake of distinguishing the one from the other; but their chief use was to distinguish them from the contending enemy. There might be other ensigns or flags, but that one which was called 'the standard' was the most considerable and conspicuous. It was regarded as the national banner, and was set up by the commander upon some prominent place, not to be lowered while the battle lasted, and above all, not to be allowed to be taken, at whatever risk defended. If the standard-bearer fell, and the standard itself was taken, confusion and rout might follow. From all the accounts, then, which have been received, whether sacred or profane, we learn the following truths respecting the use of the banner in war: It indicated the party, and specified the cause—it was the rallying point of the squadrons during the engagement—it was sometimes the telegraphic language of war—and, it was carried in the triumphal procession, as the signal of victory.

I. THE BANNER INDICATED THE PARTY, AND SPECIFIED THE CAUSE. The banner of the christian does the same. In this world there are two spiritual powers engaged in hostilities; sin against holiness, or God against Satan. This war is carried on *within* man, or in the human heart—the object of Satan being to keep God out of it, and thus to ruin it for ever; the object of God being to regain its affections, and to ensure its eternal happiness. Among the nations of this earth there are many grievous contendings. Strife of some kind sets the people against the rulers, or the rulers against the people; hence wars strictly so called. There are also intellectual combats, in which one set of opinionists essay to overthrow the lucubrations of another set; hence the war of opinions that obtains among men of science, or letters, or politics. These parties make a great noise, and cause a great confusion. Each has a leader, and each leader has some appropriate emblem by which he indicates 'his side,' and his admirers their attachment. Exciting, however, as are these clashings of carnal interests, to none of them is a christian, as such, wedded; and, indeed, in none of them does he take a very profound interest. No doubt he will have his own mind, and perhaps choose his own favourite,—Newton, for example, in the walks of natural philosophy, or Bacon in inductive science, or Adam Smith in civic economy, or any one of the illustrious statesmen of the day in politics; and he will also uphold such an ensign or banner as will publish to the world whose cause it is that he has espoused. He does this from conviction of duty, and because he knows that to hesitate or truckle must bring upon him contempt; for, as society is now constituted, he who suspends his mind in everlasting hesitancy, fearing to indicate to which side he leans, gains the respect of none, and, it may be, the scorn of all. When a mind of a high order has dared to impugn the fallacies or wisdom of antiquity, and has, in its chivalrous advances into the region of truth, scared away the night owls of ignorance, and replaced them with the lamps of knowledge, it is ennobled by the greatness of its own enterprise, and holds fast its convictions, though there be few indeed that follow it; at the same time, it expects from its professed disciples that they shall not hide these discoveries in a napkin, nor, Nicodemus-like, visit their teacher only in the night season, but make known to all their coincidence of opinions with his, and extol his excellences. No earnest *leader* cares for your '*secret*' disciples. Indeed, there have been men of that honourable spirit, who would rather confront opposition, than be tantalised with time-serving or half-hearted partisanship. 'Be either for us or against us,' is the principle on which they wish to be dealt with; if for us, say so, and say it manfully; if against us, avow it, and let us meet an open and frank antagonist.

In like manner ought the friends of Jehovah-Nissi to deal with him and his cause. It is their duty to lift up their distinctive banner before the whole world, and neither be afraid nor ashamed to do so. Now, as the Lord Jesus himself is the banner of the christian, so to set him up is just the same thing with a bold avowal that he is on Christ's side—that is, a follower of the despised Nazarene. No genuine believer, indeed, will on any account make his espousal of Christ an obscurity, or allow himself to become so afraid of the world, or so absorbed in its quarrels and projects, as to have his zeal cooled, or his adoption of the cross cast into the shade. Some there are, calling themselves christians, who allow the charms of philosophy, the hazards of politics, or the pursuits of business, so completely to occupy them, that their christian standard has been either taken from them, or it lies at their feet. No one can tell whether they are for or against Christ. Christianity seems to have no power over them; and any compliance which they affect is of a very questionable shape, too nearly resembling the conduct of the seven sons of Sceva, who took upon them to name the name of Christ over those who were possessed with devils, and to whom the evil spirit answered and said, 'Jesus I know, and Paul I know, but who are ye?' Because the claims of time are great, and in a degree to be admitted, and because there is pleasure almost amounting to intoxication in investigating truth, and in unravelling the mysterious processes of nature, many justify their temporary lowerings of the distinctive badge of christianity, and do not see that they thereby bring upon their religion the sneer of the freethinker. There are many dangerous conditions in which the precious soul of man can be placed, but there is none in which its everlasting well-being is so appallingly imperilled as in this nominal connection with Christ, while the devotedness is entirely to the idol of one's own heart. Let it be granted that this idol has the eye of beauty, still, like the cockatrice, it kills by its look; that it has the voice of soul-inspiring music, still, like the syren, that music leads to the path of death; that it has the attire and ornaments of joyous youth, still all this is only as

> 'The gilded shore
> To a most dangerous sea—the beauteous scarf
> Veiling an Indian beauty; in a word,
> The seeming truth which cunning times put on
> To entrap the wisest!'

O the power which the love of this world wields over some men! It is tremendous. In some it assumes the type of a monomania, of a kind of moral insanity, wherewith they appear to be as much monopolised as if they had been created for no other end. It is money with one, fame with another, letters with a third, pleasure with a fourth, and general philanthropy with a fifth. But it is all one what it is, if upon that one thing the soul expends its strength, and wastes its fire, to the utter exclusion of God. What a miserable breakdown is this after such flaring professions of consecrating their all to the service and glory of the Redeemer! Banners they may have, but upon the only one elevated in the centre of their operations, is inscribed the name of that carnal deity to whom they live, and by whom they are to be destroyed. Of no true soldier of the cross can these things be affirmed. JESUS is the name inscribed on their banner, in letters of life, so that whatever mistakes men may commit in judging of them otherwise, they never can mistake the Leader whom they follow, nor the cause they have espoused.

But what is this cause? It is presupposed that the christian's heart is first of all surrendered to his Lord and Master, and that, subsequent to this, the religion of the christian is adopted and advocated. The cause is christianity, or rather the progress and universal spread of christianity. The grand design of the gospel is to bring the world back to God; and this consummation is to be secured by the agency of men who are themselves saved. If they speak for Christ, it is because they have already believed in Christ; if they give to Christ, it is because they have first of all given their own selves to him; if they carry the war of truth into the region of error, it is because they are themselves enlightened and purified by that truth. It would be a ridiculous, if it were not an audacious attempt in any man to hoist the banner of Christ, while he was still its enemy. But if by that Christ he has been crucified to the world, and the world has been crucified to him, then he only acts in character when he runs to the high mountains and fixes upon their summits this solemn ensign of his faith. He indeed cannot act in character at all, unless he become an aggressor on the domain of Satan, and fight hard to reinstate his Saviour in the love and allegiance of mankind.

The cause at stake in the valley of Rephidim was God's covenant engagements with his people. Death to Amalek, therefore, was the cry, or the inscription on the standard of Israel. In like manner, the cause of Christ is the triumph of his cross over the whole earth, and, therefore, death to all systems that oppose his, is the war-cry of his friends, while the hope of success gives determination and force to their every project and appliance. Less than the conversion of a world they dare not contemplate as the object to be aimed at. It is not a mere fraction, but the whole of the globe that has revolted; and it is not a moiety, but every soul of mankind, that lie under condemnation—it is not the men of one country, but those of every era and generation, that are to be besought to repent and believe. Wherever man is found, there Christ's cross is to be lifted up; and if some new continent were to cast up at the very ends of the earth, and but one man its solitary inhabitant, to him it would behove us to carry it. So grand, so Godlike, so divine is this cause, that if all the world else were converted save this poor solitary wretch, there would be the highest propriety, yea, the most weighty necessity for bringing to bear upon his deathless spirit the hearty intercession of all saints, with the devices and sacrifices available for reaching and subduing him to the faith of the Redeemer.

In this view of the case, we may wonder that any avowed believer should feel at liberty to retire from the field of missionary action and enterprise, or refuse to go influentially forward into the thickest of the engagement. If the reader be such an one, let him immediately decipher the inscription upon his banner. Is it not, 'He loved me, and gave himself for me?' Is is not, 'Glory to God in the highest, on earth peace, and goodwill toward men?' Is it not, 'We are not our own, but bought with a price?' Is it not, 'We will follow thee whithersoever thou goest?' Are not these and such as these the appropriate devices on every standard in Israel? How comes it, then, O professed lover of Jesus, that thou art doing nothing in furtherance of the design of atoning blood? How canst thou reconcile thy alien heart, thy sordid disposition, thy inactive life, with the obligations thou hast imposed upon thyself, by carrying about with thee this banner of the Lord of hosts? O how canst thou reconcile doing nothing whatever for Christ with seeking everything precious to thy soul from Christ? Thou proclaimest before high heaven that Christ is thy banner; that is, that no less a being than thy Creator is fighting on thy side, and bleeding and dying for thee on the mysterious field of 'the reconciliation;'—and thou! where art thou? Not on his side—grudging him even a mite out of his own silver and gold—even a prayer when at his own throne of grace—even a word, one good word of acknowledgment whilst escaping underneath the broad banner of his omnipotence from the damnation of hell. O 'tell it not in Gath, publish it not in the streets of Askelon; lest the daughters of the Philistines rejoice, lest the daughters of the uncircumcised triumph.' Say not that this caricatures thy case; it is a genuine likeness —the enunciation of very truth. The Lord himself declares it: 'He that is not with me is against me. 'I know thy works, that thou art neither cold nor hot. So then, because thou art lukewarm, and neither cold nor hot, I will spue thee out of my mouth.' If, therefore, there is to be a continuance with thee of this do-nothing system, we would at once counsel thee to lower thy standard and efface its devices. Say no longer that thou art Christ's, and that he is thine, that thou art for him, and that he is for thee, or else let thy conduct be consistent with thy declarations; and while thou livest, refuse not to do all, give all, and suffer all, to extend his gospel and make his name honoured beneath every clime.

II. THE BANNER WAS THE RALLYING POINT OF THE SQUADRONS DURING AN ENGAGEMENT. If it happened, as it sometimes does in war, that any division of the army got into confusion, and if, amid the smoke and din of the battle, the standard was concealed, there was danger of defeat. But while the standard-bearer kept his ground, and so soon as the clouds rolled away, then the streaming flag was again discerned, the soldiers rallied around it, were formed into order, and anew assailed the foe. Had the banner been taken, and had no ensign of any kind remained to indicate the centre, confusion and rout must have followed. And so it is with the banner of the church. By the gospel alone is this world to be redeemed out of the hands of Satan. The cross of Christ is the central point of this gospel, and therefore the eyes and hearts of all men must be drawn hither, otherwise they remain in the slavery of sin. If this cross be hid, rebellion continues rampant. Left to itself, and left to themselves, unrestrained by the influences of Calvary, sin and sinners would speedily consummate the curse upon the earth; for not only is rebellion against God in itself war of the worst description, but in its results upon men themselves, it is terribly destructive; while its aim is to dethrone Jehovah, its immediate effect is to make men devils and to turn them against one another in implacable hate.

If the cross be not the only banner underneath which men are to be brought into reconciliation with God, then what experiment has ever been tried to arrest the fatal tendency of the race to apostacy? For four thousand years God left the heathen world to make the attempt, and what came out of it? At the time of Christ's birth, the Gentile nations were in darkness. Men were idolaters, and their souls were immolated on the altars of Moloch; men were slaves, and their lives and liberties were at the disposal of tyrants; men were children alike in religion and science, and were the dupes of every idle chimera. And when at any time the soul, struggling to possess itself of the divine light, dared to impugn the accuracy of bygone maxims, or even to hint of a sacrifice for sin, and of immortality beyond the grave, the poignard and the poisoned chalice became the reward of the embryo philosopher; while the effrontery of any speculation on the sublime laws that rule the sidereal heavens, was an iniquity to be punished by the judges. Surely four thousand years afforded a sufficiently long period for trial. Had it been shorter, the infidel might have pronounced it inadequate to the discovery of truth. Gainsaying, however, on this point, is silenced. The history of the heathen world up to the birth of Christ, is very interesting to the christian student. None of the nations kept long together; none of the mighty dynasties were perpetual; no system of morals, no principles of any kind had a long lease of life. The tendency of all men and of all things, whatever the regime under which they were placed, was to disunion, dispersion, and death. *Why?* THERE WAS NO BANNER. These nations had no rallying point around which men might meet and be incorporated. One peculiar people alone kept together, and were neither dissolved nor absorbed. Century after century passed away, and generations lived and died, and ten thousand times ten thousand interests rose and fell, but still that people 'dwelt alone,' retained all their religious and political distinctions, and were as entire when Christ was born as when Moses died. *Why?* THERE WAS A BANNER. God's truth was among them; and hence, though dispersed for a time, they always rallied again from every hidden recess of their captivities. Thus, while the wisdom of Socrates and of Plato, the military heroism of the Cæsars, the arts of the men of Nineveh, and the laws of the Ptolemies, all failed to perpetuate the integrity and the power of empires— the ark and the altar of an insignificant and downtrodden people were sublimely maintained, amid the wreck of kingdoms and the crash of intolerant philosophies. It was the attractive and centralising power of their banner that did it. It was the truth of God that did it all.

As it was then, so it is still. There is stability to no kingdom, promise to no human interest, and progress in no quarter of the globe, except where the influence of the gospel is felt. That gospel is the saviour of any, as it must be the saviour of all people. Is it not the bulwark, at this moment, of Great Britain? While continental nations lie bleeding in chains, forged by priestcraft, and are menaced every hour with some terrific revolutionary explosion, behold the solidity and tranquillity of our native land! It is the cross that rallies, consolidates, and unites us. Differences there are about mere circumstantials, but our common interest in the gospel salvation brings us all together, as into one compact Macedonian phalanx, armed at all points to defend, as one man, the palladium of our civil and religious freedom. Take down from the high places of England that pure and sacred regard for our Protestant, or rather our Christian privileges, for which we have hitherto been so highly distinguished, and it is questionable if, with all its power and prestige, this kingdom could long abide united or compact. We should then lack our common standard, and when the evil hour of contention came, we should fall to pieces like the empires of the past, and dissolve like a rope of sand as the angry tides advanced. Our safety, then, is in giving honour and prominence to the standard of the cross. If we lower it through cowardice, or compromise, then the God of mercy has no farther use for us, and will allow us to go down to the dust. If we keep it up, then we are safe; for while heaven's own banner floats over our ramparts, we are the allies of the Lord of hosts, and he will give us victory, and crown us with abundance of all good things.

But this is not all. If the banner of the gospel be the rallying point to kingdoms, even as to their secular interests, much more is it so to the church of God, in her warfare with the powers of darkness. And here it is that the christian banner is seen to highest advantage, for here it is directly used, first for the church's *purity*, and secondly for her *extension*.

1. As to her *purity*. She depends for its preservation on the divine oracles, which are her only standards. When, for instance, she suffers a relapse either as to corruption in doctrine or vitiation in morals, it can only be by the higher elevation of these standards that such errors are to be amended. Truth alone can neutralise the virus of heresy.

Hence, when heterodoxes have crept in, the unfurling of this banner has driven them out of the church. It was by this means that Luther effected the Protestant Reformation. All that was needed in his day was just the uplifting of the good old banner of 'justification by faith.' So soon as the nations saw it once more floating over the hills and the walls of Europe, their hearts were made to leap to the glorious ensign; man joined himself to man, and a short conflict was all that was necessary to overthrow Popish felonies and fictions. O but the truth, the simple truth of Jesus, has a mighty influence in the way of rectifying human systems, and sanctifying human hearts! Let but that truth have a free course, and the abettors of iniquity everywhere shall flee away. This is the grand catholicon for all errors and all woes. The edicts of kings, the anathemas of popes, and the penalties of magistrates, can do little in the domain of mind, less in the territory of morals, and nothing whatever in the region of conscience. The most these can effect is to make some men hypocrites, other men infidels, and many men dissolute. The uncompounded and untrammelled gospel of Christ has an innate power to do all its own work. Hence, when permitted to take its own way with men, it enlightens their minds, pacifies their spirits, and purifies their hearts. This is easily accounted for. God will have all the glory of converting men, and he will share it with none. He therefore repudiates the proffered arms of puny mortals. All he asks for his gospel is just that men receive it for themselves, and give it to others. As to mere earthly assistance in upholding and disseminating his own cause, he repudiates it, and requires of us that we let it work in its own way, that we give it space and time, and that we leave its efficiency to his blessing. Above all, he commands that we do not touch it with the brush, by way of freshening its complexion; nor dress it in purple and fine linen, by way of adding to its comfort; nor hang a sword by its side to give it a military air, or to help it in a quarrel; nor put a crown upon its head, and set it on a throne, to impart authority to its oracles, or to secure currency for its laws; nor, in short, in any other way to annoy and encumber it with the weapons that are carnal. Let us leave truth, then, to walk forth in its native majesty, and with appeals from its own clear running brooks, it will sling them at the forehead of gigantic infidelity, and lay it lifeless in the dust. Only give to it a sufficiently elevated position—let its banners stream from all the evangelical pulpits of the land, and from all the missionary pulpits abroad, and in a short time its divine work shall be accomplished: 'all the ends of the earth shall see the salvation of our God.' While a pure gospel is the only standard unfurled on the field, the divisions of the army are not distracted from the centre—the cross. Their eye ever rests upon it, and they contend strenuously in that direction. It is only when sectarian, or feudal, or imperial banners are added, that the true one is concealed, and disasters occur. The soldiers are then puzzled by varieties—they get off the centre—their eye is not alone on the cross, and hence they often fall into confusion, and fight against one another—rallying now around some painted device, and then around some tattered rag of men's own invention. O that the time were come when christian men would cherish unbounded confidence in the intrinsic omnipotence of Bible truth, and that no other banner save the cross were ever hoisted within the pale of the church! What a rushing of the hosts would then be towards it! what a havoc of its enemies! what a shout of triumph from every bulwark of Zion! How could it fail? Is not the banner the cross of Christ? and is not the 'foolishness of God wiser than men, and the weakness of God stronger than men?'

2. All this is equally true when affirmed of the church's *extension* or *progress*. If the simple preaching of the gospel be enough to preserve her purity, it must be equal to secure her increase. Doubts are sometimes expressed as to the capacity of gospel truth to convert the world. There are so many antagonist systems, and so many centuries have passed away while so little comparatively has been done, that many hesitate to give their assent to the proposition, that the christian religion is its own best propagator. Now, this scepticism is somewhat

inconsistent. Very few confide in mere secular or sectarian policy to preserve the *purity* of the church's doctrines, or to simplify these when they have been adulterated. It is admitted that to the church herself should be left the work of keeping her own house clean. But if this be so, why allow her an intrinsic power as to the preservation of her purity, and deny her that power as to her own propagation? It appears to be a more delicate and difficult thing to keep truth *pure* in such a world as this, than to support and extend it. Indeed, the most heroic deeds on her fields have been connected with her masterly efforts against unholy mixtures and vain traditions; and, but for the time, zeal, blood, and life she has expended on these, her advancement and captures might have been on an incalculably larger scale. When she has had nothing to do in the way of preserving her purity, she has found the rapid dissemination of her principles comparatively easy. And it is singular enough, that while stores of time and treasure have in past days been consecrated to the protection of her chastity, similar contributions towards her mere progress have been made on a much smaller scale; that is, it has taken more to retain the integrity of Truth, and to keep her free of the glosses of error, than to uphold her temple and feed her fires. If, then, the solitary banner of the cross be the only effective custodier of what is pure, let us believe in its ability also to possess the church of all the land that remains to be cultivated. Has not our Lord promised that the kingdom of his dear Son shall 'look forth as the morning, fair as the moon, clear as the sun, and terrible as an army with banners?'

III. THE BANNER WAS SOMETIMES THE TELEGRAPHIC LANGUAGE OF WAR. When Israel fought against Amalek, Moses was upon the top of the adjacent hill earnestly engaged in prayer, and the victory gained is, by most students of the passage, understood to be the answer to his prayers. This is a fair enough view of 'the lifting up of Moses' hands,' but it is not the only idea conveyed by it. From his exalted position he had a sight of the entire field of battle, and could narrowly survey the various movements of the contending parties. He thus had information which Joshua could not in active engagement acquire. Hence it has been suggested that we may consider the rod which he held in his uplifted hands, as on that day the royal standard of Israel; and that he pointed with it to this and to the other part of the enemy's forces which appeared to be most vulnerable. Thus the rising and falling of his rod was in reality the telegraph of despatches, by means of which the battle was brought to a successful issue.

How interesting the lesson here taught to the militant christian! While he espouses the cross and rallies around it his best energies, he is also instructed and encouraged by it in all his conflicts with spiritual adversaries. The gospel, in short, is at once the cause itself, and the very source of the strength and skill which are put forth in its defence. To it, therefore, he ever looks. As he looks, he receives intimation of the particular enemy that is advancing, of the time and mode of attacking him, and of the best manœuvres for surprising and discomfitting him. If it be against his own personal piety that 'fleshly lusts' are warring, he is thereby taught how and when to crucify them. If it be against the interests of the entire army of the church that hostilities are concentrated, by the same rod of God is he directed as to the sure method of defeating them. On all occasions indeed, and at every stage and crisis of the spiritual life, is his banner to him an infallible guide. It never misleads him. It never leaves him in a difficulty. He may have to continue his warfare from night to morn, as well as from morn till night, but by constantly studying the movements of this ensign, he reaches in the end the expected crown. No wonder that the christian has such confidence in the cross; that confidence has never been betrayed. Even when at times the enemy appears to be gaining ground, he has only to look once more at the banner, and his courage is braced up, and his efforts begin to tell powerfully against the foe.

The hazard of war is proverbial. Often during the same engagement does the fortune of the day seem to favour the one, and then the other party; but victory uniformly declares for the christian at the last. When Amalek prevailed against Israel, another look at the rod of Moses turned the tide in their favour. The very sight of that rod would re-invigorate the fainting; for they must all have heard of the wonderful things done by it in the land of Ham. Such like is the look of the believer at the cross of Christ. A divine energy is transmitted from it which no power in earth or in hell can resist; and this solves the mystery of the marvellous achievements of the weakest saints. Left to themselves, they are sure to fall; guided and upheld by the despatches and couriers of the gospel, they stand and conquer. What an irresistible argument for ever 'looking unto Jesus' as we 'fight the good fight of faith!' It was the first look at him that inspired the soul with energy, and excited it to action; and it is the continual looking at the same centre that secures great progress in holiness. In itself, alone, the cross of that Saviour is a complete armoury to the believer. Its truth is his girdle, its righteousness his breastplate, its peace his shoe, its faith his shield, its salvation his helmet, and its word his sword. Yea, 'the Lord his banner' is also his sun by day, which scatters before him every cloud; and his moon by night, which casts its silver rays across the dark and death-like vale where he fights. Wonderful banner! for, when hungry, it points him to the bread of life; when thirsty, it leads him to the wells of salvation; when wounded, it pours oil into his wounds;

when despairing, it reanimates him with hope; when fatigued and feeble, it gives him rest and shelter under its broad flag, and sends him forth like a giant refreshed with new wine; when dying, it supplies him with the elements of spiritual heroism; and when dead, it touches him, and he lives. O, never did weary and warworn soldier fight under banner like this! for when he is weak, then he is strong; when faint, then he pursues; when troubled on every side, then he is not distressed; when perplexed, then he is not in despair; when persecuted, then he is never forsaken; when cast down, then he is not destroyed, 'always bearing about in his body the dying of the Lord Jesus, that the life also of Christ might be made manifest in his body.'

So much to be depended upon, indeed, and so certain are the timely issues of needed counsel and answered prayers from the cross, that the feeblest christian may go up at any time against a whole generation of Amaleks; he may face the principalities of hell—he may challenge death and the grave. The looks he ever gives to that standard must nerve him up to every extremity, fortify him against all weapons, and draw him upwards to the very bosom of him who is the great High Priest of his profession. When there, he puts his ear to the throbbing of that heart which shed its blood for his life, so that, what with seeing and what with hearing, in this grand centre of his faith, he is prepared for every exigency.

Not more quickly does the telegraph convey intelligence on its lightning wing, than does the warning from the cross reassure the believer, and hasten him onward and upward to the blessed experiences of his faith; yea, to the glorious realisation of paradise regained. Valuable as are the electric wires, they are not implicitly to be trusted; they may be broken; the ocean's tides may break in upon and arrest the progress of the fluid, and he who trusted in a crisis to their infallibility, is suddenly disappointed. But no such calamity can befal the telegraphic banner of the christian. Its influence permeates all atmospheres, darts beneath all seas, flies over alpine chains, crosses eternal snows, and circulates, with equal freedom, among all elements; so that whatever vicissitudes come, whatever opposition starts up, by instant resort to, and by wise consultation of the rod, he is possessed of all the information he needs, and at his right hand, in one moment, is the entire panoply of God. Casting away, then, all carnal confidence, and removing all trust in human desires or human merit, let us hold fast the profession of our faith without wavering, 'looking unto Jesus the author and the finisher of our faith.'

IV. THE BANNER WAS USED IN THE TRIUMPHAL PROCESSION TO SYMBOLISE VICTORY. In by far the most important sense of the word, 'the victory' may be said to be gained by the sinner when he believes and is forgiven. From that hour the object of Satan is defeated. He is now one of the ransomed of the Lord, and only awaits his coronation day to receive the laurel of the conqueror. That day, however, is often far distant from the period of the sinner's conversion. He is left for a while on the field of battle, where not a few of his old antagonists, whose wounds have not yet proved fatal, continue to threaten and vex him. The first conflict, however, is never repeated; that is, he is not again subjected to the act of regeneration. A man is only once converted, after which his spiritual fights can scarce be dignified with the name of battles; they are only skirmishes with the fragments of a dispersed and a discomfitted enemy. To drop metaphor: the great matter is at first, when the soul is made to yield to God, and glory in the cross; after this its progressive sanctification occasions all the contest that goes on between the powers of nature and of grace; all the work now is just the following up, by the Spirit of God, of the great and decisive victory in the day of effectual calling. The question, therefore, is, should the christian celebrate this victory before he enters heaven? and the reply must be in the affirmative. In ancient and even in modern warfare, the signal of victory is the elevation of the banner on the captured fortress or on the battle-field. The enthusiastic warriors wait not till all the conditions of surrender are fulfilled; and the triumphal procession, amid which the gay ensigns are waving, is not postponed until every preliminary is arranged. Victory brooks not delay, therefore up to the blue sky rise the shouts of the warrior in that very moment in which the enemy is scattered and fallen.

What a fine lesson does this teach to believers! Your path, christian readers, from the moment of reconciliation to God, ought to be strewed with flowers; on your brows should be placed the verdant laurel; the banner of the cross should be carried in your hands high above your heads, and wherever you lodge, should wave over you as the signal to all that you have won the battle—that you are the Lord's. In this way you give glory to God in the highest, and thus also you proclaim the praises of the Captain of your salvation, as 'strong and mighty in battle.' Surely no christian will conceal his laurels, or hide the banner that tells to whom he is indebted for all he is and hopes for. By conscientiously manifesting his saintship, he not only gives glory to whom glory is due, but intimidates his enemies and keeps them away. Many good men are sadly tormented by their adversaries—often tempted to sin. If they would only examine themselves, they would discover that they expose themselves to all this by not lifting their banner high enough, or by not lifting it at all. When the enemy sees no banner but his own, he thinks the victory may yet be his, and while one gleam of hope remains, he relaxes no effort to gain his point. Now, to be relieved, not entirely, but to a comfortable extent, from such hostilities, the christian has only to hoist his flag high enough, and to keep it up as long as he is on the field. In other words, he must always keep glorying in the cross of Christ. By that cross he at first triumphed over his enemies, and by that cross alone he shall go on to conquer over the field till he reaches the citadel of heaven. The cross does it all, therefore of the cross they should never be ashamed. The world may laugh at such an emblem; but they must extol it as all their 'salvation and all their desire.' We mean not by this to counsel you to the superstitious use of what the Romanist calls his crucifix; for this would be to make and to worship an image; but we mean, that engraven on the tablets of your hearts, that inscribed on every action of your lives, and that placed high in all your religious confessions should be Jesus Christ and him crucified. We mean, that so decided and distinct should these confessions be, that neither man nor devil can for one moment doubt either your actual allegiance or the source to which you ascribe its existence. It is he who, disregarding all the sneers of the fool, all the wiles of the world, and all the cravings of the deceitful heart, desires all mankind to know that it is only by the grace of God that he is what he is—that it is only for Christ's sake that he is a pardoned sinner and an heir of hope—it is he who, in thorough contempt of his own paltry works, makes mention of Christ's righteousness, even of his only—it is he who, denying himself all 'ungodliness and worldly lusts, lives soberly, righteously, and godly in this present world'— it is he who, in stern and unflinching regard to the law of Christ, yields ever to his constraining love, and publishes on the house-top what he has heard in the ear; yea, who like Wisdom 'crieth without, and uttereth his voice in the streets, in the chief places of concourse, in the openings of the gates'—*this* is he who moves gallantly and rapidly forward in the divine life, his enemies being driven before the banner he carries, and before the life which he now conscientiously and consistently leads.

And when at length the field is abandoned—when all the wounds of the soldier have been healed by Jehovah-Rophi—when he is made perfect in holiness; then it is, still waving the cross in his dying hand, still glorying in it with his dying breath, still enfolding it in the arms of his immortal faith, his soul reaches the gates of the celestial city, and all the crowned victors who have preceded him rush forth to meet another brother in arms, giving him a rapturous welcome, and forming a grand procession, convey him into the immediate presence of the King, who puts the crown upon his head, the palm into his hand, and eternal songs into his mouth.

CHAPTER XIV.

JEHOVAH-SHAMMAH: THE LORD IS THERE.

PART I.

'The name of the city from that day shall be, Jehovah-Shammah;' that is, 'The Lord is there.'

EZEKIEL xlviii. 35.

THE scripture quoted above is the last sentence in the book of Ezekiel. While it is an appropriate conclusion to his prophecies, it is also suitable as a winding up of the subject of this volume. Though not the last of the prophets, Ezekiel, in the passage referred to, looks forward to times subsequent to those of Malachi. He is 'the burden of the word of the Lord' upon the future gospel church; and after describing changes in the history of the Jews of which we cannot even form a conception, he foretells the rise of a mystical city, the name of which was to be '*Jehovah-Shammah.*' In the context, the references cannot be to the return of the Jews from captivity, and consequently not to the literal Jerusalem. In other predictions upon this subject, the *literal* return is manifestly meant; but in this one there are arrangements bearing upon some great future to which nothing corresponds in actual history. The city, for instance, is not named. No mention is made of Jerusalem at all, and the whole description from first to last gives countenance to a spiritual rendering. The 'city' referred to is undoubtedly the church of Christ under the New Testament dispensation; and the name of that church is, 'The Lord is there.' Now, we think this the proper place for the consideration of this new covenant title of our Lord and Saviour, not only because it has great and comforting truth within itself, but because it is a kind of summing up of all the privileges that flow to his people from those gracious relationships in which the former titles represent him as standing to them. Is Jehovah 'the Lord our God?' his friendly disposition 'is there.' Is he Jehovah-Jireh? his actual provision for our wants 'is there.' Is he Jehovah-Tsidkenu? his justifying righteousness 'is there.' Is he Jehovah-Rophi? his healing virtue 'is there.' Is he Jehovah-Shalom? his dying legacy, even his peace, 'is there.' Is he Jehovah-Nissi? his cause 'is there.' Is he Jehovah-Shammah? he himself, in all the perfections of his Godhead and in all the blessings of his grace, 'is there,' *there* in every ordinance of Zion, in all her oracles, in all her members, in all her enterprises, and in all her interests. Emphatically and peculiarly is Jesus the Jehovah-Shammah—the God whose presence is in the church, which he hath purchased with his own blood. That church is now his dwelling place; it is his 'rest,' and he 'likes it well.' This doctrine of the *perpetual presence* of the Saviour in every age and down to the end of the world is the great bulwark of the church, but for which the gates of hell would certainly prevail against her. It is more; it is the source of her life, her joys, her advances, and her triumphs. But for this presence, indeed, there would be no church on earth at all; and if that presence were withdrawn even from heaven, its chiefest joy, if not its main attraction, would disappear. It is therefore very evident that in this title of 'Jehovah-Shammah,' as affirmative of Christ's actual inhabitation of his church, there must be substantial material for believing reflection and spiritual refreshment. This much is indicated by his latest words on earth, 'Lo I am with you always, even unto the end of the world.' Under this conviction, we shall now review in their order *the presence itself, the places of the presence, the realisation of the presence,* and then *the special seasons for its realisation.*

I. THE GRACIOUS PRESENCE OF THE LORD. 'The presence of the Lord' is a phrase frequently to be met with in the Bible. It admits of various explanations. In general, it is referable to his omnipresence: 'Whither shall I go from thy Spirit, or whither shall I flee from thy presence?' But it has also special and gracious significations. The first time we meet with it is in the account given of the fall: 'Adam and his wife hid themselves from *the presence of the Lord* amongst the trees of the garden.' The second use of the phrase is in the narrative of the banishment of Cain: 'And Cain went out from *the presence of the Lord.*' In both of these instances it is implied, that God and man had been in actual or endearing fellowship, but that in the loss of 'the presence' there was interruption to that communion. In other passages, the reference is evidently to the will or commandment of Jehovah, such as when it is said of Jonah that 'he rose to flee from the presence of the Lord.' In a third class, we have the phrase applied to the divine judgments: 'Tremble thou earth at the presence of the Lord;' 'Let the wicked perish at the presence of the Lord;' 'The earth is burnt at his presence.' In a fourth, the connection is with the promise and prospect of the goodness and mercy of God: 'And he said to Moses, My presence shall go with thee, and I will give thee rest.' In a fifth, we are directed to the throne itself on which God sits: 'I am Gabriel, that stand in the presence of God;' 'For Christ is not entered into the holy places made with hands, which are figurative of the true, but into heaven itself, now to appear in the presence of God for us.' And lastly, to the celestial blessedness the Holy Spirit applies the words, 'In thy presence is fulness of joy, and at thy right hand are pleasures for evermore.' In all these passages the phrase is evidently restricted, and of course must have limited significations. We prefer holding by the idea of that *speciality* in the divine presence which is vouchsafed to his own people, and which is altogether of a gracious character. None others enjoy it; and as it is enjoyed by them, it is one of their most precious privileges. What, then, does it imply in this restricted and spiritual application?

1. ACTUAL ABODE. This *presence* is something far better than his merely '*looking down* from heaven'—it is his coming down from his Father's house, and from the praises of eternity, to '*dwell* with him also that is of a contrite and humble spirit.' In many respects even the general truth of his omnipresence is pleasing to his people; but this they have in common with his enemies—this is given to all his creatures, irrespective of their being good or bad, rational or animal, terrestrial or celestial. His *gracious* presence is reserved for his chosen ones, and implies something in addition on a grand and imposing scale. He is 'with' them, on the very spot where they are; yea, he is 'in them,' in their very souls, to 'bless them and to do them good.' There was an *actuality* in the divine presence within the garden of Eden when he spake to our first parents, and at Horeb when he appeared in the burning bush to Moses, and within the holy place where the Shechinah dwelt between the cherubims, above the mercy-seat. God was in these places in a sense in

which he was in no other place. But his presence with his people now is more real or actual still. It is not even such a presence as his disciples enjoyed when he dwelt among them in the days of his flesh, precious and pleasing as that presence unquestionably was. It is something still more palpable, still more near and dear, still more comprehensive of the blessedness of divine communion. He is '*with them*,' not merely to witness and watch over them, but to make them, in consequence of this mysterious inhabitation of their souls, the happy recipients of his richest grace. He is 'with them always.' Having once taken up his abode, he will never quit them—it is his rest; he will never leave nor forsake them. His grace shall never be recalled, his blessing never lost, his smile never changed into a frown; for 'the gifts and callings of God are without repentance.' Jesus is 'the word of the Lord;' and the 'word of the Lord *abideth for ever.*' The phrase also implies—

2. EXERTED INFLUENCE. Not only is the Lord always with his people, but he is always with them in the actual dispensations of his divine Spirit. We cannot conceive it possible for him to take up his special abode among them, and be of no more use to them than to others with whom he does not thus reside. If he dwell with the saints, it is to *move* them by moving within them and diffusing throughout them those irresistible and pleasing influences, to which they are ever indebted for their spiritual activities

and productions. It is only when he thus dwells with his people that they are favoured with what have been called 'divine manifestations.' Such was the privilege of the first disciples : 'He that loveth me,' said Christ to them, 'shall be loved of my Father, and I will love him, and manifest myself unto him.' When Judas, not Iscariot, asked, 'How is it that thou wilt manifest thyself unto us and not unto the world?' he replied, 'We will come unto him, and make our abode with him.' Thus also in his intercessory prayer he says : 'I have manifested thy name unto the men whom thou gavest me out of the world.' These manifestations consist of those views of his favour for and mercy towards them, by which they are made to rejoice in his salvation—in those receptions of gospel comforts, by which they know themselves to be his children—in those clear and happy discernments of their adoption, by which they cry, 'Abba, Father,' and in those seasonable gifts of saving and confirming grace, by which they are cheered and invigorated in the good fight of faith. The enjoyment of such privileges greatly enhances to them all the divine ordinances, as it is for the most part in them that these manifestations are made. This indeed is the secret of the christian's attachment to 'the word, sacraments, and prayer;' and this is the grand motive under which he leads the life of godly fear. They are, therefore, always positively the better of his company. If they lodge him in their hearts, he fills these hearts with his own bread of life. If they admit him into their darkness, he dissipates it with his light. If they exalt him to the throne of their affections, he elevates them in their thoughts and desires 'to things that are in heaven.' If they entertain him at their table, he loads it with his own benefits, and causes their cup to overflow. It must indeed be the best of all blessings to have a loving and sin-pardoning God actually dwelling in the soul. Throughout all its region of thought and feeling, alike upon its active and among its passive powers, the divine afflatus is ever at work, exerting an authority which fails not to accomplish the kindness of the God and Father of our Lord Jesus, in the experience of every believer. This authority is *influence* of the right kind, exerted through the proper channel, and sent in the right direction. It is the doing and bidding of God 'pacified' towards us in Christ. It is the mercy and power of God reaching us through the mediation of Christ; and it is the grace of God abundantly given to the hungry and thirsty soul, that thereby its guilt may be cancelled, its purity promoted, its peace secured, its consolations multiplied, its safety made certain, and its eternal life placed beyond all peril. Such, indeed, are the nature and power of the influence thus exerted, that his people not only never want, but they cannot want; they are made competent, even they, frail as they are at their best estate, for every duty, trial, and temptation; no vicissitude can meet them for which they are not prepared, and no enemy whatever can oppose them whom they shall not more than conquer. Now, when we think how broad the divine commandment is, how overwhelming to poor human nature are the afflictions of this life, and how subtle, numerous, and powerful are the soul's enemies, we cannot but wonder that there is even one case of successful faith, even one instance of a human soul getting safely to heaven. But our wonder, though it may be increased in another view, is in this one diminished, when we discover that it is not the believer at all, but God's influence in and over him, that does it all from first to last. Hence the boast of every christian is, 'Not unto me, O Lord, not unto me, but unto thy name give glory, for thy mercy and for thy truth's sake.' Again, the phrase implies,

3. PREFERRED CLAIMS. God takes up his abode in the hearts of his people to state and make clear to them his claims upon their love and homage. Were he to speak to them only from a distance, or outside their hearts, they would neither listen nor consent; but his *inward* testimony is irresistible; for when it issues from his own mouth, then it comes to them in what is called ' the demonstration of the Spirit and in power.' Having done so much for them as their Saviour, he has not a mere titular but an actual right to their love and service. This right, however, only becomes *actual* when he makes them feel their obligations to him, and these they never do feel till he

himself prefers them with all the winning persuasiveness of his own presence, in addition to the eloquent appeals of his own word. Up to the day of this indwelling and inspeaking, they disregarded all his claims and remonstrances, and were in the way of being for ever lost to every sense of justice and of gratitude. He saw that it would not do to confine his plans to mere messengers and messages, so he decided to come himself, and in his own person to win them over. Having previously enlightened their eyes, he came down and presented himself to their view, saying, 'I am the Lord thy God;' that sight was enough; they then saw 'beauty in him that he should be desired,' and they constrained him, saying, 'Abide with us.' He replied, I will, but 'give me thine heart.' Were he never thus to prefer his claims, they should never be acknowledged among men—which suggests the next thought of,

4. ACKNOWLEDGED TITLES. We cannot conceive it possible that when God, in actual presence, prefers his claims, his people will resist or refuse to own them. Whenever he says, fixing his longing look upon the orphan soul, 'My son, give me thine heart,' that heart is surrendered in that very moment. There are no fascinations otherwise that can cause it to hesitate. God's own honour is now at stake; for when he goes the length of wooing in person the heart of any poor sinner, he secures for himself success. His *gracious* presence, then, cannot but

imply that his rights are always and cheerfully acknowledged, whether by the thief on the cross, or by the persecutor on the road to Damascus, or by any of the sons and daughters of men, of whatever age and stage of hard-hearted iniquity. It is indeed the loftiest music heard out of heaven—the responses of those hearts which give way to the bewitching smiles of redeeming love, as these are manifested beneath the arch of the rainbow that is round about the Saviour's head. Does he say, 'I am the Lord thy God?' they reply, 'Thou art the Lord our God.' Does he say, 'My son, give me thine heart?' their reply is, 'Our hearts, Lord, will we give;' and while this harmony is restored, and this song is singing, the recording angel writes it down in 'the book' over against each believer's name, 'Thou hast avouched the Lord this day to be thy God, and to walk in his ways,' and 'The Lord hath avouched thee this day to be his peculiar people'—which farther implies,

5. MAN RESTORED. When man is re-admitted into the presence of God, it is evident that reconciliation has taken place. His departure from God sunk him into the low estate of sin and misery, but God's presence with him re-elevates him to the high estate of holiness and peace. The presence of the Lord is sometimes a curse. It hastens the sinner still farther and farther from him. But it is otherwise with his *gracious* presence. By this he never fails to restore the sinner to his proper senses; for 'the times of re-

freshing come from the presence of the Lord.' While asunder, that sinner conceives hard things of God. But when he manifests himself as the God of love, kindly and encouraging thoughts of God return; and in proportion as these thoughts are cherished, does man go on to know and love God better and better. By such convictions, produced by such indwelling, the whole moral nature is renovated. The witness to his pardon lies within himself—it is God that tells him that his sins are forgiven. He might discredit an angel, but he must believe the Lord of angels. He might doubt a prophet or an apostle—he might be sceptical of his own spirit, but he cannot resist the testimony of God's Spirit with his spirit. The presence of the Saviour with him is his security that all shall now go well with him. It is impossible that it ever can be otherwise. Hence the sure and progressive sanctification of his soul through life; hence its completion in holiness at death, and hence its reception into heaven hereafter. When all the wicked ' shall be punished with everlasting destruction from the presence of the Lord,' all the saints shall be presented 'faultless before the presence of his glory, with exceeding joy.' And this suggests the last thought under this division of the subject, namely,—

6. GOD SATISFIED. When he condescends to come and take actual possession of the heart, we may be assured he will so adjust all within as to make it a fit place of residence for such ' an high and holy one'

as he is. He would not have come at all, but for the certainty of getting this satisfaction. He gets it. No heart ever refused his personal application, and hence it is that he ever 'sees of the travail of his soul, and is satisfied.' He is satisfied even with the very first thought of love towards him, feeble and awkward though its expression may be. He is satisfied with the first look at his cross, faint and brief as it is. He is satisfied with the inaudible whisper of a new-born faith, and the imperceptible yearning of a newly-formed heart. He is satisfied with all these, because he 'is there' himself, and sees that it is the unveiling of his own beauty, the intoning of his own mercy, and the warmth of his own grasp, that shook off the slumbers of sin, and awoke the soul to the highest sense of mediatorial love. To give to the Saviour such satisfaction as this, may be said to be the christian's 'chief end.' For this he was called of God at the first by word, by providence, and by ordinance, and when nothing else would do, for this God himself descended to enter in and take possession. But the satisfaction he receives is not so much from the immediate changes and improvements that follow his gracious residence there, as from the large promise now given of the full harvest of his people's homage and praise. When he gets admission at first, he no doubt finds all in confusion; and in comparative disorder the renewed heart remains for a long time; but there is satisfaction growing even out of this state of things, for the Saviour is never grieved by any total backgoing in the justified soul; on the contrary, he is ever pleased by the sight of its gradual assimilation to his own image—he himself takes care that he will 'perfect that which he has begun.' And none but he who shed his blood as an atonement for sin, can tell the joy experienced by a sight of sin's subjugation throughout the region of a reconciled heart. In addition, however, to all this, he has ever the satisfaction of contemplating the *end* of it all, and *that* he knows, whatever may be present imperfections, shall be perfect holiness and happiness for ever. This was the 'joy that was set before him;' in all his sufferings he had respect unto this as his 'recompense of reward;' and with this in prospect, he is content to dwell for a time with his people even in that tabernacle where 'they groan, being burdened.' But for such a prospect, he could not remain with them—he must withdraw his presence; but enjoying it as he does, he is patient with them and long-suffering, and is with them 'always.' The very fact, in short, of his dwelling with them, proves satisfaction of the highest degree; it proves great love for his people, and this love comprehends two things: approbation of, and delight in them. He *approves* of them. They have complied with his invitations, and taken him for their Lord upon his own terms; hence says our Saviour, 'If a man love me, he will keep my words, and my Father will love him, and we will come unto him, and make our abode with him.' He *delights* in them. From all eternity, he tells us, his delights were with the sons of men; and again it is written, 'The Lord taketh pleasure in them that fear him, in those that hope in his mercy,' and 'they that deal truly are his delight.' The scriptures abound with expressions of this divine complacency; but perhaps for pathos and beauty the following surpass them all: 'Can a woman forget her sucking child, that she should not have compassion on the son of her womb? yea, they may forget, yet will not I forget thee. Behold, I have graven thee upon the palms of my hands; thy walls are continually before me.' 'Thou shalt also be a crown of glory in the hand of the Lord, and a royal diadem in the hand of thy God. Thou shalt no more be termed Forsaken, neither shall thy land any more be termed Desolate; but thou shalt be called Hephzibah, and thy land Beulah, for the Lord delighteth in thee.'

II. THE PLACES WHERE THIS PRESENCE IS VOUCHSAFED. The Psalmist thus sings: 'In Judah is God known; his name is great in Israel. In Salem also is his tabernacle, and his dwelling-place in Zion;' and again, 'The Lord loveth the gates of Zion more than all the dwellings of Jacob.' From these and parallel scriptures we learn that his principal and most important dwelling place is the gospel church at large. We remark, then, in the first place, that—

I. THE LORD DWELLS IN THE CHURCH. There is but one church—the church of Christ. It is called the 'household of faith;' and all are members of this household who believe on the Lord Jesus, its divine and only 'head,'—that is, every really penitent and pardoned sinner is a christian, and none but christians are members of Christ's 'mystical body.' To be 'in Christ Jesus' is at once the status and the proof of genuine faith. To be *in the church* is just another mode of expressing the same truth; so that none are in or belong to the church who are not thus 'in Christ.' Nominal or formal adherence to a party or section of the church does not constitute membership; and difference of country, of tongue, of colour, of denominational peculiarities, if the person be 'in Christ,' does not in the slightest affect his condition or his privilege as one of the family of God; for, says the apostle, 'Ye are all the children of God by faith in Christ Jesus. For as many of you as have been baptised into Christ, have put on Christ. There is neither Jew nor Greek, there is neither bond nor free, there is neither male nor female: for ye are all one in Christ Jesus.' Now, all believers being members of Christ, are also 'members' one of another. Christ is the head, and they are his body. Whether they dwell in heaven or upon earth; whether they live now, or are to be born and live thousands of years hence, it does not affect this truth—they form but 'one body;' they constitute, and they alone, that corporation which is called '*the church*,' or 'the church catholic.' And it is within or in this church that the divine Redeemer dwells, in the manner, and for the purposes specified in the former part of this exposition. It is true, his glorified person is actually in heaven; but his real, his gracious, his divine person is as certainly in this spiritual household, in this 'holy temple.' Like his Father's house above, this temple below may have 'many mansions;' but his presence is not confined to any one of these—it fills them all with light, and truth, and joy. As the human head is the source of vitality and influence to the members of the body; or, as the vine gives sap and fruitfulness to all the branches: so does Christ, Christ himself, and Christ alone, influence vitally every member of his church. They all hold by him as 'the head,' and they all grow upon him as 'the true vine.' He dwells in this spiritual Zion as its fountain of life; he reigns there as its sole King; and his sceptre of righteousness is there extended over the mystical edifice, with all its palaces and towers—with all its prophets, priests, and kings—with all its laws, rites, and privileges—with the whole body of its people, from Adam down to the last-born saint. Thus his presence is, in this respect, universal as the church, and perpetual as its existence; and every section of it may now claim not apostolical succession merely, but Prophetic, Mosaic, Patriarchal, and Adamic descent—all the saints of these dispensations were 'in Christ,' and we 'are all one in him;' for 'there is no difference,' and there cannot be any. In this unity there is a beautiful equality among denominations of christians. They may pretend to various kinds of pre-eminence, but the fact is, and ever must be, 'they are all one in Christ Jesus.' He dwells with them as their only Head, and they dwell in him as his only or one church. How ought this great truth to draw the christian sects together into an *avowed* union! What a pity it is that they should seem to be divided when in reality they are not! 'Is Christ divided?' Let this consideration repress bigotry and spiritual self-complacency, and let it animate all who believe in the great essentials of christianity to drop their 'shibboleths,' and 'dwell together' as brethren.

2. THE LORD DWELLS IN ALL THE ORDINANCES OF THE CHURCH. They are all of his appointment. Notwithstanding they have no intrinsic efficacy, they have no might nor power in themselves to regenerate or enlighten the soul. The Bible, for instance, is the word of God, but the words of the Bible are not God. The mere reading of them does not exert saving energy. God must be in that word, or must go along with that word, whether read or heard, into the understanding and heart, otherwise the ordinance is abortive. But as the word is his, and as 'to search' it is one of his ordinances, so does he use it as one of the means by which he takes possession of the guilty soul. 'Thy word,' says David, 'hath quickened me.' The ordinance of preaching also is equally ineffectual

but for him. 'Who then is Paul, and who is Apollos, but ministers by whom ye believed, even as the Lord gave to every man? I have planted, Apollos watered, *but God gave the increase.*' Peter's pentecostal sermon could not have made one convert. It was the descent of the Holy Ghost by that sermon into their hearts that led them to the cross. No christian ministry, whatever be its nature, genius, or sanctified endowments, has virtue in itself to save souls. Hence the necessity of having the continual presence of the Lord Jesus in the ordinance of preaching. This is equally true in respect of all the other means of grace, and more especially in respect of the two symbolical institutes of the christian church, Baptism and the Lord's Supper. With whatever mystery ignorance and superstition have invested these, they are in themselves as impotent as the rest. Apart from the divine presence in them, they are, for really spiritual ends, as useless as if they were strictly human inventions. But God does use them for the good of his people. In baptism, when it pleases him, he may and often does apply the thing signified by the water, even the blood of Christ; and in the Lord's Supper he is graciously present with the believing communicant, who can then say, 'His flesh is meat indeed, and his blood is drink indeed.' But our Redeemer is not pledged to be in any of these ordinances *of necessity* to all and sundry who may observe them; he is only pledged to meet in them with, and to make them efficacious to those, who by faith discern himself as the Lord their God, and 'yield themselves his servants to obey.' It is in the ordinances *of the church*, or as observed by the church, that is, by believers, that he is ever present and makes them uniformly blissful. But when the men of *the world*, who have not believed in his name, observe these in a corporal or carnal manner, they do not find him there, because they do not seek for him there. Being content with the form, they disregard the substance. All spiritually-minded men, however, seek and find the Lord in these institutions; and hence their 'souls thirst for him, and long for him in a dry and thirsty land wherein no water is, to see his power and his glory as they have seen them in the sanctuary.' Such men alone find God in his 'word;' and hence they testify, 'The entrance of thy word giveth light; it giveth understanding unto the simple.' These alone see God in the courts of his own house; hence they prefer Jerusalem above their chief joy, and are glad when it is said unto them, 'Let us go into the house of the Lord.' These alone receive the spiritual blessing in the sacraments; hence their recorded experience, 'The cup of blessing which we bless, is it not the communion of the blood of Christ? the bread which we break, is it not the communion of the body of Christ?'

3. THE LORD DWELLS IN EACH SECTION OF THE CHURCH. He may not approve of the subdivisions

which difference of opinion on minor matters has occasioned, but neither does he on that account deny to any of them his blessing. Whatever be the character of *their* pretensions, Christ himself is impartial. He is not more with one than with another. He presides alike over the counsels and over the interests of the most modern and insignificant, as over the most ancient and illustrious churches of Europe. It is not ancestral venerability, nor pompous ritualism, nor overweening claims of orthodoxy, that at all influence his presence. It is the place which his cross occupies among them, and the degree of faith in it to which they have attained, together with the conformity to his death in their entire procedure, that commands him into the midst of them with his blessing. If he be more in one gospel church than in another, it is only where his love is more appreciated, and his glory more sincerely sought after. Even in the days of Paul, there were degrees of excellence among the churches. He had to reprove 'the foolish Galatians;' but he highly commended the church of the Thessalonians, saying of them, 'We are bound to thank God always for you, as it is meet, because that your faith groweth exceedingly, and the charity of every one of you all toward each other aboundeth; so that we ourselves glory in you in the churches of God, for your patience and faith in all your persecutions and tribulations that ye endure.' To the extent, then, only of a difference in christian love, faith, and usefulness, do we own to a difference as to the presence of Christ among the various sections of his church. But not one—not even the one most nearly approaching, in all its organisation and spirit, to the mind and pattern of Christ himself—holds a monopoly of the promise, 'Lo I am with you alway.' When Christ, then, is in every church, each church should respect and love its neighbour. When any church (falsely so called) has none of the presence of Christ, it is because it either never held the truth as it is in him, or, having held it, has drawn back and made shipwreck of its faith. A christian church should ever breathe and exemplify the spirit of Christ, being, like him, 'meek and lowly'—always ready to condescend to others of low estate, and esteeming its sisters more highly than its own self—ever prepared to hold out the hands of fellowship and charity to all who love the Lord Jesus in sincerity and in truth. A Christless church cannot be expected so to feel or act. It has the body, but not the soul of christianity. The spirit of form may hover around it, but the Spirit of Christ is not there. Hence its coldness, its barrenness, its rapid declension even from its nominal claims to be one of his witnesses. Let this blessed truth, then, that equally with the humblest and most obscure, as with the most potent and famous of the churches of Christ, is he graciously present. Do thousands of members meet around the altar of one section? Its name is Jehovah-Shammah—'the Lord is there.' Do 'two or three' only meet together in his name? Their name also is Jehovah-Shammah—he 'is there in the midst of them.' And if he, the Lord himself, be thus present, let not the lowliest church droop in the absence of mere earthly patronage; and if he, the King of kings, be present, let not the most august assembly of his people be covetous of the tribute and homage of the most illustrious of the sons of men; neither let them despise the humbler and more unpretending church beside them, though it may be so small as to meet in the house of a 'Nymphas' or of a 'Philemon.' Yes, God be thanked, he is with us all, and always present, to do to and for each of our sections what he sees to be necessary for our well-being and well-doing. As associated in his name and by his authority, he recognises every one of them as witnessing for him; and therefore he abides most graciously with them all, to keep them pure, alike in doctrine as in practice, and to excite and aid them in the work to which they are called and consecrated, of advancing the interests of his kingdom all over the earth.

4. THE LORD DWELLS IN EVERY GODLY FAMILY. He may have a preference for 'the gates of Zion,' but notwithstanding, he abides also in 'the dwellings of Jacob.' How beautiful are these declarations: 'I the Lord dwell among the children of Israel;' 'All the children of Israel had light in their dwellings;' 'I will save them out of all their dwelling places;'

'The Lord blesseth the habitation of the just;' 'The voice of rejoicing and salvation is in the tabernacles of the righteous: the right hand of the Lord doeth valiantly;' 'The Lord will create upon every dwelling place of Mount Zion, and upon her assemblies, a cloud and smoke by day, and the shining of a flaming fire by night!' What a privilege thus belongs to the house of piety! It may be a lowly hut, entered by every wind that blows, and deluged by every wintry storm. But *there* also dwells the Lord of heaven. There is 'The Angel of the Covenant,' and there are all covenant blessings. O happy beyond conception is that family with whom Jesus condescends to live! *They* can never want—*they* can never complain of solitude—*they* can never be in difficulties, never in despair. The Lord is their God, and he dwells with them. He therefore, in all their family arrangements, is recognised—in every vicissitude he is trusted—in every trial he is appealed to, and after every bereavement he is an upmaking portion. Beneath that humble roof-tree is the family altar. While it stands, evil is kept on the outside. It is only when that altar is cast down, that the enemy rushes in like a flood, and overwhelms every interest in his fury. On the contrary, 'Blessed is every one that feareth the Lord: that walketh in his ways. For thou shalt eat the labour of thine hands: happy shalt thou be, and it shall be well with thee. The Lord shall bless thee out of Zion; and thou shalt see the good of Jerusalem all the days of thy life. Yea, thou shalt see thy children's children, and peace unto Israel.'

5. GOD DWELLS IN EVERY RENEWED SOUL. Though the heaven of heavens cannot contain him, yet he dwells with the humble and contrite. The Saviour's inhabitation of the pious soul is one of the gospel mysteries; but it is a great and cheering truth. It is one of Paul's prayers for the Ephesians, 'That Christ may dwell in their hearts by faith;' and it is one of his questions to the Corinthians, 'Know ye not that ye are the temple of God, and that the Spirit of God dwelleth in you?' It is on the memorable occasion of Christ's *first* visit that the sinner becomes 'a new creature;' and if he has been growing in grace since that hour, it is because the Saviour has never left him. He has been a dweller in that soul ever since, and by means of his Holy Spirit, has carried it, and is carrying it forward in the path of life towards life everlasting. 'The temple of God!' what a solemn revelation! In itself this is a great truth. 'Know ye not your own selves,' asks the apostle, 'how that Jesus Christ is in you, except ye be reprobates?' What an alternative! If he dwells not with us, whatever our religious profession may be, we are 'reprobates.' Let us not then refuse to believe that the gracious presence of the Saviour is with each renewed heart, because to us the doctrine of such indwelling is incomprehensible. We ought to be assured of it from the effects which are produced in every in-

JEHOVAH-SHAMMAH. 319

stance of actual conversion, from the steady and sure progress of religion in every such heart, and from the impressive illustrations of holiness which the whole future life affords. And when we anticipate that 'hour and power of darkness,' even our entrance into the valley of the shadow of death, let us cherish the delightful assurance of David, and say, 'I will fear no evil; for thou art with me.' Yes, even in death this presence shall be our light, our strength, our joy; it shall go with us to our last breath, and its unveiled glory shall then burst upon the emancipated and enraptured spirit.

> 'Sun of my soul! thou Saviour dear,
> It is not night if Thou be near:
> O may no earth-born cloud arise,
> To hide Thee from thy servant's eyes.
>
> 'Abide with me from morn till eve,
> For without Thee I cannot live:
> Abide with me when night is nigh,
> For without Thee I dare not die.'   KEBLE.

CHAPTER XV.

JEHOVAH-SHAMMAH: THE LORD IS THERE.

PART II.

> 'He endured, as seeing him who is invisible.'
> HEBREWS xi. 27.

LET us now consider the uses, the positive or actual uses to which the disciples of Christ must put this cheering doctrine of his gracious presence with them always and everywhere. It is evident that they can derive no comfort from it, unless they know how to apply it to their own peculiar conditions in this life. In other words, unless they can *realise* that presence, or, as in the scripture, unless they can 'endure, as seeing him who is invisible,' the words that have been spoken are neither good nor comfortable to them. To help them to take the fullest advantage of this privilege, and to fulfil the duty connected with it, we shall, first of all, show what is implied in this realisation of Christ's gracious presence: and here we remark—

1. IT IMPLIES FAITH IN HIS DIVINE NATURE. To realise this presence is confessedly a duty, which duty, however, is a religious difficulty. The christian believes it to be a duty, but how to perform it perplexes him. It is of great consequence, then, that he have some clearly defined rule for his guidance. The simple believing of the divine omnipresence does not meet the difficulty, because we cannot associate the semblance of any creature with his essence; we are forbidden to form any likeness of him either actually from matter, as idolaters do, or mentally, as if we had any form or dimensions with which to compare him. And yet every devout man desires to bring his Lord immediately before his mind's eye, more especially when engaged in acts of worship, where it would be felt to be a great relief, if he could so realise as to address him with the most friendly familiarity, and as it were 'face to face.' Such was the attainment of Moses: 'And the Lord spake unto Moses face to face, as a man speaketh unto his friend.' There was in this case very intimate communion; but it does not exactly supply the desideratum referred to; for in the same passage we find that there was something lacking still: 'And Moses said, I beseech thee, show me thy glory;' and the Lord said, 'Thou canst not see my face; for there shall no man see me and live.' It is indeed alike the dictate of philosophy and of religion, that God 'dwelleth in light which no man can approach unto, whom no man hath seen at any time

nor can see.' But while all this is true of the divine essence, let us be thankful that, in a very encouraging sense, we are authorised to think of him as if he could be seen, or so to 'endure, as seeing him.' This is peculiarly a privilege of the New Testament church. We have revealed to us *him* who is declared to be 'the image of the invisible God,' and who said to his disciples, 'He that hath seen me hath seen the Father.' True, Christ no longer dwells among men as he did in these 'the days of his flesh;' but we can all realise the fact of his humanity—we can call up to our minds the majesty of his deportment in the working of miracles, and the sweetness of his smile in blessing the mourner. With the materials for conception with which the story of the evangelist furnishes us, we can realise a form and a glory sufficient to fill us with wonder, love, and praise. But it may be asked, are we at liberty, in thinking of a divine Redeemer, to admit the idea of his humanity at all? would it not be kin to idolatry to worship what we identify with our own nature? Most certainly it would; but to obtain the benefit referred to, this is not required. We have only to think of one who, though 'found in fashion as a man,' was in reality God; and when thus thinking of Jesus Christ, we are at liberty to fall down and adore him, not because he is 'the word of God,' but because this Word is God himself. Analyse the devout feelings of the christian in meditation or communion, and you will find, that while the thought of worshipping Christ as man is repudiated, yet the great idea of a divine presence is active there. When, for instance, we think of heaven and of the Redeemer on his throne, it is a great relief to realise God in him—very God, dispensing richest mercy. To such a mode of thought we are invited when he bids us 'honour the Son as we honour the Father.' In such an exercise there is perhaps a danger of trespassing the boundary that separates Deity from humanity, and of giving homage to the visible form of the glorified Redeemer rather than to the invisible and uncreated. Hence the necessity of godly jealousy and vigilance over our spirits. At the same time, it is not very likely that a truly pious mind will fall into such an error. It must be admitted that we are entitled to think of Christ's 'true body,' or to realise him in the form in which he was crucified, and while thus meditating, to fall down and worship this very person as 'Emmanuel, God with us,' or, God in our nature. When on earth, his personal appearance sometimes commanded the spectator into the spirit and attitude of worship. It was the impression made upon his mind by the sight of the hands and pierced side of Christ that drew from Thomas the adoring exclamation, 'My Lord and my God!' and there cannot be a doubt, but that the adoring love of the saints above waxes the more passionate, that they stand in the very presence of 'the Lamb that had been slain.' Now, though unto us still militant, this sight of Christ's glorified humanity be not given, yet it is permitted to us believingly to realise this illustrious person, to picture to our minds the glorified man Jesus Christ, and to serve and worship him accordingly.

Such a privilege as this is among the most delightful for which the christian has to bless God. It supplies a great spiritual vacuum—it satisfies a very frequent and strong thirsting in the pious mind, and to some extent meets and sets aside a painful, sometimes a distracting difficulty. Without it, while the abstract idea of a God might be entertained, the effort to realise some presence upon which the adoring soul might fix itself, must for ever have been impossible. This is a privilege, too, for which more than mankind are indebted to the scheme of mercy. All the angels of God, and for anything we can tell, all his intelligent creatures everywhere, share in this kindly help to the comfortable conception of a divine presence. That 'all the angels worship him,' we know; and we cannot fail to perceive, that in this exercise they must be greatly assisted by the actual appearance, in the midst of them, of the incarnate Son of the Highest. What those other intelligences may have of this privilege we know not, but it is far from improbable that they are indulged with some revelation of the glories of his mediatorial person.

But how could such a privilege exist at all, and how could believers use it, except upon the understanding that the Saviour is divine as well as human? Hence we say, that in order to realise him, we must have strong faith in his deity. Our conceptions of the constitution of his person must soar beyond the poor thought of the Socinian, that he is only a sinless piece of humanity; and far beyond the more ambitious thought of the Arian, that he is nothing more than the first created and most glorious of all God's creatures. We must rise into the sublime region of the great mystery of godliness, and believe him to be 'God manifest in the flesh.' In order to this, we must rectify our notions and certify our convictions by a reasonable study of the evidences of his divinity, as these are furnished abundantly in holy scripture; for while this doctrine is essential to the validity and efficacy of the atonement, it is also one of the best helps to the timid and limited minds of believing men, when they would realise his constant presence, and luxuriate in the thought of his near and intimate relationship to them. For this reason we assign to it the foremost place in our analysis of the subject.

2. IT IMPLIES THE ASSURANCE OF HIS FRIENDSHIP. We cannot realise the gracious presence of Christ unless we know and believe him to be mercifully disposed towards us. The kindly presence of an enemy is an absurdity. We may fancy his becoming our friend, but in this case it is the realisation of a fancy, not of a truth—that is, of a foe, but not of a friend. So long as we regard him as hostile, we can

only realise a hostile presence, which is disagreeable, and we rather turn away from it. So it is with the christian and his Lord. He desires no presence so much as Christ's, just because he believes that there is no one so friendly to him. He is satisfied that Christ will do him no evil, yea rather, that he will plentifully fill his cup with all good. It is only when unbelieving fears break in, or when consciousness of unholiness presses hard upon him, that the presence of Jesus becomes disagreeable, and he is disposed to say with Peter, 'Depart from me, for I am a sinful man, O Lord.' Joseph's brethren 'were troubled at his presence,' because there was uncancelled guilt on their consciences. David slipped out of the presence of Saul, because he feared his wrath. Haman was afraid at the presence of the king, because he dreaded his vengeance; and Job was distressed at the presence of God, because he meditated exclusively on his awful decrees. Thus it is only when a 'presence' is for some reason either a terror or a discomfort, that it is shunned rather than courted; but when the reverse is the case, there must be the assurance of substantial friendship. Hence, when the Psalmist expects it, he says, 'I shall yet praise him for the help of his countenance;' when he dreads its loss, he prays, 'Cast me not away from thy presence;' and when he invites all people to extol it, he sings, 'Let us come before his presence with thanksgiving.' When Christ dwelt upon the earth, his presence was often greatly desired.

'All men seek for thee,' said his disciples to him. 'Sir, we would see Jesus,' said the Greeks. 'Come down ere my son die,' said the nobleman of Capernaum; and of the two disciples of Emmaus, it is recorded, 'They constrained him, saying, Abide with us.' Thus, whatever might be the motive, it appears that his presence was much sought after by those who believed him to be able and willing to do them a service.

If, therefore, to realise Christ be a great attainment, let us cherish the conviction that he loves us, that he is our very best friend, that we can glean nothing from his countenance but the smile that reassures the heart, listen to nought that drops from his lip but 'the blessing that makes rich,' and take from his hand only the cup that overflows with new covenant mercies. There cannot indeed be any approach to this spiritual exercise independent of such convictions. It is of a privilege we are speaking; but it were no privilege to realise an object we could not trust. Yea, it is hell itself in embryo to have the conscience shaken throughout its domain at the bare thought of God; for he can be, and is realised by the wicked in the prospect of judgment. 'Our God is a consuming fire' only to those who are not 'in Christ Jesus.' To all who have fled to 'the hiding place,' he is merciful and gracious. Of what importance, then, must such kindly thoughts of Jesus be, when their influence reproduces him often to our view, and draws us into the most delightful fellowship! Here indeed you have the whole secret of a christian's life of faith upon the Son of God, and how it is that *he* is 'all his salvation, and all his desire.' The christian has cast out of his heart all suspicions of Christ's suitableness, and filled it with the most profound persuasions of his love. He has so disciplined his thoughts about Christ, that even the idea of indifference is never associated with his presence. He no doubt has his moments of compunction, and none can exceed him in godly sorrow for sin; but not on this or on any account, can he become disaffected to his Lord's society. There is no society which he prefers to it. And why? Because in it he finds salvation, and a good title to eternal life. Nay, it is when thus grieved on account of his sin, that the presence of Christ is the more valuable to him, for in him alone he sees his sacrifice of atonement, and is satisfied—in him he sees the only friend in all the world to whom such as he can go, with whom he can speak in confidence, and from whom he receives the consoling sense of pardon. Yea, by how much the more cast down he may at any time be, the more agreeable does this presence become; for Jesus cannot be seen, as a christian sees him, without the heart being filled with gladness before the approving countenance of God—then the disquieting and vexing thought is silenced, peace returns, and hope remounts her throne.

Here, then, is a recipe for all soul-disturbing

thoughts of God. Learn to realise Christ's gracious presence. Whatever ideas of the overawing majesty and holiness of Jehovah you may have entertained, never think otherwise of Jesus Christ than as your friend and advocate—not an advocate for your sins, but for the pardon thereof, and therefore such a friend of your precious souls as you can find nowhere else. If you think of God, while you believe not thus in Christ, no wonder though you tremble. But believe thus in and of Christ, and then even your 'meditations on God will be sweet'—you will experience him, all holy and all just though he be, to be a God of love, and ready to forgive. Ah, it is just that *separated thought*, that Christless conception of Deity, that fills you at present with such terror in the anticipation of judgment. You have got your lessons, no doubt, about God, but not in the school of Christ. We marvel not, then, that your countenance turns pale, and your knees smite the one against the other, at the very mention of his name. But go to Christ, as the great teacher of the great God, and he will tell you another story altogether about his Father; for 'no man knoweth the Father, save the Son, and he to whom the Son shall reveal him.' He will take these natural thoughts and *christianise* them; and the moment they undergo such a change, you will see God and live, you will embrace him as your own God and Father in him—of such mighty consequence are right ideas of Christ himself to the formation of correct and pleasing ones of that awful Being before whom we are all to appear in judgment. O think kindly, then, of Jesus Christ! It is impossible to think too kindly of him; and this will dispose you to court and realise his presence as your divine Redeemer; and when you have attained to this, he will speedily educate you in, and convince you of, the truth of the great first principle of his religion, namely, 'GOD IS LOVE.'

3. IT IMPLIES DEPENDENCE ON HIS GRACE. Grace is what all men need. Unbelieving men need it in order that the work of faith may be begun in them. By the grace of God alone can the natural heart be changed, and the new creature formed. But believing men need grace too. They can no more do without grace after, than before and at their conversion. Eminent as Saul of Tarsus became, he says, 'By the grace of God I am what I am.' Now this grace is in Christ Jesus. It cannot be had apart from him. It reposes in his arm, it is promised in his smile, and it is communicated by his hand. He must therefore be seen, and known, and trusted. Grace is not to be had as the rain descends, falling indiscriminately upon 'the evil and unthankful,' as upon the good and grateful; nor as the sun shines upon men, without respect of persons. It always comes in company with its author and finisher. This is a society that is ever entire. Wherever grace is, Christ is, and where Christ goes, grace follows. This proves that to re-

ceive grace we must admit Christ. In other words, when we 'endure as seeing him,' it is presumed that we are depending upon him for grace.

But what is grace? It is divine help and strength communicated for Christ's sake to the believing soul— help to discharge all duties, and strength to resist all temptations, and bear all trials. Grace is therefore the most precious of blessings. Without it christians would speedily lapse into condemnation. When Paul had the thorn in the flesh, and was buffetted by the messenger of Satan, he besought God importunately for deliverance, and received this answer, 'My grace is sufficient for thee, for my strength is made perfect in weakness.' It was not promised that the thorn should be extracted or that the messenger should be recalled, but that while these remained, he should be strengthened to endure them. Upon this he was reassured; and why? he relied upon the promised grace, and got it. His thorn and his tormentor might remain, but so also did his Master's presence; and hence his noble burst, 'Most gladly, therefore, will I glory in my infirmities, that the power of Christ may rest upon me. Therefore I take pleasure in infirmities, in reproaches, in necessities, in persecutions, in distress for Christ's sake; for when I am weak, then am I strong.' Here then is the illustration of our proposition. Paul earnestly sought Christ's presence for the sake of Christ's help or grace, or his grace and help for the sake of his presence; and so enraptured was he with both, that he was quite content, rather than be deprived of either of them, to smart under the thorn and be buffetted by the devil: yea, his very pleasures were drawn from his infirmities and his trials, just because these were the occasions that made Christ's presence necessary and his grace sure.

And so it is in every similar instance. All christians have their thorns and their devils; and when, under the power of faith, they realise their Saviour's presence, it is because of the grace they need and get. In fact, the very sense of his presence is grace itself; it cheers, strengthens, and emboldens them. But for this grace which they expect, what comfort could they derive even from such a presence as his; and for what other end could they desire it than its spiritual advantages? The life of faith is threefold: it is life in earnest, life in action, and life in production. *It is life in earnest.* All mere formalism is disavowed. The era of spiritual death is closed, and the voice of the Son of man has alarmed the soul into a sense of its ruin; therefore every look, word, thought, are now big with concern about that soul's salvation. *It is life in action.* The wordy or mere professional existence has lived its day; work, work, work is now the constant burden of the christian's song, and every implement of spiritual improvement is seized and plied in order to advance personal piety. *It is life in production.* The years of barrenness are past, and all manner of spiritual fruit is now yielded to the glory of God. The soul now leaps to the celestial invitation, 'Sing, O barren, thou that didst not bear; break forth into singing, and cry aloud, thou that didst not travail with child : for more are the children of the desolate than the children of the married wife, saith the Lord.' Such like being the life of faith, from whom does this earnest, active, and fruitful spirit draw its supplies ? not from within itself, for it is empty ; not from others, for they are equally poor; not from ordinances, which in themselves have no vital spark ; not from mere intellectual appreciations of the plan of mercy, which natural minds can attain to and yet despise; not from any one or anything on the earth beneath, but entirely from one in heaven above, even Jesus himself. Still, to be possessed of this there must be something more than mere rational perception of his excellence as a mediator. Simple thoughts of his glorious presence in heaven will not do ; dreamy sketchings of his enthroned majesty will not do ; and even paradisaical reveries of the inexhaustible riches of his grace will not do. It will not do for the soul to send itself away through trances like these to realms of bliss, and instead of awakening to life and action here, lullaby itself into soothing slumbers among such heavenly beatitudes. This will never do. It is this that exiles the anchorite, inspires the enthusiast, and maddens the fanatic; but this never made, never can make, a christian life. Such a life is maintained by a stern and steady realisation of Christ's presence with us, as we battle our way through this weary world.

Faith in Christ's gracious presence is, therefore, exercised for our present needs. No doubt we expect to go and be with him in his Father's house; but this only after we have fought our good fight. While thus engaged, we desire him to come to us and abide with us in 'our earthly house of this tabernacle,' because we need him, and cannot do without him. Without him every temptation would lay us in the dust, every foe would fatally wound us, on every cross we should be crucified, and by every loss we should be overwhelmed. Therefore, while in this world, we must have *his* presence; we must have it every day, every moment and everywhere. And when by faith we are thus realising him in the midst of us, it is that we may obtain his 'grace and mercy to help us in every time of need.' Great, then, is the christian's confidence in his Redeemer. He knows that in consequence this dear friend must be ever well acquainted with all his wants and woes, which is tantamount to an assurance that he can never want for any good thing. And thus it is that he ever sings, 'God is my refuge and strength; a very present help in trouble.'

4. IT IMPLIES CONFORMITY TO HIS EXAMPLE. In realising, we are 'looking unto Jesus;' but how can a believer look at *him* and not admire him? And who can admire him without being led, as it were

insensibly, to imitate him? It is written, that he 'left us an example that we should follow his steps;' but to copy an example, we must needs have it before our eyes, and to follow another implies that we see him. Now, when faith realises the Lord Jesus, it not only sees every beauty in him that he may be desired, but this very exercise of looking at or realising him is inseparable from a gradual assimilation of our nature and character to his nature and character. He is holy; we see no sin in him and no imperfection of any kind or degree; hence the believing regard of this holiness of his, has a sure reaction upon ourselves, in working within us all holy feelings and desires. He is also, as to his character, a being of matchless purity: 'He did no sin, neither was guile found in his mouth;' hence, the perpetual presentation to our minds of such an unsullied and brilliant pattern of religious and moral excellence, has the certain effect of moulding our walk and conversation so as to be a *fac simile* of his. No doubt in these believing exercises of the christian mind upon the Saviour, the divine Spirit is constantly at work to render them subservient to progressive sanctification; hence the apostle, 'We all, with open face, beholding as in a glass the glory of the Lord, are changed into the same image from glory to glory, even as by the Spirit of the Lord.' 'It is the Spirit that quickeneth.' In this mysterious co-operation, however, where the devout mind works upon a divine example, and where the divine Spirit operates through this example upon such a mind, the result never fails to be a *likeness* between the disciple and his Master. It is, indeed, the law of our nature, that we come ere long to resemble that which we very intensely love and habitually contemplate. Thus the likeness of the child to the parent is not confined to the expression or form of the countenance; it extends also to the mental habitudes and the customary manners of the parental life; and this is begotten of filial reverence and affection. In the life that is *spiritual*, the same law is in force, but on a much larger scale, and for nobler and more lasting ends. The love which the christian heart cherishes for the Redeemer, and the profound reverence with which it is filled from its meditations on, or its realisations of, his unparalleled worth, eventually controls the whole man, outer and inner, and the whole life of the man, hidden and open, social and devout; and not only so, this control is felt in every variety of condition, whether in joy or in grief, in health or in sickness, in living or in dying. Yea, so tenacious of its hold on the mind is the influence exerted from this constant 'enduring, as seeing Christ who is invisible,' that no power whatever can destroy or disengage it; it becomes a ruling passion, and is stronger than death. When death comes, the assimilation to Christ's image which has been going on is absolutely perfected; for when they 'see him as he is,' they are 'like him' in a sense and to a degree which could never be affirmed even of the most advanced stage of militant saintship.

Thus the realisation of Christ's gracious promise has an eminently practical effect. Nothing is so practical as the transformation of one's very nature into the nature of another; and such is the practical result in the process of which we speak. When, then, we consider that our 'looking unto Jesus' comprehends a believing and admiring study of his *life* as well as a cordial trust in his *death*, we should certainly be careful to give to each department its due amount of attention. We are enjoined to be 'conformed to Christ's death,' which must mean, to the *principles* on which he acted when he gave himself up to be a sacrifice for sin. And what were these principles? A strong hatred of sin, an eminent regard for holiness, a perfectly sincere love to the law and to the justice of God, and the strongest possible desire for the glory of God the Father. Now to be conformed to these principles, we must study, and constantly realise to ourselves, the *life* as well as the death of Christ; and by so doing we too shall come to imbibe them into our very being, and to transcribe them into our entire walk and conversation. We never can be so essentially religious as when we drink into the 'spirit of Christ;' and we never can be so actually religious as when we place our feet into the very prints of his steps, and follow him in the regeneration. The study of the principles of moral philosophy, and the contemplation of moral grandeur in others, may produce good effects upon our own mode of life and conduct; but these are superficial impressions at the best, and their existence is short at the longest. To resemble, as to our nature, 'the invisible God' in the scriptural, which is the *real*, sense, we must be conformed to the image of his dear Son; and to be continually reflecting as we live and move the shining beauties of his holiness, we must be 'setting the Lord continually before us.' To be unholy, or to be tardy in the growth of holiness, is altogether inconsistent with such a realisation of the Saviour's presence as we go forward to Zion. Hence it has ever followed, that christianity alone has produced what, by comparison, may be called perfect characters among men. It is in vain that we search among all the records of the past for such specimens of disinterestedness, of heroism, of purity, and of power, as are furnished out of her repositories. When her orbs approach, all other lights disappear. Every system, and every exemplification of mere human ethics, have failed to produce perfect characters. But Christ's own principles constructed his own life; and every life that is controlled by his, is an additional illustration of the intrinsic power of these principles to rear a new and a corresponding greatness in the character of believing man. Wherefore, let us cease to idolise man at his best estate, and withdrawing our eyes from all lesser luminaries, let us fix a steady and unfaltering look upon Jesus, and upon him alone.

CHAPTER XVI.

JEHOVAH-SHAMMAH: THE LORD IS THERE.

PART III.

'Thou God seest me.'
GENESIS xvi. 13.

LET us now hear the conclusion of this matter. Since the gracious presence of Jehovah-Shammah is so valuable in itself and so much an object of desire by the believer, it becomes us to be always ready to use the privilege for our spiritual comfort and profiting. This it behoves us to do at all times. But there are special seasons when the '*realisation*' of what we have been hearing is of more than ordinary importance. To notice a few of these is the object of this chapter. Christ's presence with us, then, should be realised,

1. ON THE MOUNT OF ORDINANCES. When sinful men would worship God, it must be through a mediator; and if they would have their worship accepted, that mediator must be realised; for it is written, 'No

man cometh unto the Father but by him.' And again, 'In his temple doth every one speak of *his* glory.' This being admitted, it is evident that we must have him distinctly before our minds, or 'endure as seeing him' while adoring him. Nothing, of whatever pomp and pretension, is worship which is not offered by faith in Christ. He himself often declares it: 'I am the way;' 'I am the door.' In all our approaches to God, then, whether in secret or in public, there must be positive recognition of our Surety. We must place our hands upon his head as we pass onwards to the footstool, and 'make mention of his righteousness, even of his only.' If we have no respect to his presence as mediator, then we sing, pray, preach, hear, and communicate, all in vain. There are two ways particularly in which his presence in ordinances is indispensable. It is, first, indispensable to make the religious service itself acceptable to God; and, secondly, to make it available for our own spiritual edification. What poor barren affairs are ordinances to many! They come to and go from them alike poor and blind. This is because no Saviour is ever recognised or embraced in them. They know not Jehovah-Shammah. To them the Lord is *not* there.

It is presumed that when we go to worship God we previously recognise the necessity of, and implore his presence to be with us. Is it not, then, most obviously our duty and our interest, when actually engaged, to believe that our Redeemer has heard us, and that he is actually beside us? O what a help is this to solemnity of mind, to devotedness of soul, and to spiritual improvement! It is upon the mount of ordinances that his glory and beauty are revealed; and when these are once seen, they can never be forgotten. 'O Lord, thou art my God,' the realising christian exclaims, 'early will I seek thee; my flesh longeth for thee in a dry and thirsty land, where no water is, to see thy power and thy glory so as I have seen thee in the sanctuary.' Indeed, ordinances are just profitable in proportion to the degree of faith exercised in the divine presence. Happy indeed is that christian who in his closet can so realise Christ as hearing his every whisper, and as giving, in reply, all needed grace. Happy is that man who in the courts of the Lord's house is made conscious that God himself is in the midst thereof. Happy is he who at the baptismal font, or at the Lord's table, loses all thought of the presence of others, keeps his mind apart from all sinful cares, and is fully absorbed in the grand, the thrilling conviction, that he is with Jesus, and that Jesus is with him. Such, indeed, is 'an accepted time.' Every text then becomes precious, for Christ is there; every promise is sweetness, for Christ is there; every precept is good, for Christ is there; every fellow-saint is beloved, for Christ is there; every burst of music is delicious, for Christ is there; every prayer is fervent, for Christ is there; every sermon is excellent, for Christ is there; and all the sanctuary services rise higher in his esteem, for Christ is in them all. But for this realisation, not only would not God accept the offered worship, but the entire service would be felt to be alike cumbersome and insipid. Paul himself might be the preacher; the eloquence of Apollos might fill the edifice; the doctrines taught might be sound; and all the encouragements given might be of the highest order, but if Christ be not in them, they 'become as sounding brass, or a tinkling cymbal.' Hence it is that thousands derive no benefit from ordinances. They never think of Jesus. He is to them, or in their experience, *not there.* And hence, too, it has often happened, that where all the adjuncts and appurtenances in the sanctuary have been exceedingly plain; where neither poetry nor painting are in any way employed to aid and excite devotion; where the preacher is amongst the most unpretending of men, perhaps the persecuted, though patriarch pastor of the locality; where the place of worship itself is the hole in the rock, the audience unpolished mountaineers, and the whole insignia of the service is a perfect contrast to the imposing solemnities of the cathedral—hence, we say, it has often happened that, notwithstanding, there the finest minds have been produced and educated, the noblest characters formed and developed, and the most illustrious and spiritual heroes called into being and action. CHRIST HIMSELF WAS THERE! If, then, we would get good out of ordinances; if we aspire to more devout thoughts in them; if we would acquire a greater relish for plain and faithful preaching, and for honest God-fearing and soul-loving ministers; if we would be less tormented with intruding worldly thoughts, and not so easily put about with trifling occurrences in the audience, or occasional slips in the preacher; if, in short, we would more richly and fully experience the marrow and fatness of gospel institutions, we have but one thing to do, and to do it heartily and always; we have but to invoke the presence of the Master, to exercise full assurance that he is himself among us, and is actually waiting to communicate saving grace.

2. ON THE SCENE OF TEMPTATION. Christians are more frequently and powerfully tempted than other men, and their temptations are among their bitterest afflictions. Other trials they can trace directly to their Father's hand, but these can only be forthcoming from their own depraved nature, and the artifices of 'the wicked one.' They do not consider themselves to be without sin because they believe in Christ, neither do they think that they are perfectly free of danger to their best interests. They accede to Paul that it is possible for them to 'grieve the Holy Spirit of God,' wherefore they tremble at the idea of temptation, and watch and pray that they may not enter into it. A good man is sometimes apt to think, that if he were only not tempted to sin, he never should sin; or, though he might indicate occasionally his innate depravity, yet would his errors be of a venial order, compared

with those into which he so often falls. Freedom from temptation, however, he must not expect while here. He is still in the flesh—still within the sphere of the devil's influence, and, therefore, tempted he shall be, and that often grievously.

To resist and flee from such temptation, however, is duty, and duty which is never so easily and effectually discharged as when faith brings the Saviour himself upon the darkening scene. When this is done, Satan flees, and the temptation loses its power. The solemn thought, just at the very moment of weakness, and when we are on the eve of surrender, that the eye of the Holy One of Israel is upon us, has an irresistible influence. At such a time, the remembrance of these words, 'Thou God seest me,' has stricken with terror the boldest of the soul's adversaries. The tempter may be clothed in the garb of an angel of light; the pleasures of sense, the glitter of golden heaps, the flatteries of gay deceivers may be the bribes, and the ardent passions within may all be clamorous for indulgence; but to introduce the Lord Jesus into their midst—to realise him as having groaned, and bled, and died for sins and for us—to command memory to rehearse to us the sorrows of the Lamb of God—to instruct imagination to sketch for us the bloody sweat, the pierced limbs, and the cleft heart, the haggard features, and the drooping head—to give the signal to gratitude to tell us over again the melting story of his marvellous love, and, beyond all, to issue orders for the instant admission of that lovely sufferer himself into every region of our thoughts, and more especially into those infected with the tempter's breath; and to give him freedom to enter and examine the interior of our hearts, by throwing wide open the gates of the affections there—to do all this is almost certain to slay the lust that wars against us, and to withdraw us from the spot, exclaiming with the young Hebrew, 'How can I do this great wickedness, and sin against God?' O what lover of the Son of Mary could deliberately do iniquity before his very eyes? Suppose Jesus to return to the world, and to be your daily companion, think you the thought and purpose of uncleanness could win your consent for a moment? Could you swear, steal, lie, cheat, be drunken, unchaste, or sordid? Impossible! you reply; the very consciousness of his holy look, the sight of his matchless beauty, the idea of his unparalleled pity, the pathos of his friendly voice, the very music of his footstep, and the eloquent appeal of his whole demeanour, would be enough to drive such unrighteousness far, far hence. And is sight or sense of loftier sway over your souls than the grace of faith? It ought not to be so. On the spiritual field of personal holiness, far higher exploits have been done by faith, than have ever been narrated of the mere influence of the carnal sense. It was not when Christ tabernacled among men, and when their eyes and ears actually saw and heard him, that the christian church rose into greatness, and illustrated its matchless excellence by innumerable conquests over the wildest passions of our nature. It was after his ascension, and when faith, not sight, was left to maintain the combat. If, then, we feel that in his actual presence we could not sin, let us rejoice that we hold in our possession this power of realising that presence in its most precious bearings upon our welfare, and that we thus can wield an influence against temptation which is certain to carry us untouched through the most fiery ordeals of this wilderness; 'for this is the victory which overcometh the world, even our faith.'

3. ON THE THRESHOLD OF SPIRITUAL DECLENSION. The christian is not at all times flourishing. Even his life of faith has its vicissitudes and critical periods. Upon the whole, his religion certainly makes way. Indeed there is a sense in which it never retrogrades, so that at the end of his life he will be seen to have progressed, and to be nearer to perfection, than he ever was at any former period. Still he suffers alternations. At one time all the graces are in hopeful exercise, and at other times some of them are inactive; at one time he is fully assured, at another time he cries out, 'Lord, I believe; help mine unbelief;' at one time any person may see that he is making decided progress in the beauties of holiness, and at another it would be difficult to say whether in him religion was living or dead. At one time he is very happy in his experiences, and at another he is conscious of much

spiritual discomfort. There are ups and downs in spiritual being, though in the main there is a gradual rising to the stature of perfection in Christ.

Such, however, are not the most painful and alarming of the spiritual revolutions of a good man's life. These are unimportant compared with those sad declensions of piety to which he is prone. Yes; he has seasons which, when tried beside others, exhibit a lamentable change in the wrong direction. Not only is there no progress, but it appears as if there was a strong determination to the coldness and stiffness of a worldly life, as if former professions had been insincere, former fears delusive, and former joys a cheat or a lie. This is really the most humiliating period in the history of genuine godliness; and it has often occurred, spreading confusion among the friends of religion, and making the enemies of all religion triumph over what they think to be discovered hypocrisy and contemptible cant. Perhaps there are few christians who cannot remember such periods in their past experiences, and who have not had to lament and weep over their spiritual barrenness. No doubt the declension, such as it was, was in every instance arrested, as in every instance we believe it was permitted for good. But how was it arrested? By the Good Shepherd alone, who has many ways of 'restoring the soul.' The remembrance of himself, however, is by far the most powerful of them all. 'I remembered God, and was troubled,' said Asaph. The Israelites, for their comfort, 'remembered that God was their rock, and the high God their Redeemer.' Said Jonah, 'When my soul fainted, I remembered the Lord.' When the cock crew, Peter 'remembered the words that Jesus spake.'

We must despair of any man who can resist the influence that issues from this realisation. If this does not recall the backslider, what shall? But it is impossible for a believer in Jesus to resist it. He returns from his backsliding in that moment that he occupies his mind with the love and sufferings of the Saviour, and with the remembrance of the days of sweet communion gone by. By this he receives a check to his carelessness, a chide to his ingratitude, and a spur to his obedience. To all, then, who are either conscious of such declension being begun, or who dread its approach, we would most earnestly recommend the practice of holding regular fellowship with Jehovah-Shammah. This will be to them a powerful memento of obligation, of vows, of experiences. This will shame them out of spiritual lethargy, and urge them into spiritual action. This will alarm them when stepping on the slippery places, and hasten them over to the solid and good old paths. This will emancipate them from the influences that led to the evil, and place them under the powerful attraction of the Cross.

4. IN THE NIGHT OF SPIRITUAL DARKNESS. Such a night occasionally sets in upon the people of God. And what is a night of spiritual darkness? In such a night, we may say, all men were born; for all are

by nature the 'children of darkness.' And if they are never 'born again,' their whole life is just one long, long night, in which they sleep the sleep of spiritual death, and awaken only to find themselves in the more deadly region of the lost. But when men are converted, they are translated into the kingdom of light, and for the most part their succeeding years are spent in the enjoyment of that light which God 'sows for the righteous.' They live 'in the light of his countenance'—'in his light they see light'—in God himself they dwell, 'and in him is no darkness at all.' All this is true; but so is this, that these very persons sometimes encounter a night of spiritual darkness in which they go about 'mourning as without the sun.' It is, however, a night of very different materials from that of the natural man. In his night there is no moon or star to relieve the surrounding gloom; and though it be indeed a grievous thing for hours, and even years, to drag through its dreary watches, yet are not its horrors so intolerable in consequence of its having been preceded by no day. The spiritual night of a believer is one in which he feels as if he had lost his lamp; or rather, as if his sun had gone down, leaving him to grope about in the dark, as if he had never had the benefit of his cheering rays. He has not now so palpably a sense of the love of God; he cannot plead the gracious promises as he was wont, the sweetness has gone out of them, and their strength has failed; even Calvary and its bleeding victim only unfold the darkness that once overspread the ninth hour, instead of pouring forth the meridian splendour of a finished redemption. In a word, he believes still, but his faith only torments him; he prays still, but his prayers return unto him void; he still goes up to the sanctuary, but its services are only torturing mementos of joys clean gone for ever. And all this is the more afflictive and stunning to him that he has known by experience what it is to live in the smile of reconciling love. He has seen 'the Star that came out of Jacob,' and he has gazed with faith's eagle eye upon the Sun of Righteousness itself. But if this spiritual night of his implies a previous day, which only aggravates his misery, it also promises a dawn—the dawn, too, of a morning when he shall again see his Lord, and rejoice. His spiritual necessity, then, endures but for a night; his spiritual joy comes in the morning. Such nights are generally short; and christians have it in their power, if not to prevent them, to make them less dismal, and shorten their duration. Let them only determine to realise more constantly the gracious presence of their Lord; and if they succeed, it is likely no such darkness shall ever encompass them; for what cloud can obscure that on which his smile is falling? The darkness of the christian is, after all, not the setting or absence of their sun; it is only a temporary obscuration—some ugly opaque worldly object has come in between them and it, which one ray of the 'morning star' never fails to drive away. Only let them never part company with their Lord—let them labour hard to reach the full assurance of his unalterable love for them; only let them call without ceasing upon him, and without doubting, leave the charge of all their affairs to him; and they are certain to see the clouds passing off, and soon to find themselves, in the elevations of their faith, carried far up even to the top of the high mountains, from which they descry their goodly heritage. 'The burden of Dumah! he calleth to me out of Seir, Watchman, what of the night? watchman, what of the night? The watchman said, The morning cometh, and also the night; if ye will inquire, inquire ye; return, come.'

5. IN THE SEASON OF TRIBULATION. 'Many are the afflictions of the righteous,' and many are the sources from which these spring; some from out of godly sorrow for sin, and many from the trials and vicissitudes of life. Those that issue from the former are exceedingly bitter. But there is ever one remedy sufficient to mitigate, if not to remove them. When the sense of sin oppresses a christian, it must be because he has ceased to realise Christ's presence. Let him just send and bring back his Saviour, and all his tears shall be wiped away. No believer can continue to be distracted by a sense of sin when he gazes upon the eye, and into the heart of Christ. The smile in that eye proclaims a pardon, and the blood of that heart washes out pollution. The conclusion is thus irresistible. The sorrowing penitent rises from the

ashes; he obeys the commandment, 'Be of good cheer;' and goes on 'his way again, rejoicing.'

The tribulations of christians that issue from the vicissitudes of life are indeed also very distressing, leading them to cry out, 'Is it nothing to you, all ye that pass by; behold and see if there be any sorrow like unto my sorrow, which is done unto me, wherewith the Lord hath afflicted me in the day of his fierce anger?' Yes; it is the christian that is often pierced through with many sorrows. Death sends shaft after shaft among the lambs of his fold, and the friends of his circle. Disease enfeebles, disfigures, or disables his frame; and to him are appointed many days and nights of sore weariness. Calumny also shoots out her tongue upon his reputation; adversity spoils his goods—'naked came he out of his mother's womb,' and he is likely 'naked to return thither again.' But it is remarkable that he has comfort in the midst of all. He never loses sight of his best Friend, who, though he was dead, is alive again, and never leaves nor forsakes him. He gives his body to the same Physician who has healed his soul; and so engaged is he about the cure of the latter, that he is not overanxious about the former. He sees no frown, and hears no reproof, from Christ; and though his riches may have fled away, he ever holds in his grasp 'the pearl of great price.' Thus, it is the realisation of Christ's presence that comforts and sustains him in the furnace. He can bear the loss of all things, so long as he has

Christ; yea, he is scarcely sensible of any pain while he tastes the joy of his Lord. He hesitates to admit a loss while he can call Jesus his; and his highest boast, while one wave after another dashes stormily over him, is, that though 'he passes through the waters,' Christ is with him; and 'through the rivers,' they do not overflow him; and 'through the fire,' he is not burnt; nor do the flames kindle upon him; for he exclaims, 'The Lord is my God; the Holy One of Israel is my Saviour!'

6. IN THE VALLEY OF THE SHADOW OF DEATH. It is appointed unto the righteous, as well as unto the wicked, 'once to die.' True, it is only once, but then, in that once what a complex, what an appalling work is to be done! Nature resiles from it, yea, we may say, abhors it.

> 'The weariest and most loathed worldly life
> That age, ache, penury, and imprisonment
> Can lay on nature is a paradise
> To what we fear of death.'

Not so, however, is it with the sanctified man. He has correct ideas of what death is to every one who dies 'in the Lord.' He knows Him whose death has unstung death, and whose resurrection has got the victory over the grave. Hence he is not only not afraid of it, but he says, 'I loathe it; I would not live alway;' 'I have a desire to depart and to be with Christ, which is far better.' His faith in Him who is 'the resurrection and the life,' and in that life and immortality which have been brought to light in the gospel, is just as 'good to him as the summit of Nebo was to Moses; and being fully assured of the validity of his title to a mansion in the skies, he waits, even with desire, for the approach of the messenger who is to put him into actual possession.

Still, even to good men, there is something deeply solemnising in that event which fixes their everlasting destiny; and when they at length do enter the dark vale, they would sink under the terrors of nature but for the exercises of religion. And what are these? These are, the *trust* which the soul places in Him who hath abolished death, in its cause and in its results; the *firm hold* which it takes and keeps of his rod and staff, who hath promised to be with it in the last distressing hour; the *sublime* realisation, in short, of Christ's own gracious presence with it in the final struggle, and in the impending triumph. O, there never was a genuine believer or a dying saint so beset with clouds, but the admission of Jesus instantly gave light; and if darkness still brooded, it was because this realisation was suspended. Christ is a light shining in a dark place. The valley of death is as dark a place as one can enter; but if Christ be there, all is light in the Lord.

> 'The chamber where a good man meets his fate
> Is privileged beyond the common walk
> Of virtuous life—quite on the verge of heaven.'

The extraordinary fortitude with which some meet death, and the triumphant peace in which others actually die, cannot be accounted for otherwise, than that they are spiritually seeing some glorious and powerful friend beside them. Assuredly it is no trifle for a believer to draw his latest breath—even he may cry out, 'Alas, for that day is great; it is even the time of Jacob's trouble.' But he has resources within and without himself. He has his Lord within him, 'the hope of glory.' He has his Lord above him, the evening star. He has his Lord beneath him, the sure and tried foundation. He has his Lord around him, the invulnerable shield. He has his Lord beyond him, the merciful forerunner. And he has his Lord in glory beckoning on him to arise and come away. What a splendid and comprehensive realisation is this! One feels that if able to accomplish such, we could hail death with rapture. And why not be able? When your time comes to die, O christian reader, you have not much to do to accomplish this: you have only to believe in Christ's presence with you, and *there he is*, nearer to your bedside than the dearest friend that watches and weeps over your departing spirit, and administering to your soul all those consolations which no love of man, woman, or angel could impart. Yes, *there he is*, 'in you,' and 'with you;' and *there you are*, 'in him,' and 'with him,' his strength your strength, his joy your joy, and his glory your glory. To be able to realise Him after this manner, in one's dying moment, as a friend we have long known, loved, trusted, and served, is beyond controversy one of the greatest attainments of christian piety; and you may all attain to it, if you would only set about appreciating a Saviour's boundless worth, and cultivating an endearing intimacy with him. Only cleave and cling to him now, and you will find that he will cling and cleave to you then; only study well his mediatorial work and worth now, and you will find, that on a deathbed, the learning you thus acquire shall be the only learning you will remember or care about—the only learning indeed of the slightest use to you. Erudite scholars and enthusiastic philosophers are students of perishable systems which mock their affrighted spirits as eternity draws nigh; they are only students *for life*, and so when life ends, their studies end too. But the christian studies an imperishable science, inasmuch as he is the disciple of an immortal teacher; he is therefore a student for eternity; and so when the clock of time has run out, he has the principles at hand which powerfully support him. His telescope is as useful now as ever; he used it for the survey of a spiritual world, and he can use it still. The constellations of his firmament go not out with his last breath. His powers of analysis are as much in request as ever; they were applied to the mystery of redeeming love, and into it they will still look, even after the curfew has tolled the knell of his adieu to life. His divine preceptor not only has given to him immortal truths, but *he* remains to the end their infallible exponent, so that the course of christian study is not tantalised at its close, by unexpected and mortifying discoveries of untenable theories, and is never found weeping over systems exploded by the experiments of new-born philosophies—is never found writhing under the lash of self-convicted folly in the past, and of utter hopelessness now of recovering time. Many learned men have died alike ashamed of their authorities, and of themselves the dupes thereof. They have left the world denouncing their teachers as impostors, casting away their inventions as toys which answer not the requirements of an immortal soul at such a time. But no christian can so die. In his last moments his authority is as great and infallible as ever—the imperishable nature of his hope is more evident than ever to his mind, and the truthfulness and suitableness of Jesus, while deepened in his convictions, are the grand and ever-present sources to him of that unfading hope, which, without a single falter, sublimely waits the moment that puts life and immortality into his hands.

Such is certain to be the blessed result to all who, when dying, have this learning, and this ability to realise and depend upon the Son of God. Who, then, would waste a lifetime, and spend the higher and the lower powers of the intellect upon mere evanescent curiosities in what is called literature; or upon strange and unearthly arcana in the temples of that hero-worship which has led away some of the finest minds of the age from the school of the cross, and from the feet of Him who died there? None, surely, who have power to think out a great idea like that of christianity, who have spiritual refinement enough to see the untellable worth of a deathless soul. None in whom remains one vestige of regard for the Almighty Creator, one shred of respect for their own futurity, one stray affection even, still feeling its way to some mercy-seat, still breathing, however feebly, in the fear, that after all, salvation is no dream, Christ no impostor, death no joke, and judgment no bugbear. Whosoever, therefore, would die in that peace and comfort which are but the foretastes and the forerunners of heaven, must *immediately* so think of, and so love and trust in, Jesus Christ, that to them it will be both easy and consistent to realise at once his gracious presence, and rejoice in the hope of sitting down beside him at the Lord's right hand. This, and this alone, shall dissipate the terrors of death. This, and this alone, shall tune your dying voice to the pæans of victory. This, and this alone, shall fill your hearts with untrembling fortitude, and qualify you for leaving behind you to the world, and to the church, another legacy wherewith to enrich the evidences of christianity, and wherewith to endow the spiritual temples of God, that are to be reared after your own translation to the NEW JERUSALEM.

CHAPTER XVII.

THE IMPROVEMENT.

'I flee unto thee to hide me.'
PSALM cxliii. 9.

READER! is the above exclamation of the Psalmist a truthful description of thy present feelings, now that thou hast perused these simple but sincere efforts to show unto thee the way of escape from the wrath and curse of an offended God? If it be so, then happy art thou, from this time henceforth, and for ever; for 'the Lord hath dealt bountifully with thee,' and hath fulfilled in thy gracious experience these precious words, 'I will establish my covenant with him.' If it be so, then the following analysis of thy consciousness in this matter must be held as the correct development of the spiritual process through which thou hast been passing. Whereas at the first thou wert careless about thy soul, knew not of its guilt, and sought after no Saviour from the dreadful consequences of sin, thou hast had thine eyes opened to see thine own worthlessness and helplessness, and thou art now ready to acknowledge that thou wert deservedly condemned to die, and if left to thyself, must of necessity have perished for ever: thou hast been made to fear and tremble under conscious guilt, and to cry out in great alarm about thy soul, 'What shall I do to be saved?' thou hast listened to the offers of mercy and pardon through Jesus Christ, and hast seen in his obedience and death what perfectly suits thy case, meets all the claims which divine law and justice have upon thee, and gives thee an irresistible plea with God, for the forgiveness of every sin already committed or yet to be committed, and in the end for a perfectly safe if not a perfectly peaceful death, to be followed by an eternal life of purity and joy, of honour and glory. Moreover, if it be so, thou hast given up thyself to the Lord Jesus, to be governed by him, to be used by him, and to be made 'complete in him'—to be *governed* by him in all thy thoughts, words, and actions, having no will of thine own, but delighting perpetually to do his will; to be *used* by him in the surrender of thy bodily powers, of thy spiritual energies, and of all thou hast of time, treasure, zeal, and influence, towards the promotion of his cause among those with whom thou hast to do; and to be made '*complete in him*' in submitting thine entire moral and religious nature to the sanctifying influence of his precious blood, to the enlightening power of his sacred scriptures, to the spiritualising tendency of his varied providences, to the elevating and inspiring hopes of the kingdom of heaven, and in all these things, to the teaching and blessing of the Holy Ghost sent down from above. If it be so, then thou feelest that thou art no longer 'thine own'—that thou hast no wish ever again to live as if thou wert 'thine own'—that to be Christ's is at once thy chiefest joy and most exalted privilege, thy most powerful motive to live nearer to God, and to do more for God; and thy everlasting fountain of comfort in sorrow, of strength in weakness, of counsel in difficulties, and of hope unto and beyond death and the grave. If it be so, then it is thine to overcome the love of the world, the lusts of the flesh, and the pride of life; thou art happier now in the 'liberty wherewith Christ hath made thee free,' than thou ever wert when indulging in all manner of licentiousness; and that which once truthfully described thy sensations in sinning has now become a misnomer, for to thee 'the pleasures of sin' have become tortures and humiliations of spirit, from which, with haste and terror, thou fleest unto Jesus, that he may 'hide thee.' The days of thy 'chambering and wantonness,' of thy dull and inactive life as to the requirements of religion, and of thy mad sporting with the interests of thine immortal soul, are over and gone, and now the beauties of holiness have fascinated and bound thy heart at once to the law and to the cross of Christ. This life thou feelest to be valuable only as it is used to prepare thee for the next; so absorbed art thou with an awful eternity, that the passing years seem to thee to be but 'a vapour,' or a 'weaver's shuttle,' or 'a tale that is told.' To look back is hateful, except as the past may preach to thee constant cause of repentance, and humility, and self-abnegation; to look forward is to anticipate large advancements in heavenly-mindedness during thy sojourn here, diligent application to all the means of grace, and rapturous realisation of the celestial blessedness. And if it be so, then be congratulated now on thy second birth, on thy 'translation from darkness to light, and from the power of Satan unto God.' Thy *worst*, in every sense of the word, is over; thou art now 'in Christ Jesus'—he will 'hide thee.' It matters not who pursues thee, *in him* thou art safe. When the holy law searches for thee 'in that day,' and finds thee in him—when the inflexible justice of Heaven searches for thee, and finds thee in him—when thine own conscience searches for thee, and finds thee in him—when the angels search for thee, and find thee in him—and when God himself arises and searches for thee, and finds thee in him, then by that law and justice thou shalt be pronounced 'Not Guilty;' by thy conscience thou shalt be congratulated on thy justification; by the angels thou shalt be hailed as a kindred spirit, and by the Lord God Almighty thou shalt be embraced and crowned as one of his adopted family, and as 'a joint heir' with Jesus Christ. Happy man!

let thy gratitude break forth into singing; and in the meanwhile, ever clothed with humility, yet fill thou the vault of heaven with the high praises of thy Jehovah-Jireh, who has provided all these good things for thee, and by whose grace thou art what thou art.

But what if it be not so? What if the reader remains in unbelief and impenitence? O pitiful—O shameful condition! On the supposition that thou art to live and to die in it, there remaineth for thee no other salvation. Greater is thy guilt than that of the men of Sodom and Gomorrah, and more appalling shall be thy latter end; for saith the apostle, 'If we sin wilfully after that we have received the knowledge of the truth, there remaineth no more sacrifice for sins, but a certain fearful looking for of judgment and fiery indignation, which shall devour the adversaries. He that despised Moses' law died without mercy under two or three witnesses: of how much sorer punishment, suppose ye, shall he be thought worthy, who hath trodden under foot the Son of God, and hath counted the blood of the covenant, wherewith he was sanctified, an unholy thing, and hath done despite unto the Spirit of grace?' Dear reader! be persuaded to revolve again and again the solemn and serious truths of this humble treatise, written for thy soul's good, and now urged upon thee that thou mayest live and not die—FLEE UNTO JESUS, AND HE WILL HIDE THEE! That thou hast not as yet fled to him, is a clear proof that thou art not convinced of the peril that overhangs thee—it is impossible that thou couldst thus remain insensible to the Saviour's matchless worth, if thou knewest how near is the sword of justice, how appalling are the messengers of divine vengeance, and how far thou art, in thyself, from every place of refuge. Thou wilt know the distance better when thou takest to running in the day of God's wrath. But *then*, running and fleeing must be useless; for the door of 'the hiding-place' is shut, and the deluge approaches. That door, however, is at this moment open—thou hast nothing to do but to enter, and within thou wilt find 'all things ready.' There thou wilt be welcomed by Jehovah-Jesus, whose smile will tell thee that he is 'the Lord thy God'—there Jehovah-Jireh will spread out before thee his richest promises for thy safety and comfort—there Jehovah-Tsidkenu will order for thee 'the best robe,' and put it upon thee, hiding in it the shame of thine own nakedness, and making thee 'comely in his comeliness'—there Jehovah-Rophi will wash thee in his living waters, mollify thy wounds with ointment, and heal all thy diseases—there Jehovah-Shalom will breathe upon thee, and diffuse delicious peace throughout all thy soul—there Jehovah-Nissi will spread over thee the banner of his love, and cause thee to triumph over all thine enemies—and there Jehovah-Shammah will insure thee, in his own gracious presence, to be with thee to the end of all thy warfare, through the midst of all thy trials, when thou passest through the waters of Jordan, and when thou landest on the shores of Canaan.

Say, is it not most unreasonable that in defiance of all thy necessities and of all this manifold provision for them, thou shouldest refuse to 'hide' thyself in Christ? Speak, reader, speak but one word in self-justification, and it shall be considered. Thou art silent—thou hast not one word to say on thine own behalf. No wonder; for what can be said in excuse or in palliation of a spiritual suicide like thine? Refusing to believe in Jesus, is in fact a putting to death of thy soul—while coming to and abiding in him, is to possess thyself of life everlasting; and yet thou wilt not flee. O look behind thee, and thou shalt see the avenger of blood coming hurriedly upon thee. Haste thee, sinner, else thou art lost; for quick as lightning is the divine wrath; when once its fire begins to burn, blessed are all they that are hid in him. 'Escape, then, for thy life, look not behind thee, neither stay thou in all the plain: escape to the mountain, lest thou be consumed.' Look on either side, and thou shalt see that thou art hemmed in by the unscalable walls of judicial condemnation, and cannot find escape either on the right hand or on the left. Look above thee, and the frown of an angry God, like some dark and menacing cloud, is ready to burst upon thee in its holy ire. Look beneath thee, and behold a yawning hell eager to draw thee down into its unutterable woes. But look *before* thee, and thou shalt 'behold the Lamb of God, who taketh away the sin of the world,' with arms outstretched to embrace thee, with a heart panting after thy soul to hide it beneath his mercy-seat in the ark of his covenant, and with thy blood-signed and blood-sealed title to pardon, purity and peace now, and perfect bliss hereafter, unfolded on that mercy-seat, and awaiting thine acceptance. Behold Him! He is the Son of the Highest —the Word of God—God himself—God in thy nature—God incarnate in thy stead! Behold Him! He is a man of sorrows and acquainted with grief—he is wounded for *thy* transgressions, and bruised for *thine* iniquities—he is mocked, and buffeted, and spit upon, and scourged—he is agonised, and in his agony his whole body weeps tears of blood; and all this because *thou* hast sinned and art still sinning against his God and thy God. Behold Him! He is nailed to an accursed tree—he is the laughing-stock of the brutal soldiery, and the butt of Jewish spite—he is now treading the wine-press of his Father's wrath alone— the sun hides his face, and supernatural darkness reigns over all the land—the earth quakes, the rocks are rent, the vail of the temple bursts open in the midst, and the very graves discover their loathsome tenants, while a cry more mysterious and appalling than any which ever broke upon the ear of God or of man, rises from the tortured Jesus on the cross of Calvary: 'My God, my God, why hast thou forsaken me?' Behold Him! He is now a pale and mangled corpse—his spirit is gone, and the great atonement for thy sins is made, is finished, is accepted—made by thy substitute, finished on his cross, and accepted of the righteous Lawgiver—*but refused by thee*, O infatuated man! Is it possible? Accepted of the God whom thou hast offended, and whose curse is upon thy soul, and refused by thee! Yes, Oh man, whosoever thou art, there is no such thing as infatuation in the world, if thou art not possessed of it. Think—think again and again over this thy condition, and say can there be one of greater iniquity and of more impending peril? Who is this that thou despisest and rejectest? Jesus the Son of God and the Saviour of mankind. What is it that thou refusest? The justification of thine own soul from all its sins, and the grace that is sure to rectify all its errors, remove all its pains, and fill it with the joy and peace of believing. And who art thou that darest thus to treat thy Saviour and his great salvation? A poor, wretched, blind, and naked creature—the slave every moment of debasing lusts—the sport of devils, and the football of a world lying in wickedness—yea, thou art the doomed one and the condemned—the imprisoned and helpless victim of a law that must have death for its penalty, and that can by no means clear the guilty. And is it for such an one as thou art thus to despise the riches of God's grace, and for one moment longer to turn away from the only 'hiding place' where thou art safe from all the consequences of thy sins?

God forbid! yea rather be persuaded to flee unto him, and he will 'hide thee.' Dost thou inquire, When? must it be now, or may I defer it till some more convenient season? Beware of delay, sinner. There is no promise that the door of mercy is to be open beyond the present moment—hence the emphasis of that scripture: '*Now* is the accepted time; behold *now* is the day of salvation.' Ponder these words; they distinctly tell thee that there is a time when God will accept of thee; but that time is of the smallest conceivable amount—the present moment—not the next, but *now*. They tell thee that there is a day of salvation; but it is the shortest day of which we have ever heard—just the present moment—not the next, but *now*. In other times there may be days and years, and ages—in 'the accepted time' there is but a moment. In other days there may be minutes and hours—in 'the day of salvation' there is but a moment. True, many have tried like thee to elongate God's accepted and salvation times, and have hazarded their souls upon the profane experiment, and they have perished in consequence. O foolish man, eschew the sin and fate of Felix, who bargained for a future opportunity, but to whom no such opportunity ever came. Now—at this moment—while thou readest these appeals, fall down upon thy knees, and, 'looking unto Jesus,' cry out, 'God be merciful to me a sinner.' Wait not till to-morrow; 'for thou knowest not what a day may bring forth.' Before another sun goes down, thy soul may be required of thee. Should it be so, what wilt thou do, or think, or say? Do what thou pleasest, think as thou canst, and say what thou art inclined to, it will be all in vain—*where's the hiding place?* Gone! Gone for ever! And thou wilt have thyself to blame; for thou knewest that it was only promised to thee *now*—at this moment—and thou wouldst not enter. Yea, thou wast expressly told that it might be shut to-morrow, and yet thou saidst to thy soul, 'Soul, thou hast much goods laid up for many years, take thine ease, eat, drink, and be merry.' Reader! on these rocks of procrastination and presumption, innumerable souls have been wrecked and lost; and there is a high degree of probability that thine own shall suffer the same fate, if thou dost not put on a bold resolution, and at once flee unto this wonderful Man, who is 'as an hiding place from the wind, and covert from the tempest.' May God even now fill thy soul with such a purpose, and give thee grace to arise, and swiftness of foot to flee unto him that he may 'hide thee!' O resist the temptations of Satan, and of the world, which powerfully plead for delay; cast them boldly behind thy back; and before they can return to confront thee with their impudence, and weaken thy purpose with their smiles, thou mayest be out of their reach, for ever safe and happy within thy 'hiding place.' Yes; when once there, thou mayest hear them, now gnashing their teeth with rage at thy escape, and now raising their syren voices to win thee back; but the spell of their enchantment passes not through the walls of thy divine refuge, nor can their muttered wrath injure now a single hair of thine head. Once 'in Christ Jesus,' and there is to thee 'no more condemnation;' and 'neither death, nor life, nor angels, nor principalities, nor powers, nor things present, nor things to come, nor height, nor depth, nor any other creature, shall be able to separate you from the love of God, which is in Christ Jesus our Lord.'

What, then, is thy resolution? Hast thou refused to flee? Is this sun to set upon thee still in thy unbelief—still 'out of' Christ? Then know thou, O despiser of the infinitely lovely Saviour, that thou wilt never again be so easily persuaded as thou art at this moment—thy heart is already harder, and thy conscience is more-seared by this obstinacy; and it wants but a few more such audacious and heartless refusals to make thy salvation impossible, by provoking the Almighty to shut the door of the 'HIDING PLACE' for ever.

www.ingramcontent.com/pod-product-compliance
Lightning Source LLC
Chambersburg PA
CBHW021052080526
44587CB00010B/216